Reforming Fiscal Federalism for Global Competition
A Canada–Australia Comparison

Publication No. 4 in the Series

Edited by
Paul Boothe

Western Centre for
Economic Research
at the University
of Alberta

The University of
Alberta Press

First published by
The University of Alberta Press
Athabasca Hall
Edmonton, Alberta, Canada   T6G 2E8

Copyright © The University of Alberta Press 1996

Printed in Canada   5   4   3   2   1

ISBN 0-88864-294-6

Canadian Cataloguing in Publication Data

Main entry under title:

Reforming fiscal federalism for global competition

   Proceedings of a conference held in Edmonton in October 1995.
   Includes bibliographical references.
   ISBN 0-88864-294-6

     1. Federal-provincial fiscal relations—Canada—Congresses.*
   2. Intergovernmental fiscal relations—Australia—Congresses.
   3. Fiscal policy—Canada—Congresses.   4. Fiscal policy—Australia
   —Congresses.   I. Boothe, Paul Michael, 1954-
   HC115.R43 1996   336.71   C96-910669-6

All rights reserved.

No part of this publication may be produced, stored in a retrieval system, or transmitted in any forms or by any means, electronic, mechanical, photocopying, recording, or otherwise, without the prior permission of the copyright owner.

Printed by Priority Printing Ltd., Edmonton, Alberta, Canada.

∞ Printed on acid-free paper.

COMMITTED TO THE DEVELOPMENT OF CULTURE AND THE ARTS

Contents

Preface		v
Acknowledgements		vii
1.	Introduction — Paul Boothe	1
2.	The Comparative Nature of Australian and Canadian Economic Space — Thomas J. Courchene	7
	Some Non-Policy Explanations	9
	Policy-Induced Differences in Geo-Economic Space	9
	The Role of Region in National Decision Making	12
	Globalization and the Australia/Canada Comparison	13
	Conclusions	14
	Appendix	15
3.	The Challenges of Globalisation: Lessons from Australian Experience — Cliff Walsh	23
	Lessons from Australian Experience?	25
	Hawke's New Federalism	27
	Intergovernmental Relations Under Keating	32
	Regionalism Revived	39
	Conclusions	42

4. Fiscal Federalism in Australia and Canada: A Brief Comparison of Constitutional Frameworks, Structural Features of Existing Fiscal Systems and Fiscal Institutions — Stanley L. Winer and Allan M. Maslove 45
   An Overview of Stylized Facts 47
   The Evolution of Fiscal Federalism over the Last Decade 56
   Explaining Differences in the Degree of Fiscal Centralization 59
   Conclusions 61
   Appendix 72

5. Tax Assignment and Fiscal Externalities in a Federal State — Bev Dahlby and L. S. Wilson 87
   Fiscal Externalities in a Federal State 89
   Applications to Australia and Canada 98
   Conclusions 101

6. Making a Mess of Tax Assignment: Australia as a Case Study — Cliff Walsh
   The Assignment of Taxing Powers 109
   Australia's Fiscal and Federal System in Broad Perspective 113
   The Consequences of Fiscal Imbalance 117
   The Causes of Fiscal Imbalance 124
   A Scheme for Returning Taxing Powers to the States 126
   Alternatives and Objections: Is Commonwealth Policy-Making Really Threatened? 130
   Making Fiscal Coordination a Reality 134
   Conclusions: Towards a New Approach to Promoting National Objectives 135

7. Assigning Responsibility for Regional Stabilization: Evidence from Canada and Australia — Paul Boothe and Jeffrey Petchey 141
   Previous Literature 142
   Evidence from Canada and Australia 147
   Two Case Studies of Discretionary Fiscal Policy 153
   Conclusions 159

8. The Partisan Component in Intergovernmental Transfers — Robert Young and Campbell Sharman, with Andrew Goldstein 163
   Initial Considerations 164
   Previous Studies 168
   The Results 172
   Conclusions 177
   Appendix 181

9. Preserving and Promoting the Internal Economic Union: Australia and
   Canada — Thomas J. Courchene 185
       Constitutional Provisions Relating to the Internal Economic Union 187
       International Influences 194
       Positive Integration 196
       Competitive Federalism and the Internal Economic Union 212
       Conclusions 217
       Appendix 221

10. A New Federalism for Canada
    — The Honourable Jim Dinning 223

Preface

Despite fairly similar beginnings, the Australian and Canadian federations have evolved quite differently over time. The different courses the two countries have taken have been well documented by scholars in periodic comparisons of the salient political and economic characteristics of the two nations. Over the past decade both nations have become acutely aware of the impact of increasing global competition and both are having to adapt modes of operation and institutions to prosper in a world economy that is increasingly modern and highly competitive in many of the areas of traditional strength for Australia and Canada.

While private sectors in both countries are well on in the process of adapting to the changes of global competition, progress in the public sector has lagged behind. In some areas (for example, the sharing of taxing and spending powers), relatively little progress has been made in the past decade in addressing obvious problems. It is not too great an exaggeration to say that the process of reform and adaptation seems deadlocked. At times, political leaders at both national and sub-national levels seem engaged in a dialogue of the deaf. Tired old positions are continually repeated. An injection of fresh ideas is needed to break the deadlock and re-start the process of reform.

The purpose of this volume is to enhance our understanding of the current state of fiscal federalism in Canada and Australia by examining the effects of increasing global competition on our fiscal arrangements. My colleagues and I hope that this work will contribute valuable information to policy makers and re-energize public debate on fiscal reform, leading to the consideration and ultimate adoption of practical solutions to our problems. In this way, we hope that public sectors in both countries can adapt to once again serve us well in this rapidly changing global economy.

Acknowledgements

The project began in 1993 with discussions between me (Paul Boothe of the Western Centre for Economic Research (WCER) at the University of Alberta) and then-director of the Federalism Research Centre (FRC) at Australian National University, Brian Galligan. After these preliminary discussions, external financial support was sought from the Donner Canadian Foundation with internal support being provided by WCER and FRC, which by that time had a new director in the person of John Uhr. Research projects were initiated in 1994 and continued with a Research Workshop held in Canberra in May 1995 sponsored by the FRC. The final papers were presented and discussed in Edmonton in October 1995 at the Reforming Fiscal Federalism for Global Competition conference sponsored by WCER.

Many people and organizations have contributed to the successful completion of this project. I am especially grateful to Patrick Luciani and the Donner Canadian Foundation for their interest and support of the project. As well, additional support was provided by Alberta Federal and Intergovernmental Affairs, WCER and FRC. The Economics Department of the University of Tasmania provided me with an excellent environment as I edited this volume. John Uhr of FRC contributed a great deal of time and energy and organized a very useful workshop in Canberra which included both authors and government and academic participants. Ted Chambers of WCER and Louise Edwards of the University of Alberta Economics Department worked hard to make the Edmonton conference a success. Gail Ovelson proved an invaluable administrative and secretarial assistant and Andrea Waywanko of Alberta Treasury designed and typeset the book. Glenn Rollans and Leslie Vermeer of the University of Alberta Press tied all the ends together to complete the book's publication.

A number of government officials from Canada and Australia contributed their ideas and support for the project. I would like to single out for special thanks Michael Butler from British Columbia Finance and Corporate Relations and Frank Gregg from Finance Canada for their contributions in both Canberra and Edmonton. I am grateful to Al O'Brien from Alberta Treasury and John Wright from Saskatchewan Government Insurance Corporation who served as panelists in the opening and closing sessions of the Edmonton conference. I would also like to thank our colleagues at the Australian National University and University of Alberta who served as discussants at the Canberra workshop and the Edmonton conference.

Finally, I would like to express my appreciation to the Provincial Treasurer of Alberta, the Honourable Jim Dinning, for participating in the Edmonton conference and setting out Alberta's vision of the Canadian federation of the future. Together with Mr. Dinning, I believe that our federal systems must adapt if they are to serve us well in the competitive global economy of the future. I hope that this volume will help to re-invigorate debate on reform of the vital institutions of government in our two countries, and contribute to strong and prosperous nations in the 21st century.

Introduction

1

Paul Boothe

The practice of fiscal federalism can sometimes be very different in Australia and Canada. These differences come from different histories, politics, geographies, and economic conditions. However, both countries are struggling to adapt their public institutions, as well as their economies, to the realities of increasing global competition. The main goal of this project is to understand the implications of globalization for federal systems and to consider how policies and public institutions can respond and adapt.

The studies presented in the volume are divided into two groups. The first group seeks to understand the current economic and policy environment. Differences and similarities are documented and discussed. The second group of studies focuses on fiscal arrangements. The main thrust of these studies is to examine current problems, and consider potential reforms.

Leading the first group, the study by Tom Courchene of Queen's University, identifies some key differences between Canada and Australia. Canada has greater regional disparities than Australia (roughly four times as large); Canada has larger regional variations in unemployment than Australia; Canada's transfers are more targeted to poor regions than Australia; and Canada has higher average per capita income than Australia. Much of the remainder of the Courchene paper is devoted to understanding the reasons behind these differences. Courchene ends his introductory paper with a discussion of how Canada and Australia will adapt to the growing trade and financial links between their individual regions and different parts of the world. For its part, Canada is accommodating this trend by becoming increasingly decentralized. According to Courchene, the challenge for Canada will be to maintain its internal social union in the face of further economic and fiscal decentralization. For Australia, which is relatively more centralized in areas of social policy, the challenge may be to find ways of decentralizing fiscal and economic policy to enable regions to do business with different international partners.

The second introductory paper, by Cliff Walsh of the University of Adelaide, reviews recent developments in Australian fiscal federalism since Prime Minister Hawke's *New Federalism* initiative of 1990. Walsh describes the work leading to the mutual recognition of product standards and professional qualifications by state and commonwealth governments. Although Hawke's successor, Prime Minister Keating, is viewed as favouring a highly centralized federal system for Australia, Walsh reviews progress made in the area of regulation (microeconomic reform) and the development of a common macroeconomic and fiscal outlooks by state and commonwealth governments. In addition, Mr. Keating presided over the establishment of an important intergovernmental institution, the Council of Australian Governments (COAG). Walsh concludes his introductory survey by reiterating his warning that institutions and strategies for reforming fiscal arrangements may not be easily transferred between countries. This is especially true, he argues, because the particular path taken by a country depends importantly on the goals and abilities of the national and regional political leaders of the day.

The final introductory paper, by Stan Winer and Allan Maslove of Carleton University, provides a useful comparison of the constitutional arrangements of the two federations as well as how the fiscal arrangements operate in practice. Not surprisingly, successive rounds of judicial interpretations have caused current arrangements in both federations to depart substantially from their original form as laid out in the constitution. The evidence from both countries is that other, non-constitutional forces have important effects on the evolution of fiscal arrangements in a federation. Winer and Maslove speculate on the nature of some of these other forces. They warn policy makers that constitutional changes which are inconsistent with these other forces may well be undone by compensatory adjustments elsewhere in the fiscal system.

The next five studies form the second group. The first, by Bev Dahlby and Sam Wilson of the University of Alberta, examines the effect of the

Introduction

division of tax and expenditure powers on the mix of taxes and expenditures found in Canada and Australia, and on the overall level of taxation. Dahlby and Wilson pay special attention to the potential for tax externalities, both between separate jurisdictions (like two provinces or states), which they call horizontal externalities, and between two levels of government (like federal versus provincial or commonwealth versus state governments), which they call vertical externalities. While the impacts of horizontal externalities are well known, the impacts of vertical externalities are not. Dahlby and Wilson point out that governments will tend to overtax bases which they share with other levels of government. They argue that the relatively large size and number of tax base overlaps in Canada may contribute to explaining Canada's higher level of overall taxation compared to Australia.

The next paper, by Cliff Walsh of the University of Adelaide, examines the assignment of tax bases in Australia and discusses the problems associated with Australia's high degree of vertical fiscal imbalance.[1] These problems include the centralization of decision making, the potential for conflict between commonwealth and state governments, the lost of electoral accountability, and the loss of financial market scrutiny of state financial affairs. Further, he argues that in order to discharge their constitutional spending responsibilities, Australian states have been forced to exploit narrow and somewhat artificial tax bases, which has led, in turn, to potentially serious distortions in the Australian economy. Walsh suggests that a rebalancing of tax bases might lead to a less-regressive overall tax system in Australia.

Walsh's next step is to propose a strategy for reducing the current high level of vertical fiscal imbalance in Australia by replacing a portion of commonwealth income tax with a flat tax on income levied by the states, together with a corresponding reduction in unconditional transfers to states. He goes on to discuss the benefits of the strategy and to compare it to one of its well-known alternatives. Walsh concludes by briefly discussing how the lessons from Australia might be applied to the current debate on tax assignment in Canada.

Turning to the expenditure side of fiscal policy, Paul Boothe of University of Alberta and Jeff Petchey of Murdoch University examine the impact of spending by both national and regional (i.e., provincial or state) governments on regional economic fluctuations. Three main lessons can be drawn from

---

1. Vertical fiscal imbalance is the degree to which a sub-national government's spending responsibilities are not matched by its revenue raising powers. Australia exhibits the highest degree of vertical fiscal imbalance (i.e., state expenditures financed by Commonwealth transfers rather than own revenue) of any federation in the industrialized world.

their work. First, regional economies are more similar across Australia than across Canada. Second, both federal and provincial governments in Canada run counter-cyclical fiscal policy overall. However, when fiscal policy is broken down into automatic and discretionary components, discretionary policy is almost always pro-cyclical, i.e., exaggerating rather than mitigating economic fluctuations. Lack of data on federal spending and revenue by state precludes the same type of analysis for Australia. However, for the most part state expenditure in Australia shows the same properties as provincial spending in Canada. For the small portion of commonwealth spending the authors could analyze (commonwealth grants to states), the results are mixed. The final lesson has to do with the size of fiscal presence required for an effective counter-cyclical policy. Research from the European Community indicates that only a relatively small fund is required for stabilization of the magnitude enjoyed, for example, in the US. Boothe and Petchey argue, therefore, that the need for counter-cyclical fiscal policy says little about the division of expenditure responsibilities in either federation. Given their past track records, discretionary counter-cyclical policy should be avoided by all governments.

Bob Young of the University of Western Ontario and Campbell Sharman of the University of Western Australia examine whether partisan politics affect intergovernmental transfers. Complementing existing work for Australia, Young and Sharman find that Canadian provincial governments of the same political stripe as the federal government tend to get a higher ratio of transfers to direct federal spending than provinces governed by different parties. They also find evidence that provincial governments of the same party as the federal government are likely to receive a higher ratio of transfers to government revenue collected. Finally, their results indicate that periodic changes to the equalization formula have tended to favour provinces with governments of the same party as the federal government.

Tom Courchene compares Canada's and Australia's management of their internal economic unions in the face of increasing global competition. In particular, he considers the role the courts have played in enhancing the Australian internal economic union on one hand and serving to fragment the Canadian internal economic union on the other. In Australia, the commonwealth and state governments have generally acted to enhance the economic union, while in Canada both levels of government have contributed to its fragmentation. Courchene stresses the role of external forces, such as the North American Free Trade Agreement (NAFTA), in opening up the internal economic union in Canada. The forces of globalization will probably require Australia to consider some

Introduction

decentralization in the future, while Canada will have to work to maintain the internal social union in the face of external competitive pressures.

In the final paper, the Honourable Jim Dinning, Provincial Treasurer of Alberta, argues that Canadian fiscal federalism must be reformed to reflect today's realities. He identifies three realities that must change the face of fiscal federalism: the need to reduce federal spending and the attending impact on the financing of Canadian social programs, the impact of growing government debt on Canada's ability to attract investment and create jobs, and the provinces' demonstrated ability to deliver programs effectively, cooperatively and in a fiscally-responsible manner. Dinning sees a new federalism evolving to meet the challenges posed by these three realities and lays out the characteristics that new federalism should have. Canada will have a clear division of responsibilities between federal and provincial governments to deliver government services effectively and efficiently. There will be a flexible approach to program delivery so that programs can meet the particular needs of citizens in different regions of Canada. National standards will be forged by federal and provincial governments working cooperatively to find national consensus. Finally, this new federalism will be achieved within the framework of the existing Canadian constitution. Dinning concludes with a call to all governments to accept that the world and Canada's place in it have changed. Making the changes required to remain a prosperous and unified country will be difficult, but he is confident that Canadians are up to the task.

2

The Comparative Nature of Australian and Canadian Economic Space

Thomas J. Courchene

From the first moment Canadians touch down in Australia they feel quite at home. Human nature being what it is, the typical next step, at least for academics, is to engage in Canadian-Australian comparisons and, for some of us, to undertake analyses and even to offer policy advice based largely on our Canadian environment and experiences. Some then take the further step of focusing on those Australian institutions/policies/processes that might be imported into Canada. All of this is predicated on the assumption that our nations are very similar.

On the surface, this certainly seems to be the case. We are both former British colonies and are members of the Commonwealth. We are both federal nations. We are both constitutional monarchies. Our land masses qualify us among the largest nations on earth. We are both small, open economies endowed with ample resources. We both have vast parts of our territory that are sparsely populated. Both of our nations have significant aboriginal or First Nations populations.

We do, of course, recognize some important differences. Australia does not have the equivalent of a U.S. on its border with the resulting dominant impact on both trade and cultural identity. (As an aside, Canadians' views of the U.S. probably resonate well with the New Zealanders' views of Australia. By way of a minor example, Auckland has now broken into the Australian

Rugby League in the same way as Toronto and Montreal have franchises in the U.S. national pastime.) Moreover, Canadian scholars have duly noted the differences in our upper chambers and, on more than one occasion, we have unsuccessfully attempted to convert our appointed Senate to the "triple-E" version in Australia — elected, equal and effective. We also recognize that Australia has no equivalent to Quebec — a province that is linguistically, culturally and legally (civil law vs. common law) distinct. Even recognizing these important differences we, nonetheless, tend to assume that the similarities clearly outweigh these differences.

Lest these generalizations begin to annoy Canadians and Australians alike, let me state that these were *my* priors when I first visited Australia three years ago. As my research on the Australian economy progressed, it became increasingly evident that these important and obvious similarities between our two countries effectively masked some very significant differences in the nature of the two economies and particularly in the nature of the national/sub-national economic interface. The first tangible evidence of this arose in the context of a comparison of regional (state/provincial) disparities in Canada and Australia (Courchene, 1993, Appendix 1). Because the range of rationales for these differences in regional disparities, or the differences in the nature of the geo-economic space, encompass most of the comparative analyses that follow, it seems appropriate to introduce the volume from this perspective.

Accordingly, appended to this introduction is the technical appendix on disparities alluded to earlier. Among the key features of this analysis that are relevant as backdrop for this introduction are the following:

- that regional disparities are roughly four times as large in Canada than in Australia;
- that the variation in employment rates across Canadian provinces, compared to the Australian states, is even larger;
- that in terms of after-transfer income, the regional disparities are considerably narrower, indicating that Canada's transfer system is more targeted to poor areas than is Australia's; and
- that, overall, the level of per capita GDP in Canada is higher than that in Australia (note that the differences in 1995 are less than the Appendix tables suggest for 1991 because the value of the Canadian dollar has fallen relative to the Australian dollar). This was not always the case, which, in turn, suggests that while Australia may have avoided a regional disparity problem, this may be at the expense of holding back aggregate income growth.

The issue that arises from all of this is: why are regional disparities larger in Canada?

Some Non-Policy Explanations

At the most basic, perhaps tautological, level the reason for the narrower Australian disparities is that economic activity is distributed more equally across Australian economic space. For example, every state and territory is engaged in pastoral (sheep and cattle) activity and, with its lone vineyard, the Northern Territory now joins the rest in viticulture. While not attempting to downplay the differences between industrial Victoria and resource-rich Western Australia, it is probably the case that the geographical distribution of economic activity is more marked within Canada. But this cannot be the whole story since internal migration of labour and capital mobility would provide some equilibration over time.

A second reason may relate to city size. Most of the Australian states are dominated by their capital cities and except for Hobart (Tasmania) these are large urban conglomerates. I recall some research a decade or so ago which suggested that if one compared the income level of Halifax with that of similarly-sized cities in the rest of Canada, much of the disparity in appendix Table 2.2 would disappear. Moreover, the larger the city, the higher the level of income. In Australia, five of the six states have an urban conglomerate of at least 1 million people. Hence, one ought to expect lesser disparities in Australia than one finds in Canada where the largest city in each of the five poorest provinces (the Atlantic provinces and, arguably, Saskatchewan) is much smaller than the largest city in the top five provinces. At the very least, this is a hypothesis worthy of further research.

A third difference is that Australia has no economic superpower on its border. This may help explain why aggregate income in Canada has surpassed that in Australia.

However, my interest is more in potential institutional or policy-induced influences or explanations for these differential regional disparities. To this I now turn.

Policy-Induced Differences in Geo-Economic Space

In their paper, Maslove and Winer present a comparative overview of institutional, constitutional and policy differences between Canada and Australia. What I shall do is to focus on aspects of their analysis (as well as some comparative issues that they do not touch upon) as potential explanations for the very different nature of the economic space in Australia and Canada.

Wages

The first point to note is that Australia is a "wages union" of sorts, in both the public and private sector. National wage grids exist for university professors, for example: a university English professor receives the same wage whether employed in Hobart or in Sydney. Under the "federal awards" pursuant to Australia's industrial relations system, employees of the Victorian state government cannot be denied access to these federal awards (see Courchene, this volume). In the private sector, a settlement in one industry in one state can be "transferred" across the system, so that private-sector wages are also quite similar.

This is in sharp contrast to the Canadian situation where wages can and do differ significantly across universities both within and between provinces. A recent illustration is the announcement that Ottawa's minimum wage across the country will be tied to provincial minimum wages — poles apart from the Australian reality.

There is a related aspect of wage policy that is also relevant. Thanks to the ruling of the famous *Harvester Case* in 1907, wages were to be adequate to grant a man, his wife and their three children "a living wage." A corollary of this is that the wage gradient (wage ratio of unskilled to skilled labour) is much narrower than that in Canada. Whether Australia will be able to hold to this narrow wage gradient will be dealt with later. For present purposes, the relevant point is that wage policy in Australia is part of the society's overall income-distribution strategy. In turn, they represent a powerful force underlying the egalitarianism of Australian society and probably play an important role in generating the narrower income disparities in Australia.

Equalization

Australia's equalization program is far more egalitarian than is Canada's. (For a comparative analysis, see Courchene, 1995). There are two related reasons for this. First, the Australian system equalizes for both revenue means and expenditure needs whereas Canada focuses only on the former. Second, there are no "tall poppies" in the Australian system since there is full equalization, i.e. the rich states are brought down and the poor ones brought up, unlike the Canadian system where the three "have" provinces pocket any own-source revenues above and beyond the five-province standard. In other words, Australia equalizes net fiscal benefits across all states.

What this means is that there can be no Alberta-type energy boom in Australia. Were this to occur in Australia, the "lucky" state would only pocket its population share (adjusted for fiscal need) of any revenue boom. Alternatively, all states would share equally in any revenue bonanza.

Thus, there is no way that an energy boom could ever be *capitalized* in wages or land rents in a particular state because there is precious little differential left to capitalize. This is, of course, consistent with the maintenance of a wages union — if Australia were to have a Canadian-style equalization program they would not be able to maintain their uniform wage policy. This, too, probably contributes to the narrowness of regional disparities in Australia.

As a passing aside, this may be part of the reason why Boothe and Petchey find that, unlike the case in Canada, business cycles across Australian states tend to be synchronous.

Social Expenditures

Unlike Canada, where welfare benefits in New Brunswick are roughly 40-50 percent of the levels in Ontario, welfare benefits in Australia are delivered federally and, therefore, equal across all states. (As an aside that I shall highlight later, Australia has no equivalent of Canada's unemployment insurance and, therefore, no "regional" component to UI.) This, too, supports the underlying egalitarianism and is consistent with both the Australian form of equalization and the wages union. It also means that Canada's concern with the portability of welfare benefits is a non-issue in Australia.

Vertical Fiscal Imbalance and the Centralization/Decentralization Mix

Dahlby and Wilson present evidence on the allocation of taxing powers between the federal and provincial/state governments, replete with the critical observation that sharing a tax base may lead to over-taxation in much the same way that a common property fishery will lead to over-fishing. In his paper, Walsh focuses in more detail on Australia's vertical fiscal imbalance and also places it in the context of micro-economic reform initiatives, of intergovernmental financial relations and of the underlying institutional and constitutional framework. I want to use the fact that Canadian provinces have much more own-source-revenue fiscal room than Australian states to make the point that the Canadian system is far more decentralized. Actually, one could also approach this from the formal distribution of powers, as I do in my own contribution to this volume. In any event, the key point is that the Canadian provinces have significantly more freedom to legislate as they wish across a wide variety of fronts. One result of this is that there is much more leeway for the provinces to fragment the internal common market. However, it is also the case that Ottawa has much more freedom to fragment Canadian economic space than does the Commonwealth government in Australia. The constitutional underpinnings of all of this are dealt with in my later paper.

However, the greater tax autonomy of the Canadian provinces and their greater powers do resonate well with the observation that federal-provincial transfers in Canada are increasingly unconditional whereas the majority of Commonwealth-state transfers in Australia are now conditional. In turn, this contributes to the diversity of provincial programs across Canadian economic space (competitive federalism) and, in tandem with earlier features, may well serve to explain both the greater degree of regional disparity across Canada and the fact this flexibility has ensured that, in the aggregate, Canadian income growth has not been constrained to the same degree as in Australia.

The Role of Region in National Decision Making

By way of implications arising from the above analysis, I want to focus first on the one issue that will immediately strike any Canadian visiting Australia, namely the lack of an explicit regional component to Commonwealth policy making. In contrast, hardly a day can pass in Canada without some reference to how federal policy x or y will impact on Canada's regions. With the above analysis as backdrop, this is, I think, relatively easy to explain. With welfare a national responsibility, with a wages union providing equal access to employment income, with the equalization program ensuring full equality in terms of access to public goods and services and with conditional grants tying the hands of state governments, the regional concerns are *fully covered* as it were. To this, my political science colleagues may want to add that the presence of a triple-E Senate means that, unlike Canada, the states are intricately involved in national decision-making. In any event, the key point is that the "regional" or "state" implications of Commonwealth policy tend not to loom large, if they loom at all, in any ensuing public/political debate.

The opposite is true in Canada. Ottawa is first and foremost a "redistributive" agent. Every policy is tinged with an overtone of regionalism and/or provincialism. In terms of the above analysis, the proximate cause is obvious. Equalization does not attempt to equalize provincial net fiscal benefits. Thus, it does not prevent capitalization of provincial revenues in terms of wages and rents. Welfare rates vary quite dramatically across provinces. Because this constellation of constitutional, institutional and policy frameworks does not generate regional "equity" (however defined), the result is that the regional component of Canadian federal policy is never far from the surface.

One result of this is that Canada has fallen into what I have elsewhere referred to as the "transfer dependency" trap. There must be a special regional or "have-not" province component to much of so-called national policy. The UI program is probably the best example. With preferential entry and benefits for areas of high unemployment and with special provisions for fishers, the federal legislators were no doubt well-intentioned in the policy design. Yet, even a smattering of economics would suggest that such policies would exacerbate and probably entrench any existing regional disparities. Indeed, they have. Thus, the persistence of Canada's regional disparities are "policy induced." Phrased differently, policy measures have created a regional "equilibrium" characterized by persistent disparities.

Lest one opt for the Australian system, the comparable comment is that while Australia has dodged the bullet of regional disparity, it may have fallen into a different problem: the regional egalitarianism may well have prevented the national economy in Australia from adjusting to the emerging pressures from the global economy. In the final section of this introduction, I want to offer a few comments on the range of challenges that globalization will pose for the Australian and Canadian federal systems.

To conclude this section, I simply want to express my sympathy with the valiant effort by Young and Campbell which attempts a focus on a common political component in government transfers in Canada and Australia.

Globalization and the Australia/Canada Comparison

By way of both a conclusion to the above analysis as well as a looking forward in terms of how global integration might impact on the two federations, I offer three general observations.

The first is that there appears to be an *internal inconsistency* to each federation's range of policies. For example, were one to introduce Canadian-style equalization into the Australian context, the entire system would literally blow apart, since this would be inconsistent with the wages union, nationally delivered welfare, etc. Likewise the introduction of Australian equalization into the Canadian system would cause similar havoc. In this sense, it is important to recognize that particular policies or programs are not easily "importable" across systems unless one takes account of the overall institutional and economic context of which these policies or programs are a component part.

The second observation relates to the on-going tendency of federal systems everywhere to "decentralize," writ large. In Canada's case, this takes the form of federal *downsizing* (reduction of the federal civil service by 45,000 jobs), of *devolution* to markets (privatization, deregulation and contracting out) and of *decentralization* (the Canada Health and Social Transfer). In Australia, the emphasis is on devolution of power to markets. Indeed, as my later paper notes, the Commonwealth government has engineered a competitive initiative that requires the states to devolve powers to markets as well (e.g., enhancing competition for the state utilities — electricity, gas, and water). In lieu of Canadian-style decentralization, the Commonwealth government is instead bringing the states more into decision-making at the centre. One of the vehicles for this is executive federalism. Arguably, it is now the Australians rather than the Canadians who are perfecting executive federalism as part of the art of federal governance. The main point, however, is that Australia is not undergoing Canadian-style decentralization.

The final observation is at the same time the most important and the most speculative. How are the forces of global integration influencing the nature of these two federal systems? As I document later in this volume, the provincial/regional economies of Canada are increasingly integrating north-south. What is occurring in Australia is that the states are developing quite different relationships to each other and to the outside world. Perth and Western Australia, for example, are rapidly expanding their international linkages, via increasing export surpluses, with little change in their economic linkages with the rest of the Australian states. In this sense, Western Australia may not differ much from British Columbia.

The essential comparative point is that Canada appears to be accommodating this via decentralization — allowing the provinces greater leeway to pursue their economic fortunes in terms of a regional-international interface. The challenge here is at the same time to maintain an internal social union.

For its part, Australia is nothing if not a social union. But with the income-distribution implications of globalization (income polarization and the disappearing middle class) its social union may be in trouble. Moreover, the inherent centralization of Australia may present impediments to the variety of ways in which the states are integrating with each other and internationally. If Canada has too much in the way of competitive federalism, Australia probably has too little.

Conclusions

This analysis was motivated by the fact that regional disparities in Australia appear to be far narrower than those of Canada. In turn, this must have some implications for or about the nature of economic space in the two countries. Accordingly, the analysis then delved into a comparison of various policy and institutional differences between Canada and Australia. In terms of the papers that follow, most of which focus on specific areas, the hope is that my focus on aspects of the comparative economic space will provide a broader framework within which the papers can be assessed and appreciated.

Appendix: Regional Disparities in Australia and Canada

GDP Disparity Relatives

Tables 2.1 and 2.2 present 1991 data on regional disparity "relatives" for the Australian states and Canadian provinces respectively. Underpinning the first four columns in each table is the following identity:

$$Y/P \equiv Y/E \times E/LF \times LF/P \qquad (1)$$

where Y/P = gross domestic (provincial/state) product per capita;

Y/E = gross domestic product per employed person, E;

E/LF = the employment rate, where LF is the labour force. This equals unity minus the unemployment rate, expressed relative to the national average value of E/LF;

LF/P = the labour force as a proportion of the total population. Essentially this is the product of the participation rate, LF/LFA (where LFA is the labour-force-age population) and the inverse of the dependency ratio, LFA/P (where the difference between LFA and P relates to those not of labour-force age, e.g. the children and the elderly).

The figures in these four columns are not raw data. Rather they are "relatives" or percentages of the all-provinces or all-states averages. Given that equation (1) is an identity, the value for Y/E has been calculated residually in both tables. Note that finally, that equation (1) is formulated in such a way that the greater the values in columns (2) through (4), *ceteris paribus*, the larger will be the value of GDP per capita (Y/P) in column (1). Thus, the larger is income per employed person (Y/E), the larger is the employment rate (E/LF), and the larger is the labour force as a percentage of total population (LF/P), the larger will be GDP per capita (Y/E).

Focussing on column (1) of both tables, one is immediately struck by these minimal variations across Australian states relative to Canadian provinces in terms of GDP-per-capita relatives. The high/low ratio for the six Australian states is 1.30 or 130 percent (with Victoria on the high end and Tasmania on the low end). This is in sharp contrast to the 179 percent high/low figure for Canada (with Alberta on the high end and Prince Edward Island on the low end, although Newfoundland would do as well on the low

Table 2.1
Regional Disparity Relatives
Australia 1991

	(1) Y/P	(2) Y/E	(3) E/LF	(4) LF/P	(5) HDI/Y	(6) HDI/P	(7) A.W.E.
New South Wales	1.035	1.047	1.008	0.981	1.035	1.018	1.022
Victoria	1.053	1.051	0.991	1.010	0.984	1.043	1.008
Queensland	0.888	0.891	0.989	1.008	1.001	0.891	0.931
South Australia	0.883	0.889	0.990	0.974	1.048	0.926	0.952
Western Australia	1.037	1.020	0.981	1.036	0.858	0.889	1.005
Tasmania	0.810	0.850	0.982	0.970	1.061	0.859	0.968
Northern Territory	1.224	1.154	1.002	1.059	0.841	1.030	1.153
Australian Capital Territory	1.193	1.028	1.032	1.125	1.020	1.217	1.122
Australia	1.00	1.00	1.00	1.00	1.00	1.00	1.00
Australia (raw data)	$21,753	$49,464	0.905	0.486	0.64	$13,923	$494
High/Low[1]	1.30	1.24	1.03	1.07	1.24	1.21	1.10
High/Low[2]	1.51	1.36	1.05	1.16	1.26	1.42	1.31

Notes:
1. for the six states.
2. for the six states and two territories.

Sources: ABS, *The Labour Force, Australia* (July 1991), 6203.0; *Australian National Accounts, 1990-91, State Accounts,* 5220.0; *Estimated Resident Population by Sex and Age, States and Territories of Australia* (June 1990 and Preliminary June 1991), 3201.1; *Distribution and Composition of Employees, Earnings and Hours, Australia* (May 1991), 6306.0.

side). If the territories are included in the Australian data, the disparities are considerably larger - 151 percent. Intriguingly, this arises because the Northern Territory weighs in with the highest, not the lowest, Y/P. Unfortunately, I have not included the two Canadian territories (Yukon and the Northwest Territories) in Table 2.2. However, given that the equalization formula for these two territories is many times more generous than that for the provinces, they would also not be on the low end in terms of column (1).[1]

In terms of the components of Y/P, the evidence for Newfoundland, for example, indicates that its low value for Y/P arises because it has low values for *all* of Y/E, E/LF and LF/P. In other words, while Newfoundland's value for "income per employed person" is a fairly respectable 85 percent of the national average, its value for Y/P falls to 64 percent because it also has the lowest relative employment rate and the highest dependency ratio (lowest value for LF/P). Indeed, all five provinces east of Ontario (the top five

---

1. Newfoundland, the poorest province, received $1,524 per capita in equalization for 1991/92. The comparable figures for the Yukon and Northwest Territories were $8,170 and $14,690 per capita respectively (Courchene, 1994, Table 14).

Table 2.2
Regional Disparity Relatives
Canada 1991

	(1) Y/P	(2) Y/E	(3) E/LF	(4) LF/P	(5) PDI/Y	(6) PDI/P	(7) A.W.E.	(8) T/WS
Newfoundland	0.64	0.85	0.91	0.82	1.21	0.78	0.94	2.20
Prince Edward Island	0.63	0.71	0.93	0.96	1.24	0.79	0.81	1.92
Nova Scotia	0.78	0.86	0.98	0.92	1.08	0.84	0.90	1.40
New Brunswick	0.75	0.87	0.97	0.88	1.08	0.82	0.90	1.50
Quebec	0.91	0.95	0.98	0.97	1.00	0.91	0.98	1.19
Ontario	1.10	1.05	1.01	1.04	1.01	1.12	1.05	0.80
Manitoba	0.85	0.86	1.02	0.98	1.04	0.88	0.90	1.19
Saskatchewan	0.80	0.81	1.03	0.96	1.02	0.83	0.88	1.47
Alberta	1.13	1.04	1.02	1.06	0.89	1.01	1.00	0.84
British Columbia	1.03	1.02	1.00	1.01	0.99	1.03	1.01	0.98
Canada	1.00	1.00	1.00	1.00	1.00	1.00	1.00	1.00
Canada (raw data)	$25,156	$55,040	0.897	0.509	0.69	$17,385	$531	0.29
High/Low	1.79	1.48	1.13	1.29	1.39	1.44	1.30	2.75

Source: Statistics Canada, various publications.

provinces in Table 2.2) have values for columns (2) to (4) that are all below the national average. For Australia, this is true for South Australia and Tasmania, but the deviations below the average for these states are really quite minimal for columns (3) and (4).

The generalization applicable to Canada is that there is much less disparity in Y/E than there is in Y/P, because much of the disparity in Y/P arises from high unemployment and high dependency rates. These latter two categories of relatives are remarkably similar across Australian states — from the comparable high/low rows, 1.03 and 1.07 for Australian states and 1.13 and 1.29 for the Canadian provinces, or roughly four times as much disparity in Canada.

For the Australian territories, the reason for the high Y/P for the Northern Territory relates primarily to its high income per employed person (115.4 percent of the Australian average) and for the Australian Capital Territory it relates to its low dependency rate or high value of LF/P (112.5 percent of the national average).

These data relate to a single point in time — 1991. Had 1990 been chosen as the reference date, for example, British Columbia would have come off much better because its unemployment rate nearly doubled over the early 1990s. But Ontario would have looked much more rosy as well, given that the recession in both countries took a heavy toll on the industrial regions.

Because these tables are a snapshot in time, they say little or nothing about "convergence" over time of regional disparities. Harris and Harris (1993), for example, demonstrate that Australian disparities are positively related to the business cycle. The major Canadian story, however, is one of longstanding regional disparities in the sense that if one were to rework this table for 1980 a similar pattern would appear.

In order to make some absolute comparisons, the aggregate "raw" data for these countries appear in the row prior to the high/low comparisons. Thus, converted to Australian dollars at the then (1990) current exchange rate (roughly $A112 equals $C100), the Y/P for Canada would be just over $28,000 or nearly one-third larger than Australian Y/P. (These differences are much less today because the Australian and Canadian dollars are much closer to parity with each other). These raw data also reveal that overall unemployment rates were quite similar in both countries in 1990 - 9.5 percent for Australia and 10.3 percent in Canada. This makes the fourfold difference in the high/low ratios of E/LF, namely 1.03 and 1.13, even more startling.

Personal Income Relatives

Column (6) of the tables presents relatives on per capita personal disposable income, PDI/P, for Canada and per capita household disposable income, HDI/P, for Australia, where the assumption is that PDI and HDI are roughly similar concepts. Once again, one can fall back on an identity (utilizing HDI to encompass PDI):

$$\underline{HDI/P} = Y/P \times HDI/Y, \qquad (2)$$

where HDI/Y is the ratio of personal income to GDP, expressed relative to the national average value.

Thus column (6) equals column (1) multiplied by column (5). What emerges very clearly from these column (6) figures is that the Canadian disparities in PDI/P are much narrower than those for Y/P (1.44 vs 1.79) while Australian disparities in HDI/P are reduced to a lesser extent both absolutely and proportionally (1.21 vs 1.30). As an important aside, the reason that Western Australia is well above the national average for Y/P but well below the national average for HDI/P is that, except for dividends to domestic residents, resource profits do not flow through to individuals and, therefore, to HDI. Nor do crown royalties. At the other end of the spectrum, the Australian Capital Territory records a 1.217 value for HDI/P. This is what one would expect since the overwhelming proportion of Australian Capital Territory income is in the form of wages and salaries which is part (after tax) of HDI. Indeed, the high/low ratio for HDI/P including the territories is 1.42 - above the Canadian range, although the comparison is flawed because the Canadian table excludes the two Canadian territories.

What all of this means is that Canada has a relatively more generous system of federal transfers to individuals, particularly to individuals in the poorer provinces. (Note that transfers to persons enter PDI or HDI but not Y.) This is evident from columns (5), HDI/Y or PDI/Y, where the relatives for Prince Edward Island and Newfoundland are 1.24 and 1.21 respectively. To emphasize this point, column (8) of Table 2.2 presents data for the ratio of personal transfers to wages and salaries. The relatives for the Atlantic provinces range from 1.40 for Nova Scotia to 2.20 for Newfoundland. Indeed (although not shown in Table 2.2), for at least two provinces (Newfoundland and Prince Edward Island) personal income (household income, in Australian terms) *exceeds* gross provincial product! For no Australian state is this even close to being the case. This is part and parcel of what in Canada has come to be termed "transfer dependency."

The remainder of this appendix will be devoted to focusing, superficially, on the comparative political economics of the two nations with an eye toward rationalizing regional disparity differences. At the outset one must recognize that the provincial/state level may not be the appropriate vantage point for viewing disparities. In a recent paper, Findlay, Wu and Watson (1995) observe that, for China, the economic fortunes of the various provinces are converging, but that the within-province disparities are increasing. More relevant to the present analysis, the Australian National University's Bob Gregory, in an address to the National Press Club in Canberra (April 26, 1995), drew on ongoing research with colleague Boyd Hunter (1995) indicating income disparities *within* Australian cities have increased markedly, indeed alarmingly, over the 1976-1991 period. Both these studies suggest the possibility that the real disparity story for Australia may not appear in Table 2.1 but rather *within* each of the states. Presumably, however, this would also apply to the provincial data in Table 2.2.

As stated above, the reason for the narrower Australian disparities is that economic activity is distributed more equally across Australian economic space. An important reason for this relative lack of disparity is the fact that the richer Australian states cannot fully "capitalize" this advantage in higher wages and/or better state government services because the states have a very limited access to taxation (see Part III below), the operations of the centralized industrial relations system generates relatively equal wage grids across the country and even applies to state governments, and the centralized operations of social security, including what Canadians would call social assistance or welfare, means that the less fortunate levels of the Australian population are treated identically, regardless of their state of residence.

Canada differs markedly in terms of these last three elements. In effect the federal government has channelled massive transfers into the poorer provinces, particularly to the four Atlantic provinces and Quebec. Consider the operations of Canada's Unemployment Insurance (UI) program, a program that does not even exist in Australia. Self-employed fishermen are eligible for unemployment insurance in the off-season, but not self-employed farmers. The result is obvious: the prairie farms have increased in size manyfold while much of the Atlantic fishing remains in the old one-person/one boat tradition. More generally, the qualifying period for UI eligibility is only ten weeks in the Atlantic provinces and this generates benefits for the remaining 42 weeks of the year.[2] This has become so entrenched as a lifestyle that many companies have accepted as "normal" that they will have a rotating ten-week labour force. In 1991, UI benefits in Newfoundland exceeded contributions by a factor of 4.35, for a net inflow of $1,300 per capita (Courchene, 1994, Table 8). Not surprisingly, what has evolved over time is a tendency for wages in these provinces to rise toward the national average (from column (7) of Table 2.2, the average weekly wage in Newfoundland is 94 percent of the national average whereas Y/P is only 64 percent), *and* for unemployment to remain very high as well (E/LF is 91 percent of the national average for Newfoundland whereas the lowest relative for an Australian state is 98.1 percent). This is the "transfer dependency" syndrome. In effect, these entrenched disparities in the Atlantic provinces are the result of a *policy-induced equilibrium*. Canada could afford this in the "good old days" because, like Australia, it was living off resource rents and behind protective walls and also because these provinces were small in terms of the overall population. With the collapse of industrial Ontario, this policy is progressively no longer viable and Canadians are currently wrestling with rethinking and reworking their east-west social contract.

Australia has not fallen into this version of the "regional" transfer dependency trap. However, it may well have fallen into another version — namely a "national" transfer of policy dependency trap. From its lofty perch atop the global Y/P rankings earlier this century, Australia has fallen way

---

2. These were the UI parameters in force when Table 2.2 was constructed. Recently, the minimum entry requirement has been raised to 12 weeks which, in a region with an unemployment rate above 16 percent, will lead to 32 weeks of UI benefits. In a low unemployment region (less than six per cent) it takes 20 weeks to qualify and in order to receive 32 weeks of benefits a person must have worked for 48 weeks (Courchene, 1994, Table 37).

back. On the other hand, despite its regional transfer dependency problem, Canada has moved up the ladder. Indeed, the raw data in the tables suggest a rather wide divergence between Australia and Canada in terms of per capita income and wage aggregates. Arguably, the legacy of Deakinism (protection, national wage bargaining and patterning and egalitarianism) has so rigidified the Australian economy that it has not been able to maintain its position in the pecking order of nations.

3

The Challenges of Globalisation: Lessons from Australian Experience

Cliff Walsh

Although this project has a particular focus on fiscal federalism — and on the nature of intergovernmental relations that shape and reshape fiscal arrangements — it is important to view these issues within the context of the broader challenges that globalisation poses for economic and political structures and relationships.

At the very broadest level, the challenges of globalisation to national and regional decision-making include three particularly important issues:

1. Improved international competitiveness is becoming increasingly essential to the growth of national and regional economies. This requires new approaches to economic policy, business policy, and even the involvement of governments in the development of best practice by business. New approaches to social policy are also required as a result of fundamental changes to the economic framework within which governments are operating, but these new policies have not yet been designed: indeed, they have barely been discussed.

2. Policy autonomy — economic and social — for national and state level governments is now more constrained by the influence of international market reactions, the role of international institutions and so forth.

In fact, policy sometimes is now driven by international institutions —
for example, in relation to the treatment of indigenous peoples,
environmental management issues and such where the capacity of
groups to appeal to the international community through international
organisations has sometimes completely reshaped national or regional
policies.

3. Democratic participation by national and regional citizens/voters is
being challenged by increasing internationalisation of decision making.
Treaties, agreements, conventions and such like, entered into collectively
by national governments, pass power to international organisations to a
significant extent. Individual voters in countries that have participated
in these treaties, agreements or conventions do not have direct access to
the international institutions: in fact, their interests often are claimed to
be represented by interest groups which may themselves be non-
democratic in composition, structure, membership, and so on.

Within these broad challenges, there are specific implications for
economic and fiscal policy in a globalised world. Among many areas that
are in need of reform, or at least review, some of the most obvious are:

- governments already have been forced by external pressures, including
  participation in international agreements, to reform or reduce their
  external barriers to trade;
- in addition, and particularly significant to federal systems of
  government where decision-making powers may be sub-divided,
  governments are also being obliged to focus on the importance of
  reforming or reducing internal barriers to trade — on the need for
  strengthening the nature of economic union, seeking to achieve a single
  economic market by reforming regulatory and legislative frameworks;
- there is also an increasing focus and increasing need among
  governments — especially, again in federal systems where powers are
  divided —to restructure their tax systems to be more growth and trade
  supportive: where they fail to do so, the erosion of tax bases that apply
  to mobile transactions, factors of production or outputs, for example,
  will eventually force governments to rethink their attitudes towards their
  tax policies;
- governments are also having to more sharply focus on the performance
  of business enterprises owned by the public sector, especially those
  providing key services such as power, water, transport and so on: this
  includes putting them on a more competitive and commercial basis as

suppliers of essential infrastructure services, subjecting them to benchmarking, subjecting them to competition policy frameworks, and such; and
- improving the efficiency and effectiveness of public sector service delivery is being re-emphasised by the forces of globalisation, to ensure that the public sector call on productive resources is minimised and also to ensure that social objectives are met within contracting fiscal resources: outsourcing of service management or delivery to private sector organisations, strengthened performance orientation within public sector organisations, comparative benchmarking and the like, are all being required of public sector institutions in order to ensure that services are delivered as efficiently and effectively as possible.

These, of course, represent only some of the very many challenges to governments and to citizens — challenges that are particularly strong within federal systems — arising out of the pressures of globalisation, of increased competitiveness, world wide. But they are indicative of some of the major changes facing all nations, and federations in particular.

Lessons from Australian Experience?

In what follows, I point to some of the lessons that may be of relevance to Canada from Australian processes established to deal with some of the implications of globalisation for intergovernmental relations and arrangements.

In doing so, I should preface my remarks with the observation that while learning from the experiences of others and examining the processes by which others have achieved change or reform often can be very valuable, there are substantial dangers in what might be termed constitution shopping, institution shopping and process shopping. It needs to be emphasised that history, values and culture, matter very much to the outcomes of, or the workability of, constitutional and institutional arrangements, and processes for reform of them, in different societies.

To give some context to this particular observation, I might point out that the Australian Constitution, adopted in 1901, was very much US-style in its articulation of the division and sharing of powers. That is, the federal (Commonwealth) government's powers were established as largely concurrent with the states and the residual powers are defined as resting with the states. However, in those areas where the Commonwealth does have concurrent powers, its legislation ultimately is paramount; and the Commonwealth also has a grant power, under Section 96 of the Constitution, which enables it to enter into the fields that are exclusively those of the states by setting conditions on its provision of financial support for State activities in those fields. High Court decisions — especially, for example, in relation to external affairs — have been supportive of the extension of the Commonwealth's legislative role into areas that appear to be the exclusive province of the states where the Commonwealth has entered into international agreements. In addition, the States are precluded by High Court interpretations of Section 90 of the Constitution from imposing sales taxes, and the Commonwealth has come to dominate completely income tax.

As a consequence of the particular history, the particular culture, the particular economic and fiscal developments in Australia, a distinctly different pattern of the distribution of revenue-raising powers and expenditure decision-making has evolved in Australia from that which is evident in the United States. In Australia, the degree of revenue-raising centralisation is the greatest of all among the mature federations — the degree of vertical fiscal imbalance is very substantial, despite the fact that Australia has a Constitution like that in the United States which might have been expected to maintain a degree of decentralisation of decision making in Australia similar to that in the United States.

On the other hand, although there is a very strong appearance of federal dominance in the Australian federal system, in reality, the federal government, despite capturing substantial revenue-raising powers from the states, has found it difficult to completely dominate: even grant-cutting as a way of attempting to control the expenditure of the states, and to control economic policy within Australia, has its political limits. An important aspect of an understanding of the workings of the Australian federal system relevant to this last observation is that while the political parties in Australia are at one level national — the major parties in federal parliament are also the major parties in all of the state parliaments — their internal structures are essentially federal: that is, the federal parties are essentially confederations or federations of the individual state parties, and much of the constraint that applies to the federal government when it is tempted to utilize its fiscal dominance to achieve its way actually comes from resistance within its own political party to decisions that would have significant impacts on political decision-making within the states.

With those remarks as a preface and a warning about comparing constitutions, institutions and processes, let me now turn to offer an overview of the reform processes, and the outcomes of those processes, that have been employed in Australia in recent years and which may be relevant to Canada.

Hawke's New Federalism

Beginning in 1990, then Labor Prime Minister Bob Hawke initiated a major review of Australia's intergovernmental arrangements. At the time he proposed this review as a cooperative process between the Commonwealth and the leaders of all state and territory governments, the Prime Minister mentioned the possibility that constitutional reform might be brought onto the agenda eventually, too, but he emphasised that the first and critical step was to work within the existing constitution to improve intergovernmental arrangements, processes and outcomes. In proposing that this be a review directed towards making the federal system work better, Hawke became the first Australian Labor Prime Minister to popularise and promote Australian federalism, rather than seeking to destroy it.

Quite why Bob Hawke chose to initiate a process of reforming intergovernmental relations — a reform process that contained many dangers as well as abundant opportunities — remains something of a matter for speculation (Fletcher and Walsh, 1992). The objectives of the review of Australian federalism initiated by Hawke, broadly speaking, were articulated as

- to create a truly single national economy to improve Australia's international competitiveness by, for example, reforming Commonwealth and state regulatory systems impacting on the mobility of goods, services, labour and capital, and improving the competitiveness and efficiency of public sector business enterprises;
- to improve the quality and delivery of public sector services by reviewing and realigning roles and responsibilities of all governments in Australia in order to increase well-being and improve social justice, as well as to release resources to more productive uses; and
- to review federal fiscal arrangements, with a view especially to seeking to reduce the proportion of state funds provided in the form of tied grants and possibly also leading to proposals that would reduce the extent of vertical fiscal imbalance.

After a long period of unilaterally applying fiscal pressure to the states, the Commonwealth came to see an opportunity to encompass the states cooperatively in achieving structural reforms in the Australian economy that lay outside Commonwealth jurisdiction, but which were important to its economic and political objectives, including to achieve increased competitiveness of the Australian economy in international markets. It also saw the capacity through these processes to encompass the states in the promotion of social reforms in the delivery of education services, housing services, health services and the like.

By the same token, the states saw an opportunity, through participation in this process, to regain greater control over major policy areas such as housing, education and health, which they regarded as lying essentially within their sphere of constitutional power, and greater control over the resources necessary to fund them. They also saw that a mutually supportive approach to the reform of government business enterprises and state regulatory regimes would enable them to achieve a greater degree of reform at a lesser political pain.

The process by which the Hawke new federalism proceeded was explicitly cooperative. Although it was initiated by the Commonwealth, it was neither completely top down nor completely bottom up: all spheres of government participated in what turned out to be a remarkable cooperative exercise in which even local government was given a role as a participant, represented by the President of the Australian Local Government Association.

A new intergovernmental forum was established, an on-going Special Premiers' Conference, that met as required to establish the agenda and priorities, to oversee the processes, to deal with key issues, and to try to ensure that a whole of government and whole of national perspective was maintained within each constituent government and between them.[1] This Special Premiers' Conference series, in which the heads of governments were the principal participants, was supported by a senior officials' group, comprised of the heads of the premier's departments or Cabinet departments in each of the states and territories and at Commonwealth level, who provided support for and coordination of the process, maintained the pace of work, and undertook key pieces of analysis.[2] At least to some extent, the traditional Ministerial Councils, established to provide forums for Commonwealth-state coordination in functional areas, were sidelined or made more subordinate to heads of governments than previously. This, of course, created substantial tensions from ministers and bureaucrats at all levels of government, who saw their traditional power bases being undermined. At the beginning of the process, one of the premiers, alert to the

---

1. In Australia, for historical reasons, the meetings of what Canadians would call First Ministers have retained the name Premiers' Conferences. Even though, since 1992, what Hawke called Special Premiers' Conferences have been renamed as meetings of the Council of Australian Governments (COAG), the annual meeting of leaders to deal with financial matters is still known as the Premiers' Conference.
2. Since the leaders group was referred to as the HOGS (Heads of Governments), the senior officials group came to be known as the PIGLETS!

risks from line ministers and other interest groups, referred to the possibility that "the empires would strike back" and, indeed, they eventually did.

Nonetheless, over a period that, in the event, turned out to last only 18 months, substantial outcomes were achieved by the Hawke new federalism initiative. Illustrative examples of the outcomes might be usefully categorised under a number of separate headings, even though the divisions are to some extent arbitrary.

Improved IGR Processes

Aspects of the processes by which the Hawke new federalism initiative was pursued, and of the outcomes to which it gave rise, can be seen effectively as having made the intergovernmental relations process as a whole work considerably better. The fact that the Special Premiers' Conferences, with all political leaders involved, drove reform cooperatively gave an entirely different tone to intergovernmental relations as a whole in Australia. In fact, the Special Premiers' Conferences made decisions that helped to make the traditional annual Premiers' Conferences work better in dealing with financial issues. There was agreement, for example, that the States would receive early warning of the Commonwealth's financial offer to them, and more cooperative approaches to fiscal issues by Commonwealth and state treasuries were agreed upon.

At a slightly different level, but still relating to IGR processes, we saw the emergence of a number of new intergovernmental agreements. The first, and arguably still one of the most significant, was an Intergovernmental Agreement on the Environment — an agreement between the Commonwealth and the states about what their roles and responsibilities were in environmental matters, which attempted to accommodate the fact that environmental issues can be variously local, regional, national and international and require different approaches to different issues.

Regulatory Reform

Under the Hawke new federalism, a number of regulatory regimes where differences existed between the states were tackled and substantial progress was made in achieving a greater degree of consistency, though not necessarily uniformity, between the states. The principal of these was the agreement by the states (if needs be, doing it without participation of the Commonwealth) to enact legislation to provide mutual recognition of product standards and of occupational licensing and professional qualifications. Although it took some time to get participation by all states in the relevant legislation, it now has been enacted throughout Australia with the states adopting legislation which mirrors a legislative framework mutually agreed between them and initially passed by the Commonwealth Parliament. Other aspects of regulatory reform included agreement to establish a new regulatory framework, and a new structure of fees, for the national road transport system and so on.

Government Business Enterprise Reform

The Hawke new federalism process also established at least the beginnings of a substantial new approach to reform of public sector business enterprises across all levels of government. Perhaps most striking of all was an agreement by a number of states to contribute their non-metropolitan railway assets into the establishment of a National Rail Corporation, in which the Commonwealth also took an equity position and which is managed jointly by the Commonwealth and the states. This is designed, for the first time, to provide a national system to improve the efficiency of the operation of freight rail freight services rail throughout Australia. Equally significant, although still (several years after initial agreement) not formally operational, was an agreement to establish, at least among the majority of states, a National Electricity Grid. A national grid management authority was established in 1991 (again with Commonwealth participation) and, progressively, that management authority and the state electricity authorities and other agencies have been working towards initiation of the national grid, with New South Wales, Victoria and South Australia as initial partners, but with proposals that both Queensland and Tasmania also be eventually interconnected to and participants in the grid.

Progress was also started in a number of other areas where government business enterprises had a strong role and monopolistic influence — for example, gas, water and ports — and monitoring and benchmarking exercises were established at a national level for government enterprises throughout all states: the Industry Commission has been given an ongoing role in producing monitoring and benchmarking reports across all government business enterprises, and the Bureau of Industry Economics has been engaged in producing studies of particular areas of government business enterprise where reforms would be of particular value.

General Public Sector Services

Despite the inclusion of issues concerning the roles and responsibilities of different governments in service delivery as one of the major agenda items established by Hawke and the premiers, with emphasis given from the very start to public sector housing, health, education and so on, little progress was made during the Hawke period (and, as we will see later, even subsequently) on resolution of these issues. One area where there was agreement that was achieved effectively as a result of the processes established by Hawke, though it was finalised only later, was in the area of vocational education and training, where it was agreed that an Australian National Training Authority (ANTA), jointly appointed by the Commonwealth and the states and territories, be established to coordinate approaches to the development of new vocational education and training curricula to help to determine funding priorities and to provide a mechanism through which the Commonwealth would distribute growth funds to support the vocational education and training activities of the states.

Fiscal Issues

Again, despite some prominence given to fiscal issues in the original articulation of the objectives of the Hawke new federalism processes, little progress was made in relation to restructuring Australia's federal fiscal system. Despite a clear understanding between the Commonwealth and the states that a major objective of the exercise was to try to reduce the proportion of grants to the states that were "tied" (i.e., conditional), no progress was made on this issue. A report on roles and responsibilities and tied grants for the Special Premiers' Conference was shelved without ever having been delivered to the premiers by the time the processes came to an end. Moreover, despite the release of a Treasury Officers' report that was supportive of reform to achieve a greater degree of vertical fiscal balance (a report that was supported by the Commonwealth Treasury), there was no effective progress on reducing vertical fiscal imbalance except that, at the very beginning of the process, as a sign of its good will and good intentions, the Commonwealth did agree to transfer a form of taxation of financial transactions, called the Bank Accounts Debits tax, to the states.

In fairness, it ought to be said that although no progress was specifically made in relation to reducing tied grants, there were moves being made toward the reform of tied grants themselves through a greater emphasis on performance or outcomes rather than on inputs or specific quantitative financial requirements on the states. But the first of the major reforms here — a new program called Building Better Cities — actually antagonised the states because the Commonwealth announced it as an untied capital program. The program had so many conditions attached to it that it was clear to all it was unquestionably a tied grant program.

It also needs to be conceded that the greater degree of interaction and cooperation between the Treasury departments across the states and with the Commonwealth saw the beginnings of some processes that have subsequently resulted in a greater degree of attention to the coordination of fiscal policy and improved procedures through the Australian Loan Council for approving and reporting on levels of borrowings by various governments.

General Benefits

One of the most significant benefits from the Hawke new federalism process arguably was that the states, in effect, rediscovered their role in the federation — rediscovered their potency if they acted collectively in their dealings with the Commonwealth. Indeed, in the end, when the process that Hawke had set up was put under threat by Paul Keating (a then former Commonwealth Treasurer), the states and territories actually agreed to hold a meeting among themselves in which they advanced a number of the items on the Special Premiers' Conference agenda, including a decision to go ahead with mutual recognition. The meeting also set out a series of principles which the states and territories had decided were appropriate, for discussion purposes at least, on how decisions should be made about roles and responsibilities; and state leaders continued to press the Commonwealth for greater access to taxing powers to create a higher degree of fiscal balance in the federation.

Unfortunately, however, having started in a period when there appeared to be a fair degree of political stability in Australia within the states and within the Commonwealth government, an unstable political atmosphere was established in the federal parliamentary Labor Party when former Treasurer Keating made clear his determination to seek the Prime Ministership. In that atmosphere, the process of negotiating the new federalism deal with the states contributed to the downfall of Hawke and his replacement by Keating on a platform that was antagonistic to Hawke's processes and particularly antagonistic to some of his objectives, such as the reduction of vertical fiscal imbalance. Indeed, it was a speech by challenger Keating to the National Press Club about the dangers of Hawke's new federalism for Commonwealth policy-making power that led, in effect, to an end of the Hawke-initiated processes and eventually to the Hawke Prime Ministership.

Intergovernmental Relations Under Keating

When Keating took over the Prime Ministership in December 1991, he spent several months preparing a major statement under the title *One Nation* as his principal initial contribution to a redirection of the approach of the Commonwealth government. The *One Nation* statement was an economic plan drawn up by the Commonwealth in consultation, but not cooperation, with the states. Its emphasis was on the need to build or rebuild the nation's economic infrastructure and to redesign labour market and training programs to improve Australia's competitiveness.

One Nation was, in fact, the first of what would become a series of major economic and other statements that have become characteristic of the Keating government in action. The statements, and the preparation for them, have been used by the Commonwealth to discover, shape and reshape its role in developing "national policy," by which Paul Keating has always meant Commonwealth domination of policy formulation.

While Keating might have wished he could avoid re-engaging, and consulting and cooperating with, the political leaders of the states and territories, the old intergovernmental relations system in which the Commonwealth attempted to behave unilaterally in a dominant role was now gone. The new system of intergovernmental relations initiated in the Hawke regime proved to be highly resilient: the premiers had rediscovered their place in the federation as a whole and federalism had become part of the public agenda for business and community groups as well as for politicians and political scientists. Eventually, in May 1992, a Heads of Government meeting was called by Prime Minister Keating, at which it was agreed to establish a new ongoing forum for peak level interactions between the Commonwealth and the states, a forum under the name of the Council of Australian Governments (COAG). This new forum, and the support apparatus that went with it in the form of high level working groups of officials, is similar in appearance to the Hawke process of Special Premiers' Conferences and, at one level, the overall objectives of the processes established are very similar. But, in operation, COAG and the processes involved have been much more top down, much more Commonwealth dominated, Commonwealth driven, in line with the character of the Prime Minister. Importantly, too, in functional areas, the roles of Ministerial Councils have experienced something of a revival compared with the approaches adopted under Hawke.

In effect, what Keating had come to recognize as Prime Minister was not only that, as a practical matter of day-to-day politics, he could not operate without including the states and their leaders in the process, but also that much of the policy framework that he wanted to work on, in the interests of improving Australia's international competitiveness and changing the nature of service delivery in a number of important social areas, was under the control of the states — so much so that they could not be ignored or simply brow-beaten into change.

During his second term in government, Keating produced another in the series of major statements, this one under the title *Working Nation*. This document showed his government gaining a realistic appreciation of the federal system, of the Commonwealth's role in it and the power the Commonwealth could exert. Clearly evident in that statement is a balance between a further direct extension of the Commonwealth's direct administrative and policy influence in regional Australia and the need to link with the states and their agencies in implementing the Commonwealth's employment, training and business development agendas.

The COAG process that was established by Paul Keating has, over the period of his Prime Ministership, produced a number of significant outcomes. For example, one of the earliest issues tackled by the premiers related not so much to Australia's international competitiveness as to the issue of Austalia's indigenous peoples. The issue of native title, following the so called Mabo decision of the High Court, was discussed and debated extensively with the premiers — in fact, somewhat acrimoniously debated with the premiers. This may have been an unfortunate start for Keating's COAG process. The issues involved in native title — which, in effect, created the capacity for Australia's Aboriginal communities to claim a form of title over extensive areas of Crown land and possibly over areas leased for pastoral and mining purposes — inevitably involved conflict between the Commonwealth and the states. While the peak forum of intergovernmental relations was inevitably the place in which resolution of this conflict had to be sought, for this issue to be high on the agenda early perhaps set a pattern for relations which swayed the behaviour of the Prime Minister and the premiers in COAG context towards the more conflictual end of the spectrum. Nonetheless, even if with some difficulty, and probably with more difficulty than Hawke might have had in achieving the outcomes, a number of significant outcomes have been produced and achieved.

For example, the coordination of increased expenditure on vocational and educational training and the establishment of the Australian National Training Authority was finally negotiated and set in place under Keating. More importantly, and in the end, more significantly was the fact that a National Competition Policy was discussed and agreement was eventually reached, over a lengthy series of meetings between the premiers and the Prime Minister. This National Competition Policy involves agreement that state government business enterprises and other agencies, and unincorporated enterprises trading exclusively within state boundaries (which would not otherwise fall under jurisdiction of the Commonwealth government) would be included in the scope of a revamped Trade Practices Act (which proscribes anti-competitive *conduct*) and a revamped Trade Practices Commission (renamed as the Australian Competition and Consumers Commission); and that a new overarching body, the National Competition Council, would be established to undertake analysis and provide guidance and advice.

As a result of the debate about the implementation of a national competition policy, it was eventually agreed also that a system of rewards or potential penalties would be put in place in exchange for the states' agreement to participate. A major analysis of the benefits of national competition policy reforms undertaken by the Industry Commission indicated that there were substantial revenue benefits to all governments but that the bulk of them, under Australia's current division of taxing powers, would accrue to the Commonwealth government despite the fact that the vast majority of the reform effort and the political pain would be borne by the states. As part of the implementation deal, the Commonwealth agreed that it would make additional transfers to the states, rising eventually to $600 million a year extra between them, as the states completed certain steps in the development of implementation strategies for the national competition policy.

Agreement to implement a National Competition Policy Agreement is a remarkable achievement, although the style in which it was achieved again reflects more the nature of processes under the Keating government than the sort of approach to intergovernment relations that had become familiar under Bob Hawke. Several of the meetings of the Premiers and Prime Minister ended acrimoniously rather than with friendly agreements to undertake further work collaboratively. The further work was done, nonetheless, at official level, but even at that level it was clear that the Prime Minister was strongly influencing the capacity of senior Commonwealth public servants to even discuss some options for dealing with some of the difficult issues that were involved as far as the states were concerned. At the end of the process, when agreement had been reached, the Prime Minister could not resist saying to the premiers and territory leaders (even within the confines of the cabinet room where the issues had been discussed behind closed doors) words to the effect that "the Commonwealth is the leader in microeconomic reform and the states merely camp followers."

Nonetheless, agreement to a national competition policy was a major achievement — one about which all political leaders in Australia could feel a substantial degree of pride. Related to it, but in effect continuing the reform thrusts that had been established under Bob Hawke in relation to the creation of a more competitive, single national economy, further progress also was promoted in electricity reform, with more impetus given towards the establishment of the National Grid; in the reform of the gas industry and third-party access to gas pipelines; and in relation to road transport and to water supply. In all cases, the Commonwealth and the states were establishing not only new thrusts in relation to the behaviour of the public utilities or authorities involved but also new mechanisms for monitoring of processes and of progress in changing the behaviour of these organisations.

Substantial work had been undertaken, for example, on benchmarking and comparing the performance of different organisations.

In relation to public sector services more generally, however, reforms in intergovernmental arrangements still are considerably lagging, even at the end of what now is more than four years of reform effort. Work is being undertaken, again by the Industry Commission, on measuring outputs and outcomes for major social expenditures — education, health, correctional services and so on — that will provide highly valuable information to enable the states to improve the relative efficiency of their service delivery. But in the context of attempting to improve the inter-relationships between the Commonwealth and the states, and to remove unnecessary overlap and rigidities in the design of programs or in formulas for grants, very little progress has yet been made. In part that appears to be the result of the Commonwealth insisting on dominance in the process, as it has been doing, for example, in relation to health. In part, however, it also reflects a lack of urgency being transmitted from the political leaders to their ministers and bureaucrats in particular service delivery areas. Consumed by the core debates about Native Title and National Competition Policy, the leaders have left Ministerial Councils to make slow progress on other areas, such as a new Commonwealth-state agreement on housing that would achieve substantial reforms if and when it is implemented.

In relation to a number of other issues that were on the original agenda, the extent of progress is more difficult to assess fully, but at least impressions can be given. For example, the often repeated objective of achieving a reduction in the proportion of grants that are tied has not resulted in substantial progress overall. While intra-urban and local roads grants have now been largely absorbed into financial assistant grants (general revenue grants), they remain in most cases identified in terms of their purpose: that is, to a substantial extent, they are still tagged as being for roads, even though, in a formal sense, they are no longer strictly required to be spent only on roads. The particularly tricky issue of vertical fiscal imbalance, while it has been raised frequently by the premiers in terms of access to fair shares of revenues, has been largely held off the agenda by Paul Keating's determination that there should be no significant change in the extent of the Commonwealth's dominance of revenues. (In relation to National Competition Policy, this proved to be one of the potential major stumbling blocks: had there been a reasonable sharing arrangement for access to revenues, the question of the imbalance in shares of the revenue benefits from National Competition Policy would not have been the major stumbling block that it proved to be, and a special deal or special agreement about redistributing some of the revenue benefits of Competition Policy would not have been required.)

There has, however, been further progress made on a number of other issues that have significance to the management of economic policy and international competitiveness in a globalised world. In particular, there has been substantial development of what has now come to be known as the *National Fiscal Outlook*. This represents a joint assessment by all Treasuries, state and Commonwealth, of trends expected in outlays, revenues and financing requirements over a three-year projection period for all levels of government, at least at the general government level (that is, excluding the government business enterprise sector). While this document has not yet been used formally or forcefully as a means of achieving changes in likely fiscal outcomes, it certainly has been used as a basis for understanding and approving financing requirements annually. These "approvals" are not binding, but new procedures agreed by the Loan Council provide greater transparency and accountability, including through a requirement that states report variations outside narrow tolerance bands in their borrowing levels. Here exists the potential basis on which a more formal coordinated approach to national fiscal policy could be pursued; and even without the formality of an agreed procedure for determining jointly an appropriate outcome, the information that is provided in these documents certainly has enabled effective external scrutiny of the contributions of different governments to the nation's future borrowing requirements and expenditure levels.

State Responses

The responses of state and territory governments to the style of intergovernment relations at peak level under Paul Keating as Prime Minister have been mixed, but on the whole reflect the states' dissatisfaction with the current way in which intergovernment relations are being conducted by the Commonwealth. Unlike earlier periods, however, the way in which states have responded reflects a greater degree of confidence in their own capacities to shape or reshape the system and a higher level of intellectual input through advisers and others into the states' thinking about intergovernment relations.

Among the more obvious of those responses has been, for example, the establishment of a so called Leaders' Forum. This Forum is explicitly for the state premiers and the territory chief ministers to meet to promote a number of different sorts of issues without the Commonwealth being involved. Some are a matter of them setting their own cooperative agenda for undertaking new approaches to a particular areas of policy in which the Commonwealth is not necessary as a partner. To date, the principal example has been in the joint development by the states and territories of a national crime policy. The premiers have also used the Forum to promote ideas about how the COAG processes should be added to or amended. In this context, perhaps the most notable proposal from the premiers has been that a Treaties Council should be established as a subset of the activities of the COAG to review all treaties which the Commonwealth proposes to sign in future. This would give the states a much more formal and institutionalised input into the discussion of issues that arise from the Commonwealth signing treaties concerning areas of jurisdiction that constitutionally are essentially under the states. The third aspect of the establishment of the Leaders' Forum has been its use by premiers and chief ministers as a mechanism for achieving coordinated approaches between themselves on issues that are on the COAG agenda, where there is some conflict between the states' position(s) and that of the Commonwealth. Here the prime example, arguably, is in relation to the negotiation of national competition policy where, in early 1995, discussions between the premiers and chief ministers on the outstanding issues enabled them to agree on positions which involved modifications to the approaches of some of the states, such that the opportunity of achieving a compromise with the Commonwealth was substantially increased.

A further reflection of the increased maturity of the states' participation in and debate about the intergovernmental relations system, the Australian federal system and their role in it has been an increased level of input through public speeches from state premiers. Here the principal example in the Keating (Labor government) period has perhaps been Queensland (Labor) Premier Wayne Goss, who on several occasions, including in the lead up to a recent state election, has argued that there is a need for the states to be taken seriously as partners in the Australian federation by the Commonwealth government, and that if they are not to be taken seriously they might as well be scrapped. While Goss is clearly somewhat overstating the position, his characterisation of the nature of intergovernmental interactions in Australia as they have emerged under Keating and his repeated emphasis on the importance of establishing principles in guiding decisions about roles and responsibilities in the federal system (based on work undertaken earlier by all of the states and territories) represents and reflects an important development in the intellectual environment in which discussion is occurring about intergovernmental relations in Australia. Notably, part of the most recent contribution by Goss to the debate was a leaking of the results of research which the states and territories had funded between themselves on attitudes towards the federal system among Australians and on areas of the intergovernmental arrangements and the nature of the federation that required significant and serious attention.

The fact that the states have been collaboratively engaged in promoting research on issues such as these is an additional indication of the importance of the way in which the states and territories have now come together: their work on redefining and reasserting their own role in the federation is another valuable result of the establishment of a Leaders' Forum.

Despite all that has been achieved, promoted or induced by the changing character of intergovernmental interactions over the last five years in Australia, there is an important sense in which, as of the second half of 1995, we are waiting for some new developments to help take the processes forward in a more constructive way. With a federal election due soon in Australia at the time of writing, there is an opportunity for some thinking to go on in the major parties about how they do handle the remaining big issues for Australia. These now probably relate primarily to major social policy areas, health in particular, and possibly education, community services and housing, but also, importantly, include the nature of fiscal relationships.

In my view, there is a need and an opportunity now for an agreement to be reached between the Commonwealth and states and territory leaders about the principles by which they are going to manage and approach future intergovernmental processes and intergovernmental arrangements. The principles I have in mind involve both the way in which governments will deal with one another as partners in a federation (emphasising mutual respect, the essential roles of both responsibility-sharing and autonomy the importance of maintaining a capacity for diversity and experimentation as well as the need, sometimes, for greater consistency in policy and regulatory frameworks) and also about how they will decide what are appropriate roles and responsibilities for different spheres of government in relation to different policy areas.

The very process of negotiating an intergovernmental agreement or accord which sets out those principles would make a valuable contribution to improving intergovernmental relations in Australia — giving them a status and demanding a degree of professionalism in their conduct at least as high as is expected of Australia's international relations. Without wishing to be seen as yet another "instant expert" about the problems faced by others, my impression is that Canada may need such an agreement or accord, and an associated agenda for action, at least as badly as does Australia and possibly more so.

Regionalism Revived

A further development in Australia worth at least brief mention in the context of the challenges of globalisation is the emergence (or, rather, re-emergence for the first time since the mid 1970s) of a serious regional policy thrust by the Commonwealth government. This is most clearly seen in the Commonwealth's major statement *Working Nation*. In that statement, funds were quite explicitly identified as being available for supporting the activities of regional development organisations which the Commonwealth wished to encourage separately from any support given by the states. It also provided modest support for regionally targeted infrastructure and other programs. The amounts of money involved were relatively small and extended over a three-year period but, taken together with increasing emphases on the regional organization of labour market programs funded by the Commonwealth government and a number of other Commonwealth programs, they amount to the establishment of a significant new direct attachment to regional Australia by the Commonwealth government.

While the *Working Nation* statement gave the clearest indication of this new attachment, the origins of a regional emphasis by the Commonwealth actually go back substantially further than that. Following a by-election in the seat of Wills that the Labor party lost to an independent candidate running on the adverse impacts of the Commonwealth's new microeconomic reform strategies on regional areas, the Commonwealth had established an Industry Commission Inquiry into Impediments to Regional Adjustment of Industry, and it had established an Office of Regional Development in 1993 which provided support to the Kelty Task Force which investigated broader regional economic development issues in Australia.

Even before the establishment of those inquiries, the results of which fed directly into the *Working Nation* statement, a (small) Commonwealth Office of Local Government had established a modest regional development program. Commonwealth agencies involved with employment, training and health, in particular, had been progressively regionalizing their approaches and their administrative structures, and a major focus on Australia's big cities as key regional areas had been a feature of the Commonwealth Housing Department's activities.

The thrust of the new Commonwealth regionalism is still in an early evolutionary stage and the funding levels are modest, but, at the margin, the activities currently being promoted by the Commonwealth will give the national government leverage in state development patterns. This appears to be the principal reason for the Commonwealth attaching itself to economic regions (as distinct from the states): that is, an understanding by the Commonwealth that regional patterns of economic development are increasingly driven by different forces as a result of opening up of national economies to the forces of globalisation. The future pattern of national economic development in this environment is increasingly likely to be driven by what is happening in the regions, and this has led the Commonwealth to attempt to establish its own beachhead in the regions so that it can have a significant or even dominant influence on regional development.

This differentiates the current regional thrust of the Commonwealth government from the last significant attempt on the Commonwealth's part to develop a regional approach. Under Labor Prime Minister Whitlam in the early to mid 1970s, substantial "administrative regionalism" was established by the Commonwealth, especially for the promotion of hospital and social welfare programs and policies, and links were made directly to local government. The Whitlam strategy represented an attempt by the Commonwealth to ensure that its social policy priorities could be pursued independently of the states' willingness to participate. The fact that the states were able to fight back eventually undermined Whitlam's attempt at regionalism — a lesson from which the current Commonwealth government may need to be sure it has learned something. However, it seems clear that while there is an administrative decentralisation component in the regionalism currently being pursued by the Commonwealth, its central thrust relates to regional economic development, with the Commonwealth attempting to establish for itself a more significant role in shaping regional economic evolutions. Combined with the fact that the Commonwealth now has a more significant influence in the Australian context over vocational education and training, in principle it is establishing itself in a potentially powerful position to shape the economic destinies of regions in Australia.

This new regionalism could be conceived as being part of a pincer movement by the Commonwealth. That is, along with the growth of national policies and national institutions that have been established by the Special Premiers' Conferences and COAG processes to give the Commonwealth a more substantial role in influencing key elements of state economic policy and service delivery, the regional economic development thrust represents another mechanism which the Commonwealth is using to attempt to obtain greater leverage over regional as well as national economic development. This, arguably, reflects a response to a recognition by the Commonwealth of a loss of power at national level through more traditional policy levers such as trade policy, macroeconomic management and so on, which are increasingly less available to national governments in a globablised world.

To date, the states have been slow to recognise the full implications of the Commonwealth's agenda apparently implied by its increasing involvement in education and training, in regional infrastructure issues, in the structure and competitiveness of government business enterprises and so on. These are now much more shared areas of policy influence than used to be the case, and, at the same time, the Commonwealth has been extending its administrative infrastructure to encompass regional development issues in the broadest sense. While it might be important that the states recognise what the Commonwealth strategy appears to be, it also has to be said that, in the end, the Commonwealth agencies located in the states are tied as much to the interests of the states as to those of the Commonwealth, suggesting that a degree of federal balance will be sustained notwithstanding an important new thrust by the Commonwealth government to obtain power and influence in regional Australia.

Conclusions

Since the initiation of the Hawke new federalism initiative in 1990, there is no question that governments in Australia have learned a lot more about the nature of the Australian federal system and its way of working. All governments in Australia have developed a much stronger focus on the nature of the challenges of globalisation to existing policy structures, and to existing intergovernmental arrangements.

Considerable progress has been made in tackling some of the key issues — in particular, in dealing with requirements implied by greater international competitiveness for achieving a more coordinated national economy, a single national market.

Much less progress has been made in attempting to modify intergovernmental arrangements and frameworks in relation to social policy — to remove unnecessary administrative duplication and to develop more effective policy frameworks to reflect shared interests. This is an area in which great challenges lie ahead. The consequences for social policy of the new economic and fiscal frameworks within which we are all being forced to work as a result of globalisation is an area to which least attention has been paid by analysts or policy makers. There is no doubt that substantial differences in outcomes for different groups in society are likely to be involved as we make the transition towards a more globalised economy, although many of those differences might be reduced once we get into a new dynamic steady-state. Governments that fail to find the social policy frameworks to underpin their new economic and fiscal policy frameworks will find themselves under increasing political challenge.

While recent developments in Australia in attempting to address some of these issues may contain useful lessons for other federal nations, Canada in particular, it needs to be observed once again that the approaches may not be totally transferable from one nation to another; certainly the experience in Australia indicates how important attitudes and perceptions of national leaders can be to the reform processes. For example, it would appear likely that had Paul Keating rather than Bob Hawke had control of the initiation of intergovernmental reforms in Australia, we would almost certainly have made less progress than we actually have achieved. Hawke as the initiator of the process, using a cooperative approach with the states, not only helped to give momentum to new approaches, he also (though probably unintentionally) helped to build the collective confidence of the States as participants in that process. On the other hand, the need to modify intergovernmental arrangements to accommodate the challenges of globalisation, in the end, presumably, will be recognised as compelling for all federal systems.

Canada's particular context — as a participant in NAFTA, for example — might have been expected to lead to even more pressure for, *inter alia*, tackling cooperatively national economic, fiscal and social policy issues, than was the case for Australia. That it appears not to have led to cooperative intergovernmental reforms to date may reflect the distractions of the Quebec situation. But unless some progress is made on them soon, Canada may find itself facing other explosive situations within its federal system.

Fiscal Federalism in Australia and Canada:

A Brief Comparison of Constitutional Frameworks, Structural Features of Existing Fiscal Systems and Fiscal Institutions

Stanley L. Winer and Allan M. Maslove

At first glance, there are strong similarities between Australia and Canada. Both are organized as federations with adaptations of the British Parliamentary model of government. They emerged as independent countries at roughly the same time. Both are small, open economies with strong resource bases. Yet the public sector in Canada has evolved as a highly decentralized federal system, while that of Australia has become highly centralized. In this paper we compare the federal dimension of the fiscal systems in the two countries and consider the reasons why the degree of centralization is so different.

We begin by setting out as succinctly as possible the stylized facts describing the existing nature of fiscal federalism in Australia and Canada. By fiscal federalism, we mean those aspects of the constitutional framework, actual fiscal structure, and fiscal institutions that bear importantly upon or relate directly to the federal dimension of the fiscal system in each country.

Interesting comparisons of Australia and Canada have of course been provided before (see, for example, Bird 1986; Hayes 1982; Mathews ed. 1982; Mathews 1985; Herperger 1991; Rounds 1992; Barrie 1992; Vaillancourt 1992; Alexander and Galligan eds. 1992; and Sharman ed. 1994). However, the comparative work that deals with the features of fiscal structure typically has a much narrower focus than we attempt to provide here, while much work that deals with constitutions, institutions and policy processes does not usually discuss fiscal choices. By including all three dimensions of fiscal federalism listed above in our comparative analysis, we hope to provide a brief overview that will be a useful complement to the existing literature.[1]

Stylized facts relevant to fiscal federalism are presented in Section 2 in a set of three tables. Table 4.1 summarizes aspects of the current constitutions in Australia and Canada that bear importantly on the assignment of fiscal powers between levels of government. This table incorporates judicial interpretation of the original constitution in both countries as well as the revision of the Canadian Constitution in 1982. Table 4.2 provides an overview of the federal dimension of existing fiscal structure in the two countries, and Table 4.3 deals with the federal dimension of fiscal institutions and policy processes. The stylized facts presented in all three tables are arranged by major fiscal instrument. The tables cover, in turn, selected aspects of the primary fiscal instruments: taxation; public debt; and public expenditure. Also recorded in the tables are some important special features of each federation that do not fall neatly into the previous categories. It is important to note that selecting the stylized facts listed in the tables is a subjective exercise. The "facts" we present here represent our judgment about what is most relevant to an understanding of fiscal federalism in the two countries.

Perhaps the single most important stylized fact that emerges from the comparison in Table 4.2 of the actual state of fiscal federalism in Australia and Canada, is that the Australian federation is much more centralized, especially with respect to the power to tax. Such a conclusion has often been reached before, but is no less important for that. The difference in the degree of fiscal centralization appears to be reflected in the nature of fiscal institutions in the two countries, as Table 4.3 records.

This substantial difference in the degree of fiscal centralization between Australia and Canada is difficult to predict on the basis of a comparison of the formal constitutional assignments of fiscal powers, even after taking into account judicial interpretations that have accumulated over the years. Constitutions may slow down the process of fiscal evolution. But it seems that, as Breton and Scott (1978) have argued, the formal fiscal structure of a constitution does not prevent an effective reassignment between levels of government of revenue sources and expenditure responsibilities in ways that are hard to predict on the basis of a study of the written constitution alone.

---

1. Of course there is a trade-off between the level of detail that can be achieved in describing any one aspect of fiscal federalism and the breadth of the inquiry.

The apparent fluidity of the effective assignment of fiscal powers suggests that our understanding of fiscal federalism in the two countries will be enhanced by a study of how federalism evolves over time. A complete account of the fiscal history of both federations would take us far beyond the scope of the present paper.[2] However, in Section 3 we are able to provide a brief overview of the comparative evolution of fiscal federalism in Australia and Canada during the last decade or so. During this period there was considerable fluidity in fiscal arrangements and institutions in Canada, probably leading to even more decentralization. While institutions in Australia were more stable, developments that did occur increased centralization.

An obvious question that presents itself to anyone who considers the sort of information provided in the tables is why fiscal federalism in the two countries has evolved so differently, especially with respect to the degree of fiscal centralization. As we have suggested above, it is unlikely that the explanation is to be found in a study of the written constitutions. In the fourth section of the paper we speculate on the underlying, non-constitutional reasons for the difference in the degree of fiscal centralization. While one cannot "explain" in any definitive way, we identify as important factors the facts of Canada's greater ethnic diversity (particularly the "French fact") and its regional dimensions, and regional differences in resource endowments. An additional factor is the more concentrated urbanization of Australia. In the final section, we draw some tentative conclusions from the comparative analysis as a whole.

An Overview of Stylized Facts

The Constitutional Framework of Fiscal Federalism in Australia and Canada

While it has been said that Australia is the federation that most closely resembles Canada (e.g., Hayes 1980:21), the federal dimension of the fiscal structure specified by the constitutions of Australia and Canada are different in several important ways. That this is so should not come as a surprise. The framers of the Australian constitution of 1900 (in the debates of 1891 and 1897-98) were able to — and did — consider the British North America Act (1867), as the Canadian constitution was then called, and explicitly rejected

---

2. A preliminary attempt to deal with the evolution of the effective assignment of the power to tax in the Canadian federation over a longer time span is given in Winer (1992), with associated comments by Breton (1992) and by Scott (1992). See also Breton and Scott (1978) and Gillespie (1991). For a comprehensive study of the evolution of the power to tax in Australia, see Smith (1993).

this constitution as a model.[3] The rejection is not readily apparent in the treatment of the major tax revenue source at the time the constitutions were enacted, namely the tariff. As noted in Table 4.1, in both countries customs duties are reserved for the senior government.

The rejection of the Canadian model by the framers of the Australian constitution is more obvious in the manner in which fiscal powers of the different governments are generally specified. The British North America Act explicitly assigns taxing powers and expenditure responsibilities to both federal and provincial governments, and there is a clause assigning any residual power to the federal government. However, the smaller states' delegates to the constitutional discussions in Australia were wary of any proposition which could diminish the relative powers of the states (Warden 1992:14). Since delimiting state fiscal power appears to have been considered tantamount to limiting it, no explicit list of taxing or spending powers or responsibilities of the state governments is included in the Australian constitution, as noted in the table, and there is no statement about which level of government is to receive any residual power. Moreover, the taxing and spending powers of the Commonwealth (as the federal government in Australia is called), and the states are constitutionally concurrent in most cases, with the notable exception of indirect taxation (as discussed below). There is an allowance for Commonwealth paramountcy where there is an explicit conflict of legislation. (The exact wording of those parts of the Australian and Canadian constitution that are particularly relevant to fiscal federalism, including the division of fiscal powers discussed above, are provided in the Appendix.)

Other aspects of the constitutions in the two countries that bear directly on the use of specific fiscal instruments also differ, most notably with respect to the power to issue public debt and to tax indirectly, though the latter difference developed only gradually over the years as states and provinces attempted to exercise their fiscal powers. Concerning public debt, in the Australian constitution there is explicit allowance for state debt and borrowing to be taken over by the Commonwealth. In the British North America Act and its successor, the Constitution Act of 1982, in contrast, formal coordination of debt issue is neither allowed for nor expressly prohibited.[4]

---

3. In 1982, the BNA Act was amended and renamed the Constitution Act of 1867, and as such forms part of the major revision of the Constitution in 1982 that included a Charter of Rights and an amendment formula.
4. The federal government did, however, assume most of the outstanding debt of the provinces at the time of Confederation.

Indirect taxation has a constitutional history that is long and complicated in both countries, and we shall not review these histories here.[5] We simply report that subsequent judicial interpretation of the constitution in Australia has not favoured the states' power to tax indirectly, though the exercise of this power is not explicitly or implicitly constrained by the constitution of 1900.[6] In Canada, by way of contrast, although the initial assignment (in 1867) of taxing powers to the provinces clearly did not include indirect taxation, judicial interpretation of the British North America Act in the 1920s and 1930s, as well as the constitutional revision of 1982, has left the provinces with more or less unrestricted powers of indirect taxation including, since 1982, indirect taxation of natural resources.

In view of the importance that intergovernmental grants have assumed over the years in both Australia and Canada, and as a final major point concerning the constitutional assignment of fiscal instruments among levels of government, it should be noted that neither constitution now seriously restricts either the amount or the national distribution of funds that may be transferred to the states or provinces by the central government. The Australian constitution of 1900 explicitly forbids the Commonwealth to discriminate between the states. But, by judicial interpretations over the years, this restriction was held not to apply to Commonwealth grants to the states. In Canada, federal spending power was not originally restricted with respect to its distributional effect across the provinces, and subsequent judicial interpretation has not seriously weakened this power. The 1982 revision does impose an obligation on the federal government to make equalization payments to the provinces. But neither the magnitude of the total resources to be devoted to equalizing the fiscal positions of the provinces nor the degree of equalization that is to be achieved is specified.[7]

---

5. For the Canadian history see, for example, La Forest (1981) and Gillespie (1991). For the Australian story see, for example, Smith (1992) and Smith (1993).
6. Although not directly concerned with the assignment of fiscal powers, note should also be taken of the Engineer's case in Austrialia (1920), in which it was held that Commonwealth power should be interpreted without regard to the amount of power left to the states. The decision allowed the Commonwealth to make laws that were binding on the states, and no doubt helped to further shift the general constitutional balance towards the Commonwealth in a manner that the framers had not intended. One should also note that since judicial interpretation is itself influenced by many societal forces, a list of contitutional interpretations cannot serve as a deep explanation for the evolution of the constitutional assignment of fiscal powers.
7. For a more detailed overview of the grant system in Australia see, for example, James (1992) and Mathews (1985). The Canadian situation is discussed in Boadway and Hobson (1993).

Structural Features of Existing Fiscal Systems: The Federal Dimension

A comparison of the constitutional assignment of fiscal powers in Table 4.1 with the corresponding effective or actual fiscal structure outlined in Table 4.2 reveals an interesting similarity, of a sort, between fiscal federal arrangements in Australia and Canada: it is hard to understand how the observed, effective assignment of fiscal functions in each country was shaped by, or emerged from, the formal constitutional framework. In particular, it is not at all clear how the much greater degree of fiscal centralization in Australia that now exists (reported in Table 4.2 and discussed below) could be predicted on the basis of the constitutional assignment of functions alone. Taking constitutional interpretations over the decades, such as those concerning indirect taxation, into account only softens this conclusion to some extent. Greater fiscal centralization in Australia than in Canada can be observed in the effective distribution of tax bases, in the extent of tax harmonization that reduces the cost to sub-central governments of collecting taxes, and in the importance of central government grants as a source of state or provincial revenues. Concerning the effective exercise of the power to tax, Table 4.2 records that only the federal government in Australia levies income taxation, though the constitution allows for (and constitutional interpretation has not altered) the power of income taxation at the state level. That the states would completely withdraw from the major tax source of the second half of the twentieth century is not something that could be predicted on the basis of the constitutional assignment of fiscal powers outlined in Table 4.1.

In Canada, in marked contrast to the history of income taxation in Australia, all provinces levy their own personal and corporate income taxes (and have their own Income Tax Acts as well). These provincial taxes are levied on almost identical bases as used by the federal government, and in most cases are collected at low cost to the provinces by the federal government under formal tax collection agreements (Alberta, Ontario and Quebec collect their own corporate income tax, while only Quebec also collects its own personal income tax).

There are also substantial differences between countries in the use of consumption and natural resource tax bases favouring the Commonwealth in Australia and the provinces in Canada. As we pointed out in the discussion of Table 4.1, the states in Australia have been blocked in the courts when seeking broader access to general consumption taxation although the constitution of 1900 did not prohibit such taxes. Consequently, at present the states levy only selective excises and narrowly defined transaction taxes. On the other hand, judicial interpretation in Canada has permitted and, as shown in Table 4.2, the provinces have levied broad based sales taxes. With respect to resource taxation, in Canada it is primarily a provincial revenue source, while in Australia it is shared more equally between the federal government and the states.

Still further evidence of the greater degree of fiscal centralization in Australia is provided by the differential nature of the access that state and provincial governments have to capital markets. In Australia, state borrowing is constrained to some extent by the Commonwealth through the Loan Council (more about which below). In Canada, provincial borrowing has never been regulated in any way by the federal government, and the provinces borrow internationally on their own account to a greater extent (relative to their total debt issue) than does the federal government.

As a result of the differences in the distribution of taxing and borrowing powers outlined above, the Commonwealth in Australia raises (in 1992/93) about 70 percent of all government revenues from own sources, while in Canada the federal government share of all revenues is about 45 percent.[8] Not surprisingly, in view of the distribution of taxing powers, the Commonwealth is directly responsible for more spending on goods and services than is the federal government in Canada; Commonwealth own-purpose outlays or expenditures (excluding transfers to other governments) are about 50 percent of the total own-purpose expenditures for all governments in Australia, while the Canadian federal government is directly responsible for about 40 percent of all government spending on goods and services.

A large part of the difference between revenues raised by the central governments and their direct or own-purpose expenditures represents grants to lower levels of government. Such transfers are a higher percentage of

---

8. The figures cited immediately below are for 1992/93, and are taken from Year Book Australia, 1995 (Canberra: ABS), The National Finances, various years (Toronto: The Canadian Tax Foundation) and Perry (1994). A useful data summary is found in Table 3 of Courchene (1995a).

It may be of interest that the aggregate tax mix in the two countries, which is not reported in Table 4.2, is similar with the following major exceptions (figures are for 1992 and are from Perry (1994)): (i) Australia relies more heavily on corporate taxation (14.5 percent of all taxes vs. 4.8 percent of all taxes in Canada); (ii) Only Canada has explicit social security taxes (16.5 percent of all taxes, mostly at the federal level), but note that Australia has payroll taxes at the state level (24 percent of state tax revenue or about 5 percent of all tax revenue) while payroll taxes are minor revenue sources at the provincial level; (iii) Only Canada has a value added tax, the GST at the federal level (about 12 percent of federal tax revenue), although reliance on consumption taxes of all kinds as a percent of all taxes is about the same in both countries (in the 26 percent to 28 percent range).

Concerning the aggregate size of government: total expenditures of all governments are substantially larger in Canada than in Australia (about 51 percent of GDP in Canada vs. 43 percent in Australia. See Walsh 1996 *(this volume)*.

central government total spending in Australia than in Canada and are also more important for the recipient governments; this is, of course, one more indication that Australia is fiscally more centralized than Canada. Commonwealth transfers of all kinds to the states constitute about 50 percent of total state expenditures. In Canada, on the other hand, transfers of all kinds from the federal government to the provinces now constitute less than 30 percent of total provincial expenditures.[9]

Table 4.2 also records the roles of the central, state/provincial and local governments in education, health, social services and transport and communications. The difference in the degree of fiscal centralization between the countries can be seen here too. The provinces generally play a bigger role in Canada than the states play in Australia. Moreover, local government own-purpose or direct spending is also more important in Canada, so that decentralization in Canada may be said to be more complete with respect to the three main levels of government, as well greater in overall magnitude.

In Australia, education is primarily a state function (90 percent of total own-purpose expenditures) while in Canada, where the local government sector is three times as large in terms of its share of own-purpose expenditures (about 15 percent versus 5 percent), education is shared by provincial (33 percent) and local (66 percent) governments.[10] Health in Australia is shared between the Commonwealth (43 percent), which funds the Medicare system and private hospitals, and the states (56 percent) which are responsible for public hospitals and other services. In Canada, health is almost exclusively a provincial function (90 percent). Social services in Australia, including pensions, are primarily delivered by the Commonwealth. In Canada this function is conducted by the federal government which provides unemployment insurance, pensions and old age assistance payments, while the provinces and municipalities are largely responsible for social assistance (80 percent provincial and 20 percent local). Transportation and communication expenditures are the responsibility of the states (60 percent) and the local governments (30 percent) in Australia, but are more or less equally shared by all governments in Canada.

---

9. In view of the ratios of grants to state/provincial direct spending, it is often said that "vertical fiscal imbalance" is greater in Australia than in Canada. However, this is a pejorative statement about fiscal arrangements in a federation that may or may not be warranted. The fact that each level of government in a federation does not itself raise all the money it spends does not by itself indicate that the federation is in some important sense "unbalanced." See, for example, Breton and Scott (1978).

10. These and the other figures for the distribution of own-purpose expenditures by level of government, given below and in Table 4.2, are for 1987. They are taken from McMillan (1993:Table 3).

No comparison of fiscal systems in federations can be complete without consideration of the way in which fiscal disparities between states or provinces are addressed. As in almost all federal countries, both Australia and Canada have developed systems of intergovernmental grants designed to equalize the fiscal capacities (as distinct from actual fiscal outcomes) of the states and provinces. But the structure of the equalization program is substantially more comprehensive in Australia than it is in Canada. Poorer states in Australia are equalized by transfers from the Commonwealth up to a national average as in Canada, and, in addition, richer states are also equalized down to this average.[11] Moreover, the equalization formula in Australia, but not in Canada, takes into account inequalities in expected expenditure needs as well as in potential revenue sources.[12] The Australian equalization system also includes allowance for cost of living differences between states. It may be true that the disparities between states in per-capita incomes are smaller than in Canada (Courchene, 1995:Table 1). Nonetheless, the more comprehensive system of equalization in Australia reduces whatever differences there are between states to a greater extent than is accomplished by the equalization system in Canada.

Finally we consider the comparative nature of conditional grants provided by the central governments. Perhaps the most important point to make in comparing the grant systems is that the conditions attached to the receipt of federal grants-in-aid by the provinces in Canada generally leave the provinces with much more discretion than do Commonwealth grants-in-aid to the states. To take an extreme example, in Canada there is explicit allowance for the provinces to opt out of federal grant programs with compensation, but no corresponding provision in Australia.[13] The comparison of the conditional grant systems in Australia and Canada reinforces the general conclusion that the fiscal system in Australia is substantially more centralized by almost any measure.

Fiscal Policy Processes and Fiscal Institutions

We noted earlier that the constitutional and effective assignments of fiscal instruments in the two federations do not appear to be related in an

---

11. For a comparative description and numerical comparisons of the extent of equalization in Australia and Canada, see Courchene (1995).
12. Expenditures of a capital nature are not taken into account in the Australian system of equalization payments.
13. Only the province of Quebec takes advantage of this unique feature of the Canadian fiscal system which, no doubt, was expressly provided to allow Quebec increased flexibility in adjusting to the introduction of federal conditional grant programs. Nonetheless, it remains a feasible option for the other provinces.

obvious or simple manner. However, while it seems difficult to link the constitutional facts in Table 4.1 to the effective assignment of fiscal instruments in Table 4.2, a relationship between Table 4.2 and the nature of fiscal processes summarized in Table 4.3 seems to be more readily apparent. Differences in the nature of existing policy processes and fiscal institutions between the two countries appear to be consistent with the substantial difference in the degree of fiscal centralization.

In both countries there are regular and substantive meetings of both cabinet ministers and senior officials in most areas of shared jurisdiction, a process that in Canada is labeled "executive federalism" (Smiley 1980). But the nature of executive federalism is not at all the same in Australia and Canada. Cabinet ministers from different provinces in Canada meet with counterpart ministers of the federal government on a more-or-less equal basis in many cases, and the relationship between officials of the two levels of government has even been compared to diplomacy between sovereign nations (Simeon 1972). Tax sharing arrangements, for example, may be said to be negotiated between equals even if they are subsequently 'recorded' in federal legislation. The conditions embedded in federal shared cost or conditional grant programs is another example of fiscal arrangements that emerge after vigorous federal-provincial bargaining.[14]

In Australia, by way of contrast, and especially as the financial power of the Commonwealth has grown relative to that of the states, intergovernmental meetings such as the Premiers' Conferences are often seen as opportunities for the states to argue for an increase in the size of their Commonwealth grants rather than a method of, or venue for, cooperation with the central government as in Canada (James, 1992:63). Tax sharing arrangements, when they have arisen, have been unilaterally offered to the states by the Commonwealth, and after adoption have been unilaterally terminated as well.

Perhaps the most interesting difference noted in Table 4.3 is that in Australia there are formal, quasi-independent commissions that play a key role in Commonwealth-state financial relations, while in Canada all negotiations are of a more or less informal nature even though some of the negotiations may end in federal legislation.[15] This difference too is consistent

---

14. On the role of the provinces in the determination of the terms of federal shared cost or conditional grant programs, see, for example, Bella (1979).
15. The independence of the Commisions in Australia can be said to result from one or more of the following: constitutional status (in one case discussed below); a formal voting procedure for a governing body that is based on participation by the states and the Commonwealth; the existence of a secretariat separate from the administration of the participating governments. The Australian fiscal institutions are described more fully in James (1992), Saunders (1990), and various unpublished documents of the Council of Australian Governments.

with the stronger fiscal position that the central government in Australia has attained, though it may not seem to be so at first glance.

The distribution of equalization grants or revenue assistance in Australia is normally determined by a quasi-independent Commonwealth Grants Commission, on which the states are formally represented. The total amount of equalization payments to be divided up by the Commission is, however, determined unilaterally by the Commonwealth. Although the advice of the Commission concerning the interstate distribution of equalization grants is rarely rejected, there is no constitutional obligation for the Commonwealth to accept it, and all the cheques are actually written by the Commonwealth.

It is useful to compare the Grants Council to the Ontario Council on University Affairs in the province of Ontario. This Council performs a role analogous to that of the Grants Commission, advising the provincial government on how to divide up a provincially determined total allocation among universities in the province. The universities have formal representation on the Council, as the states do on the Grants Commission. But it is fair to say that the Council's independence is merely a convenience for the province, isolating the continuing bickering between the universities from day-to-day government operations, and it is clear that the universities gain very little financial independence as a result of the Council's existence. The comparison of the Grants Commission and the Council on University Affairs suggests that such agencies are essentially agents of a strong central authority.

State borrowing has been constrained to some extent over the years by the Australian Loan Council, another quasi-independent body, which operates under a global borrowing constraint imposed by the Commonwealth. As Saunders (1990) point out, effective control by the Commonwealth of state borrowing has ebbed and flowed over the years. The states have been able to bypass the Loan Council to a considerable extent by borrowing through semi-governmental agencies. The Commonwealth has responded to these manoeuvers in various ways, and, perhaps as a result of the increasing difficulty of controlling state borrowing, the Loan Council has recently been reconstituted (1993). States will now borrow in their own right rather than via the Commonwealth or through state agencies. But the revised Loan Council is still going to monitor and co-ordinate state borrowing with that of the Commonwealth, as well as exercise some control over the total amount and interstate distribution of state borrowing. It has been pointed out before that in Canada, there is no formal attempt at coordination of provincial and federal borrowing.[16]

As a final point concerning the relationship between institutions and fiscal structure, it is important to acknowledge that establishing the consistency of institutional arrangements with the actual degree of fiscal centralization does not establish causality. It may be that the way federal fiscal institutions work in each country affects the evolution of the effective assignment of powers, or vice-versa, or causality may be bi-directional. To the best of our knowledge, there is at present no systematic empirical evidence on this complicated matter, and it remains an interesting topic for future research.

The Evolution of Fiscal Federalism over the Last Decade

Fiscal arrangements in Canada as they have developed in the post-war period have, by and large, been in the direction of increasing the level of decentralization in the federation. Generally speaking, the provincial governments have increased their expenditure responsibilities and own-revenue resources (mainly through increasing their share of personal income tax revenues) relative to the federal government. To illustrate, in 1960 federal revenues were 63 percent of all government revenues; by 1985 the federal share had dropped to 45 percent. In 1960, total provincial own revenues amounted to 34 percent of federal own revenues; by 1985 the ratio was 91 percent. Further, over this period, conditions tied to federal grants to the provinces have become progressively fewer and less binding.

Over the last decade, spurred mainly by the stresses created by high deficits, the pattern of fiscal arrangements has been altered in various ways,

---

16. A third quasi-independent institution of interest is the Interstate Commission, although this agency, provision for which is in the Australian constitution, is not directly concerned with fiscal matters. Originally intended to monitor and maintain the internal market, this Commission and its operations have been effectively restructured in various ways over the years. It is not functioning at this time, though this does not mean that the economic union in Australia is in much danger. The courts have continually reinforced the common market provisions of the common market (Zines 1990). Also the Council of Australian Governments (COAG), established in 1992, appears to be evolving into a formal institution that will be primarily concerned with micro-economic reforms including those involving reductions in regulatory and other barriers to internal trade, though at this time its influence is unclear. More about COAG below.

The Interstate Commission, COAG, and the constitutional provision for and judicial enforcement of the common market in Australia stands in contrast to Canada where the original (1867) constitutional guarantee of factor mobility has been watered down in the 1982 revision by allowance for regional development policies. Recent inter-provincial negotiation has led to the development of an Internal Trade Agreement (1994) and the establishment of an Internal Trade Secretariat. Whether these developments foreshadow a more "Australian" type of institutionalized protection for the Canadian common market remains to be seen.

sometimes by unilateral federal decisions and sometimes by agreement. The impact of these recent changes has been to create a rather fluid situation in federal-provincial fiscal relations at the current time (one is tempted to say that the established equilibrium has been disturbed and the system has not yet settled at a new equilibrium structure). While there are both centralizing and decentralizing elements in these recent changes, our judgment is that, on balance, they are likely to result in further decentralization of the Canadian federation.

Four aspects of this recent evolution are noted.[17] First, federal transfers to the provinces are becoming both less generous and less tied. The announcement in the federal budget of February 1995 of a consolidated block grant (the proposed Canada Health and Social Transfer) relating to social policy programs will directly and indirectly diminish the federal presence relative to that of the provinces. Directly, the removal of federal program guidelines (in particular in the area of social assistance) may well result in greater interprovincial variation in social programming. Indirectly, the declining value of the transfer will diminish the ability of the federal government to exert moral suasion over the provinces. Second, the federal government has or appears prepared to vacate some of its spending activities in favour of the provinces. Perhaps foremost among these is the area of training which has historically been funded and delivered by both orders of government. Under budgetary pressures and in response to ongoing pressure from several provinces (primarily Quebec) the federal government has signaled that devolving its training activities may be in the offing.

Two other major developments could arguably be regarded as centralizing. In 1991, the federal government replaced a narrowly based commodities tax levied at the manufacturer's level with the Goods and Services Tax (GST), a broadly based, value-added tax. From some provinces' perspective this constituted a federal invasion of the retail sales tax field that had traditionally (though not constitutionally) been reserved for them. In that sense, the GST represented the establishment of the federal government in a new tax base, but it is important to note that the balance of revenues generated by the two orders of government did not change. The other development was the entry into a free trade arrangement with the United States (1989) and later (1993) with Mexico as well. What these agreements did was restrict the scope for government intervention in the economy, limiting the use of policy instruments available at both the federal and provincial levels. The trade agreements may turn out to be centralizing if the policy instruments that are most constrained (e.g., direct subsidies,

---

17. For further discussion, see Boadway and Flatters (1991) and Phillips (1995).

procurement policies) are those that provincial governments tend to utilize more. However, the federal government requires the cooperation of the provinces to implement and enforce these international agreements.[18]

To summarize, while important components of fiscal federalism in Canada are currently in flux, there do not appear to be any significant developments in play that would clearly suggest the reversal of long-standing trends towards increasing decentralization. If anything, it is our judgment that the resolution of the current issues, combined with continuing efforts to accommodate Quebec, will result in further decentralization.

In the last decade developments in Australia, though more limited, stand in stark contrast.[19] In 1985-86, the Commonwealth government did not renew the tax sharing arrangements then in place and instead determined revenue sharing grants unilaterally in light of its own expenditure priorities. In the early 1990s, a joint Commonwealth-state review of intergovernmental arrangements was launched. Though the process was halted before completion, it did appear to reaffirm federal dominance in public finances, ostensibly for reasons of macroeconomic stabilization.

Federal dominance in terms of revenues and control over economic policy was solidified. Mathews and Grewal note that institutional arrangements, many of long standing, were dismantled if they stood in the way of centralized policy making. This was particularly true in the areas of taxing authority (e.g., the repeal of the tax-sharing agreements, removal of state power to impose tax surcharges) and revenue sharing. Institutions were eliminated (e.g., Advisory Council for Inter-government Relations, Special Premiers' Conference).

Perhaps the only institutional innovation that could be read as countering this trend was the creation of the Council of Australian Governments (COAG) in 1992. This body, with first ministers as the representatives of their governments, has begun to meet twice per year to deal with a broad range of financial and non-financial issues (including relatively minor matters such as determining common dates for the observance of statutory holidays). Though formal communiqués are issued following each meeting of COAG, it is not a formal decision-making body in the sense that the governments are not bound to implement any decisions. Overall, while COAG provides a new institutional mechanism for federal-state consultations, it does not represent a significant check on the powers of the Commonwealth government nor on its dominance of fiscal arrangements in the Australian federation.

---

18. See Courchene (1995b) for discussion of the relationship between broader globalization trends and the internal balance of fiscal powers.
19. For further discussion see Smith (1993) and Mathews and Grewal (1995).

Explaining Differences in the Degree of Fiscal Centralization

We have seen that the two federal countries are in fact quite different in terms of the effective assignment of fiscal powers. Recent developments, moreover, provide no substantial evidence that they are moving closer, and suggests that they may well be continuing to diverge. Australia is centralized and its allocation of responsibilities seems to quite stable; Canada is decentralized and its recent evolution suggests that it is becoming more decentralized.

Several "explanations" which immediately come to mind are not sufficient. One might point to the distribution of the power to tax in Australia and Canada to explain why Australia is so much more centralized than Canada. The states in Australia do not collect income taxes, a major tax source in all developed countries. However, this simply pushes the question back one step: one then needs to explain the distribution of the power to tax in the federation.

Another observation relates to the distribution of spending responsibilities for health, education and welfare. These have been the major growth areas of government spending in the post-war period. With a given assignment of responsibilities, one might expect the jurisdiction assigned these responsibilities to become more dominant in absolute and relative terms. However, such an explanation is not complete because the effective assignment of functions is not fixed. As we have seen from the comparison of Tables 4.1 and 4.2, the constitution does not greatly constrain the effective exercise or assignment of fiscal instruments in a federation over the decades. So like an explanation that relies on the distribution of the power to tax, this one too merely pushes the question back one step.

One explanation of the relative weakness of the states is that the Australian Senate is viewed as a House of the States. Voters may opt for greater fiscal centralization if their regional interests are "protected" by their elected Senate representatives in Canberra. But the Senate has not generally acted as house of the states or a safeguard of states' rights (Uhr 1989).

The answer has to be found elsewhere. While a definitive explanation lies far beyond the scope of this paper, it is possible to point to factors which underlie the dramatically different nature of fiscal federalism in the two countries. We briefly note several such demographic and economic factors.

Canada is notably more ethnically heterogeneous than Australia. About 23 percent of the Canadian population is French, and of course concentrated in Quebec. In addition, depending upon how people are asked to identify their ethnic origins, a further third or more of the population identify themselves as being not of "British" origin. In addition, key ethnic groupings tend to be regionally concentrated. In Australia, by contrast, approximately two-thirds of the population identify as "Anglo-Australian" in origin.

The "French fact" in Canada is clearly a highly significant factor. Indeed, when one considers the confederation compromises dating from 1867, it seems reasonable to conclude that had it not been for Quebec, Canada would have developed as a much more centralized federation. However, Quebec aside, Canada is still more ethnically diverse than Australia. If federal systems are invented to accommodate differing tastes for public services, and if ethnic differences give rise to these taste differences, one might expect that a "stronger" federalism would emerge to accommodate these differences. This would be further advanced if the ethnic groups tended to concentrate regionally, as is this case to some extent in Canada.

Another notable difference between the two countries is urbanization and the concentration of population. Canada's population distribution is often described in terms of a narrow band along the American border. But that is diffuse compared to Australia. Most of the Australian population lives in a narrow strip along the east and south coasts, and another less populous strip along the west coast. The five largest metropolitan areas in each country contain about 10 million people (1990 Australian data, 1991 Canadian); in Australia this represents 60 percent of the total population, while in Canada the corresponding proportion is 38 percent. In each country just under two-thirds of the population live in cities of 100,000 or more; in Australia this represents 13 cities, in Canada 30.

Why might more concentrated urbanization in Australia lead to more centralization? One possibility is that with population concentrated in a small number of urban centres, administrative decentralization represents a relatively easy way to accommodate diversity, thus mitigating the demand for strong constitutional decentralization. Second, dominant policy concerns in urban areas (beyond issues of management of the urban infrastructure itself) include issues such as economic development (including trade policy and financial regulation) which are largely in the federal domain. If state/provincial legislatures are more likely to be dominated by rural and more traditional interests, urban centres might be expected to push against the constraint of being units of the province/state. They would attempt to establish direct links with central governments rather than work through less sympathetic sub-national governments. A greater concentration of population in relatively few urban areas may therefore be a factor in the centralization of the Australian federation.

Canada also exhibits much more regional economic disparity than does Australia. To illustrate these regional differences one can point to the greater variations in (un)employment rates across Canadian provinces than Australian states, and to the greater variations in income averages (Courchene 1995a, Tables 1 & 2). While one might argue that the larger differences in Canada are in part, the effects of policies that subsidize regions, it is clearly the case that Canadian regions are more distinguished than Australian regions in terms of differing resource endowments and locational (dis)advantages (though the latter may be becoming less important over time). Further, the economic regions of Canada to a significant extent coincide with or are contained within provinces (e.g., manufacturing in Ontario and Quebec, oil and gas in Alberta, fish in the Atlantic provinces, agriculture in the prairies, forests in B.C.). Over time provincial governments have, therefore, emerged as the voices of the regional economic interests. Moreover, as a result of the significant regional disparities, regional economic issues are dominant factors in national policy debates.

Conclusions

The dominant stylized fact that emerges from a comparison of fiscal federalism in Australia and Canada concerns the degree of centralization: the Australian federation is fiscally more centralized than is Canada by almost any measure. Moreover, there is no indication in recent developments that this difference is diminishing. This fact, which is reflected in the effective use of all major fiscal instruments, has often been noted before. But it must continue to play a central role in any comparative analysis of fiscal federalism in the two countries.

Observed differences in fiscal policy processes and institutions in the two countries are consistent with the difference in the effective assignment of fiscal powers. Provinces bargain as equals with the federal government in Canada, while state-Commonwealth negotiations are more tightly structured by institutions that are clearly subject to the exercise of the Commonwealth's substantial power to tax. The nature of causality between the effective assignment of fiscal powers in the federation and the nature of fiscal institutions remains to be established.

The emergence of a considerable difference between the two countries in the actual degree of fiscal centralization cannot be easily explained by reference to differences in the constitutional assignment of fiscal powers. The constitutional assignment of powers in either country and the actual or effective assignment may be consistent with each other as far as the courts are concerned. But a study of the constitutional frameworks does not explain why the states in Australia do not make use of the income tax, the dominant tax source of the post World War II era, even though the Australian constitution permits them to do so. It does not explain why the federal government in Canada has not assumed a greater role in the delivery of public services even though its constitutional spending powers are substantial. In both countries, it appears that the constitutional assignment of fiscal powers does not preclude an effective reassignment of powers between levels of government over time.

The observation that there is a substantial gap between the constitutional and effective assignment of powers in both Australia and Canada leads to a number of obvious questions. What role has the constitutional assignment of fiscal powers actually played in determining the existing nature of fiscal federalism? Would the effective assignment of powers in either country have been different if there was no statement about fiscal powers in either constitution, or even if Australia and Canada had exchanged constitutions? And, in view of the fluidity of the effective division of fiscal powers, is it worthwhile to use substantial resources debating and reforming the *constitutional* framework?

We have speculated on the underlying forces that have been responsible for the evolution of fiscal federal arrangements in both countries, including, most notably, the greater cultural and geophysical heterogeneity in Canada than in Australia. While much work remains to be done in explaining the observed fiscal patterns recorded in the tables, the following cautionary note seems warranted, especially for those intent on reforming fiscal arrangements. Over the medium to long term it seems likely that trends in the development of the fiscal structure of the federations are determined by basic factors that are difficult to alter. To the extent that this is so, changes that are not consistent with the underlying long-run trends in the evolution of fiscal arrangements are likely to be undone sooner rather than later by compensatory adjustments elsewhere in the fiscal system.

Table 4.1
The Constitutional Framework of Fiscal Federalism in Australia and Canada 1995*

	Australia	Canada
Taxation: Direct	Commonwealth and states have similar access to direct tax bases	Federal government and provinces have similar access to direct tax bases
Indirect	State access to indirect tax bases is constrained relative to the Commonwealth, and only the Commonwealth may levy customs duties	Provinces and federal government have similar access to indirect tax bases, and only the federal government may levy customs duties
Taxation by One Level of Government of Another	Prohibited	Prohibited
Public Debt:	Explicit allowance for state debt and borrowing to be taken over by the Commonwealth	No formal coordination of the level or structure of federal and provincial borrowing
Public Expenditure: Distribution of Spending Powers	General rule: concurrent Commonwealth/state responsibility, with Commonwealth paramountcy when powers conflict	General rule: exclusivity of powers assigned to federal and provincial governments, with federal paramountcy when powers conflict
	Commonwealth exclusivity in some areas (eg. defence, immigration)	Federal exclusivity in some areas (e.g., defence, unemployment insurance, old age security)
		Concurrent federal/provincial responsibility in a few areas (e.g., agriculture, immigration, environment)
		Concurrent federal/provincial responsibility with provincial paramountcy in a very few areas (e.g., contributory pensions)
	Local government not mentioned in constitution	Provincial exclusivity in some areas (eg. health, education, welfare, property, civil rights and local government)
Inter-governmental Grants	Commonwealth power to transfer funds to the states explicitly unrestricted	Federal power to transfer funds to the provinces effectively unrestricted

Continued...

Table 4.1

(continued)

The Constitutional Framework of Fiscal Federalism in Australia and Canada 1995*

	Australia	Canada
Special Features: Listing of Fiscal Powers	**Federal**: yes **State**: no (but limited by judicial interpretation to powers not assigned to Commonwealth) **Local**: no	**Federal**: yes **Provincial**: yes **Local**: no
Residual Power	Not explicitly assigned	Assigned to federal government
Ownership of Natural Resources	Shared by Commonwealth and states	Exclusively provincial
Promotion of Inter-regional Equity	No constitutional obligation for Commonwealth to insure interregional equity	Joint obligation for federal government and provinces to insure interregional equality of opportunities and public services (1982). Equality not defined Obligation in principle for federal government to equalize fiscal capacities of the provinces (1982). Equalization not defined
Customs Union	Guarantee of free internal trade with monitoring by quasi-independent commission	Provision for interregional mobility of goods and factors, but not for monitoring
	Commonwealth explicitly forbidden to discriminate between states	Explicit exception for federal and provincial policies aimed at regional development (1982)

* Notes to Table 4.1:

Table 4.1 incorporates judicial interpretation and amendments of the constitutions with respect to the assignment of taxing and spending powers.

Table 4.2
Structural Features of Existing Fiscal Systems: The Federal Dimension

	Australia	Canada
Taxation: Tax Sovereignty	States exercise much less tax sovereignty than does the Commonwealth	Provinces and federal government exercise similar degree of tax sovereignty
Distribution of Tax Sources:		
• Income	Levied only by Commonwealth	Levied by provinces as well as federal government
• Consumption	Levied by Commonwealth and states without coordination. State taxation narrowly based on selected excises and transactions	Levied by federal and provincial governments mostly without coordination. Provincial taxation broadly based on retail sales. Federal vat(GST) harmonized with Quebec vat.
• Natural Resources	Levied by Commonwealth and states	Almost exclusively a provincial revenue source
• Payroll	Mostly at state level (largest own-source revenue of states)	Used at provincial level but not a major source
• Social Security	None	At provincial and federal levels
Tax Collection Agreements and Harmonization	Very limited	Extensive Personal income tax: Provincial tax levied as a 'tax on a tax' and collected by federal government on condition that bases are identical. Rates vary across country. Some provincial special provisions administered federally by mutual agreement Quebec collects its own personal income tax Corporation income tax: Provincial tax collected by federal government and shared using formula apportionment on condition that bases are similar. Rates similar across country Ontario, Quebec and Alberta collect own corporate income tax using almost identical base

Continued ...

Table 4.2

(continued)

Structural Features of Existing Fiscal Systems: The Federal Dimension

	Australia	Canada
Public Debt:	State borrowing constrained and coordinated to some extent by the Commonwealth	No federal regulation of provincial access to foreign or domestic capital markets
Public Expenditure:	Commonwealth predominates	Federal and provincial sectors roughly of equal size
Relative Size of Central Government Sector (1992)	Total expenditures *including grants* by Commonwealth about 70% of total government spending; total direct spending by Commonwealth *excluding grants* about 50% of total	Total expenditures *including grants* by federal government about 45% of total government spending; total *direct* spending by federal government *excluding grants* about 40% of total
Relative Size of spending State/Provincial Sector (1992)	States/provincial share of total spending similar in both countries (about 40%)	States/provincial share of total similar in both countries (about 40%)
Relative Size of Local Government Sector (1992)	Local government sector small (direct spending about 5% of total)	Local government sector important (direct spending about 18% of total)
Role of Grants in State/Provincial Finances (1992)	Commonwealth transfers about 50% of total state spending	Federal transfers about 30% of provincial total spending
Distribution of Specific Functions:		
• Education	Primarily a state function	Shared by provincial (1/3) and local governments (2/3)
• Health	Shared about equally by Commonwealth and states	Primarily a provincial function
• Welfare	Primarily a Commonwealth function	Primarily a provincial function
• Transport & Communications	Shared mostly by state (about 2/3) and local governments (about 1/3)	Shared about equally by all levels of government

Continued ...

Table 4.2

(continued)

Structural Features of Existing Fiscal Systems: The Federal Dimension

	Australia	Canada
Intergovernmental Grants:		
• Equalization Grants	Formula comprehensive: (i) Both taxes and expenditures equalized (ii) States equalized down as well as up to national average (iii) Explicit allowance made of cost differentials	Formula not comprehensive: (i) Only tax sources equalized (ii) Only poorer provinces equalized up to a 5 province standard (iii) No allowance for cost differentials
• Conditional Grants-in-Aid	Commonwealth grants conditional on state expenditure patterns	Federal grants conditional on provincial program designs, and leave provinces with substantial discretion
• Opting Out Provisions	No "opting out" with compensation	"Opting-out" with compensation available, but only Quebec opts out of federal programs for health, education and (partly) welfare.
Special Features:		
Regional Variation in Per Capita Incomes	"Low"	"High"

Table 4.3
The Fiscal Federal Dimension of Policy Process and Institutions

	Australia	Canada
Taxation:	Extent of tax-sharing unilaterally determined by Commonwealth	Federal-provincial taxation agreements periodically re-negotiated
Public Debt:	State borrowing co-ordinated and controlled, to some extent, by Commonwealth through Commonwealth/State Loan Council	Uncoordinated
Public Expenditure:	Commonwealth exerts strong influence on state spending via unilaterally determined conditional grants	Federal grant formulas and conditions are, to some extent, negotiated with the provinces. Threat of taxation without grants-in-aid if province refuses to join in some national programs (eg. health care)
Special Features:		
Executive Federalism	Yes. Commonwealth dominates at meetings with states	Yes. Federal government and provinces bargain more or less as equals
Quasi-independent Intergovernmental Agencies	Yes. Commonwealth Grants Commission; Loan Council	None

References

Alexander, Malcolm and Brian Galligan (eds.). 1992. *Comparative Political Studies*, Pitman.

Barrie, Doreen. 1992. "Environmental Protection in Federal States: Interjurisdictional Cooperation in Canada and Australia," *Discussion Paper No. 18*, Canberra: Federalism Research Centre, Australian National University.

Bella, Leslie. 1979. "The Provincial Role in the Canadian Welfare State: The Influence of Provincial Social Policy Initiatives on the Design of the Canada Assistance Plan," *Canadian Public Administration 22*, 439-452.

Bird, Richard. 1986. *Federal Finance in Comparative Perspective*, Canadian Tax Foundation.

Boadway, Robin and Paul A. R. Hobson. 1993. "Intergovernmental Fiscal Relations in Canada," *Canadian Tax Paper No. 96*, Canadian Tax Foundation.

Boadway, Robin and Frank Flatters. 1991. "Federal-Provincial Relations Revisited: Some Consequences of Recent Constitutional and Policy Developments," M. McMillan (ed.), *Provincial Public Finances: Plaudits, Problems and Prospects*, Canadian Tax Foundation, 87-121.

Brennan, Geoffrey (ed.). 1987. "Constitutional Reform and Fiscal Federalism," *Discussion Paper No. 42*, Canberra: Federalism Research Centre, Australian National University.

Breton, Albert and Anthony Scott. 1982. *The Economic Constitution of Federal States*, Toronto: University of Toronto Press.

Courchene, Thomas J. 1985. *Economic Management and the Division of Powers*, Toronto: University of Toronto Press with the Royal Commission on the Economic Union and Development Prospects for Canada.

Courchene, Thomas J. 1995a. *Fiscal Federalism and the Management of Economic Space: An Australian-Canadian Comparison*, Federalism Research Centre, Australian National University, unpublished.

Courchene, Thomas J. 1995b. "Celebrating Flexibility: An Interpretive Essay on the Evolution of Canadian Federalism," Benefactor's Lecture, C. D. Howe Institute, October 1995.

Gillespie, W. Irwin. 1991. *Tax Borrow and Spend: Financing Federal Spending in Canada, 1867-1990*, Ottawa: Carleton University Press.

Hayes, John A. 1982. *Economic Mobility in Canada: A Comparative Study*, Ottawa: Supply and Services Canada.

Herperger, Dwight. 1991. *Distribution of Powers and Functions in Federal Systems*, Ottawa: Supply and Services Canada.

Hogg, Peter W. 1992. *Constitutional Law of Canada*, 3rd edition, Carswell.
James, Denis W. 1992. *Intergovernmental Fiscal Relations In Australia, Information Series No. 3*, Sydney: Australian Tax Research Foundation.
James, Denis W. 1993. "The Australian Loan Council (2nd ed.)," Department of the Parliamentary Library, Parliament of the Commonwealth of Australia, November.
La Forest, G. V. 1981. "The Allocation of Taxing Power Under the Canadian Constitution," *Canadian Tax Paper No. 65*, 2nd ed., Canadian Tax Foundation.
McMillan, Melville. 1993. *A Local Perspective on Fiscal Federalism Practices, Experiences and Lessons From Developed Countries*, unpublished, December.
Mathews, R. L. ed. 1982. *Public Policies in Two Federal Countries: Canada and Australia*, Canberra: Federalism Research Centre, Australian National University.
Mathews, R. L. 1985. "Comparative Systems of Fiscal Federalism: Australia, Canada and the USA," *Reprint Series No. 69*, Canberra: Federalism Research Centre, Australian National University.
Mathews, R. L. & Bhajan Grewal. 1995. *Fiscal Federalism in Australia: From Whitlam to Keating*, Centre for Strategic Economic Studies, Victoria University.
Perry, David B. 1994. "International Tax Comparisons, 1993," *Canadian Tax Journal 42(6)*, 1675-1683.
Phillips, Susan D. 1995. *The Canada Health and Social Transfer: Fiscal Federalism in Search of a Vision*, School of Public Administration, Carleton University, manuscript.
Rounds, Taryn A. 1992. "Tax Harmonization and Tax Competition: Contrasting Views and Policy Issues in Three Federations," *Discussion Paper No. 15*, Canberra: Federalism Research Centre, Australian National University.
Sharman, Campbell ed. 1994. *Parties and Federalism in Australia and Canada*, Canberra: Federalism Research Centre, Australian National University.
Simeon, Richard. 1972. *Federal-Provincial Diplomacy*, Toronto: University of Toronto Press.
Smiley, Donald V. 1980. *Canada in Question: Federalism in the Eighties*, McGraw-Hill Ryerson.
Smith, Julie P. 1992. *Fiscal Federalism in Australia: A Twentieth Century Chronology*, Canberra: Federalism Research Centre, Australian National University.
Smith, Julie P. 1993. *Taxing Popularity: The Story of Taxation in Australia*, Canberra: Federalism Research Centre, Australian National University.

Saunders, Cheryl. 1990. "Government Borrowing in Australia," *Publius 20(4)*, 35-52.
Saunders, Cheryl. 1992. "Fiscal Federalism - A General and Unholy Scramble," G. Craven (ed.), *Australian Federation: Towards the Second Century*, Melbourne University Press, 101-130.
The Australian Constitution (as altered to 30 April 1991), Canberra: Parliamentary Education Office.
The Constitution of Canada (including the Constitution Act of 1982 and the Constitution Act of 1867), Ottawa: Supply and Services Canada, 1982.
The British North America Acts, 1867 to 1975: Ottawa, Department of Justice.
Uhr, John. 1989. "The Canadian and Australian Senates: Comparing Federal Political Institutions," B. Hodgins (ed.), *Federalism in Canada and Australia*, Peterborough, 130-146.
Vaillancourt, Francois. 1992. "Subnational Tax Harmonization in Australia and Comparisons with Canada and the United States," *Discussion Paper No. 17*, Canberra: Federalism Research Centre, Australian National University.
Walsh, Cliff. 1987. "The Distribution of Taxing Powers Between Levels of Government: The Possibility of State Income Taxation Reconsidered," *Occasional Paper No. 42*, Canberra: Federalism Research Centre, Australian National University.
Walsh, Cliff. 1996. "Making a Mess of Tax Assignment: Australia as a Case Study," *this volume*.
Warden, James. 1992. "Federalism and the Design of the Australian Constitution," *Discussion Paper No. 19*, Canberra: Federalism Research Centre, Australian National University.
Winer, Stanley L. 1992. "Taxation and Federalism in a Changing World," Richard Bird and Jack Mintz (eds.), *Taxation to 2000 and Beyond, Canadian Tax Paper No. 93*, Canadian Tax Foundation, 343-368. With Comments by Albert Breton (369-371) and Anthony Scott (372-380).
Zines, Leslie. 1990. "Federal Constitutional Control Over the Economy," *Publius 20(4)*, 19-34.

Appendix: Constitutional Provisions Related to Fiscal Federalism in Australia and Canada

This appendix lists those parts of the Australian and Canadian constitutions that are related to the federal fiscal structure in each country. As far as possible, similar provisions in the two countries are found side by side each other.

The list of excerpts from the Australian consitution is based on James (1992:Appendix 3). The corresponding excerpts from the Canadian constitution, along with additions to the list in James, was drawn up by Ted Reed.

Provisions Extracted from The Australian Constitution as altered to 30 April 1991 together with Statue of Westminster Adoption Act 1942, and the Australia Act 1986.(1)

CHAPTER 1.

THE PARLIAMENT.

PART V. - POWERS OF THE PARLIAMENT

51. The Parliament shall, subject to this Constitution, have power to make laws for the peace, order, and good government of the Commonwealth with respect to:-

Acts of 1867 (formerly) The British North American Act, 1867) together with amendments made to it since its enactment, and The Constitution Act, 1982 including the Charter of Rights and Freedoms and Other New Provisions, including the procedure for amending the Constitution of Canada.(2)

VI. DISTRIBUTION OF LEGISLATIVE POWERS

91. It shall be lawful for the Queen, by and with the Advice and Consent of the Senate and House of Commons, to make Laws for the Peace, Order, and good Government of Canada, in relation to all Matters not coming within the Classes of Subjects by this Act assigned exclusively to the Legislatures of the Provinces; and for greater Certainty, but not so as to restrict the Generality of the foregoing Terms of this Section, [it is hereby declared that (notwithstanding anything in this Act)] the exclusive Legislative Authority of the Parliament of Canada extends to all Matters coming within the Classes of Subjects next hereinafter enumerated; that is to say, --

(i) Trade and commerce with other countries, and among the States:

91(2). The Regulation of Trade and Commerce.

(ii) Taxation; but so as not to discriminate between States or parts of States:

91(2A). Unemployment insurance.

Fiscal Federalism in Australia and Canada

(iii) Bounties on the production or export of goods, but so that such bounties shall be uniform throughout the Commonwealth:

(iv) Borrowing money on the public credit of the Commonwealth:

(xii) Currency, coinage, and legal tender.

(xiii) Banking, other than State banking; also State banking extending beyond the limits of the State concerned, the incorporation of banks, and the issue of paper money:

(xxiv) The service and execution throughout the Commonwealth of the civil and criminal process and the judgements of the courts of the States:

(xvi) Bills of exchange and promissory notes:

(xx) Foreign corporations, and trading or financial corporations formed within the limits of the Commonwealth:

(xxiii) Invalid and old-age pensions:

91(3). The raising of Money by any Mode or System of Taxation.

92A.(4) In each province, the legislature may make laws in relation to the raising of money by any mode or system of taxation in respect of

(a) non-renewable natural resources and forestry resources in the province and the primary production therefrom, and

(b) sites and facilities in the province for the generation of electrical energy and the production therefrom,

whether or not such production is exported in whole or in part from the province, but such laws may not authorize or provide for taxation that differentiates between production not exported from the province.

91(4). The borrowing of Money on the Public Credit.

91(14). Currency and Coinage.

91(15). Banking, Incorporation of Banks, and the Issue of Paper Money.

91(19). Interest.

91(20). Legal Tender.

91(27). The Criminal Law, except the Constitution of Courts of Criminal Jurisdiction, but including the Procedure in Criminal Matters.

91(18). Bills of Exchange and Promissory Notes.

94A. The Parliament of Canada may make laws in relation to old age pensions and supplementary benefits, including survivors, and disability benefits irrespective of age, but no such law shall affect the operation of any law present or future of a provincial legislature in relation to any such matter. (51)

(xxiii) The provision of maternity allowances, widows' pensions, child endowment, unemployment, pharmaceutical sickness and hospital benefits, medical and dental services (but not so as to authorize any form of civil conscription), benefits to students and family allowances:

(xxix) External affairs:

132. The Parliament and Government of Canada shall have all Powers necessary or proper for performing the Obligations of Canada or of any Province thereof, as Part of the British Empire, towards Foreign Countries, arising under Treaties between the Empire and such Foreign Countries.

(xxxi) The acquisition of property on just terms from any State or person for any purpose in respect of which the Parliament has power to make laws:

92(10). Local Works and Undertakings other than such as are of the following Classes:--

(a) Lines of Steam or other Ships, Railways, Canals, Telegraphs, and other Works and Undertakings connecting the Province with any other or others of the Provinces, or extending beyond the Limits of the Province;
(b) Lines of Steam Ships between the Province and any British or Foreign Country;
(c) Such works as, although wholly situate within the Province, are before or after their Execution declared by the Parliament of Canada to be for the general Advantage of Canada or for the Advantage of Two or more of the Provinces.

(xxiii) The acquisition, with the consent of a State, of any railways of the State on terms arranged between the Commonwealth and the State.

(xxxvii) Matters referred to the Parliament of the Commonwealth by the Parliament or Parliaments of any State or States, but so that the law shall extend only to States by whose Parliaments the matter is referred, or which afterwards adopt the law:

52. The Parliament shall, subject to this Constitution, have <u>exclusive power</u> to make laws for the peace, order, and good government of the Commonwealth with respect to --

(i) The seat of government of the Commonwealth, and all places acquired by the Commonwealth for public purposes:

(ii) Matters relating to any department of the public service the control of which is by this Constitution transferred to the Executive Government of the Commonwealth:

53. Proposed laws appropriating revenue or moneys, or imposing taxation, shall not originate in the Senate. But a proposed law shall not be taken to appropriate revenue or moneys, or to impose taxation, by reason only of its containing provisions for the imposition or appropriation of fines or other pecuniary penalties, or for the demand or payment or appropriation of fees for licences, or fees for services under the proposed law.

The Senate may not amend proposed laws imposing taxation, or proposed laws appropriating revenue or moneys for the ordinary annual services of the Government.

The Senate may not amend any proposed law so as to increase any proposed charge or burden on the people.

The Senate may at any stage return to the House of Representatives any proposed law which the Senate may not amend, requesting, by message, the omission or amendment of any items or provisions therein. And the House of Representatives may, if it thinks fit, make any of such omissions or amendments, with or without modifications.

Except as provided in this section, the Senate shall have equal power with the House of Representatives in respect of all proposed laws.

117. The several Provinces shall retain all their respective Public Property not otherwise disposed of in this Act, subject to the Right of Canada to assume any Lands or Public Property required for Fortifications or for the Defence of the Country.

Money Votes: Royal Assent

53. Bills for appropriating any Part of the Public Revenue, or for imposing any Tax or Impost, shall originate in the House of Commons.

54. The proposed law which appropriates revenue or moneys for the ordinary annual services of the Government shall deal only with such appropriation.

55. Laws imposing taxation shall deal only with the imposition of taxation, and any provision therein dealing with any other matter shall be of no effect.

Laws imposing taxation, except laws imposing duties of customs or of excise, shall deal with one subject of taxation only: but laws imposing duties of customs shall deal with duties of customs only, and laws imposing duties of excise shall deal with duties of excise only.

56. A vote, resolution, or proposed law for the appropriation of revenue or moneys shall not be passed unless the purpose of the appropriation has in the same session been recommended by message of the Governor-General to the House in which the proposal originated.

54. It shall not be lawful for the House of Commons to adopt or pass any Vote, Resolution, Address, or Bill for the Appropriation of any Part of the Public Revenue, or of any Tax or Impost, to any Purpose that has not been first recommended to that House by Message of the Governor General in the Session in which such Vote, Resolution, Address, or Bill is proposed.

90. The following Provisions of this Act respecting the Parliament of Canada, namely, -- the Provisions relating to Appropriation and Tax Bills, the Recommendation of Money Votes, the Assent to Bills, the Disallowance of Acts, and the Signification of Pleasure on Bills reserved, -- shall extend and apply to the Legislatures of the several Provinces as if those Provisions were here re-enacted and made applicable in Terms to the respective Provinces and the Legislatures thereof, with the Substitution of the Lieutenant Governor of the Province for the Governor General, of the Governor General for the Queen and for a Secretary of State, of One Year for Two Years, and of the Province of Canada.

101. The Parliament of Canada may, notwithstanding anything in this Act, from Time to Time provide for the Constitution, Maintenance, and Organization of a General Court of Appeal for Canada, and for the

CHAPTER III. - THE JUDICATURE.

71. The judicial power of the Commonwealth shall be vested in a Federal Supreme Court, to be called the High Court of Australia, and in such other federal courts as the Parliament creates, and in such other courts as it invests with federal jurisdiction. The High Court shall consist of a Chief Justice, and so many other Justices, not less than two, as the Parliament prescribes.

72. The Justices of the High Court and of the other courts created by the Parliament --

(i) Shall be appointed by the Governor-General in Council:

(ii) Shall not be removed except by the Governor-General in Council, on an address from both Houses of the Parliament in the same session, praying for such removal on the ground of proved misbehaviour or in a capacity:

(iii) Shall receive such remuneration as the Parliament may fix; but the remuneration shall not be diminished during their continuance in office.

CHAPTER IV. - FINANCE AND TRADE.

81. All revenues or moneys raised or received by the Executive Government of the Commonwealth shall form one Consolidated Revenue Fund, to be appropriated for the purposes of the Commonwealth in the manner and subject to the charges and liabilities imposed by this Constitution.

Establishment of any additional Courts for the better Administration of the Laws of Canada.

VII.--JUDICATURE.

96. The Governor General shall appoint the Judges of the Superior, District, and County Courts in each Province, except those of the Courts of Probate in Nova Scotia and New Brunswick.

99.(1) Subject to subsection two of this section, the Judges of the Superior Courts shall hold office during good behaviour, but shall be removable by the Governor General on Address of the Senate and House of Commons.

VIII.--REVENUES; DEBTS; ASSETS; TAXATION.

102. All Duties and Revenues over which the respective Legislatures of Canada, Nova Scotia, and New Brunswick before and at the Union had and have Power of Appropriation, except such Portions thereof as are by this Act reserved to the respective Legislatures of the Provinces, or are raised by them in accordance with the special Powers conferred on them by this Act, shall form One Consolidated Revenue Fund, to be appropriated for the Public Service of Canada in the Manner and subject to the Charges of this Act provided.

82. The costs, charges, and expenses incident to the collection, management, and receipt of the Consolidated Revenue Fund shall form the first charge thereon; and the revenue of the Commonwealth shall in the first instance be applied to the payment of the expenditure of the Commonwealth.

83. No money shall be drawn from the Treasury of the Commonwealth except under appropriation made by law.

86. On the establishment of the Commonwealth, the collection and control of duties of customs and of excise, and the control of the payment of bounties, shall pass to the Executive Government of the Commonwealth.

87. During a period of ten years after the establishment of the Commonwealth and thereafter until the Parliament otherwise provides, of the net revenue of the Commonwealth from duties of customs and of excise not more than one-fourth shall be applied annually by the Commonwealth towards its expenditure.

The balance shall, in accordance with this Constitution, be paid to the several States, or applied towards the payment of interest on debts of the several States taken over by the Commonwealth.

88. Uniform duties of customs shall be imposed within two years after the establishment of the Commonwealth.

126. Such Portions of the Duties and Revenues over which the respective Legislatures of Canada, Nova Scotia, and New Brunswick had before the Union Power of Appropriation as are by this Act reserved to the respective Governments or Legislatures of the Provinces, and all Duties and Revenues raised by them in accordance with the special Powers conferred upon them by this Act, shall in each Province form One Consolidated Revenue Fund to be appropriated for the Public Service of the Province.

103. The Consolidated Revenue Fund of Canada shall be permanently charged with the Costs, Charges, and Expenses incident to the Collection, Management, and Receipt thereof, and the same shall form the First Charge thereon, subject to be reviewed and audited in such Manner as shall be ordered by the Governor General in Council until the Parliament otherwise provides.

90. On the imposition of uniform duties of customs the power of the Parliament to impose duties of customs and of excise, and to grant bounties on the production or export of goods, shall become exclusive.

91. Nothing in this Constitution prohibits a State from granting any aid to or bounty on mining for gold, silver, or other metals, not from granting, with the consent of both Houses of the Parliament of the Commonwealth expressed by resolution, any aid to or bounty on the production or export of goods.

109. All Lands, Mines, Minerals, and Royalties belonging to the several Provinces of Canada, Nova Scotia, and New Brunswick at the Union, and all Sums then due or payable tor such Lands, Mines, Minerals, or Royalties, shall belong to the several Provinces of Ontario, Quebec, Nova Scotia, and New Brunswick in which the same are situate or arise, subject to any Trusts existing in respect thereof, and to any Interest other than that of the Province in the same.

Non-Renewable Natural Resources, Forestry Resources and Electrical Energy

92A.(1) In each province, the legislature may exclusively make laws in relation to

(a) exploration for non-renewable natural resources in the province;
(b) development, conservation and management of non-renewable natural resources and forestry resources in the province, including laws in relation to the rate of primary production therefrom; and
(c) development, conservation and management of sites and facilities in the province for the generation and production of electrical energy.

92. On the imposition of uniform duties of customs, trade, commerce, and intercourse among the States, whether by means of internal carriage or ocean navigation, shall be absolutely free.

94. After five years from the imposition of uniform duties of customs, the Parliament may provide, on such basis as it deems fair, for the monthly payment to the several States of all surplus revenue of the Commonwealth.

121. All Articles of the Growth, Produce, or Manufacture of any one of the Provinces shall, from and after the Union, be admitted free into each of the other Provinces.

SCHEDULE B, CONSTITUTION ACT, 1982

PART III

EQUALIZATION AND REGIONAL DISPARITIES

96. During a period of ten years after the establishment of the Commonwealth and thereafter until the Parliament otherwise provides, the Parliament may grant financial assistance to any State on such terms and conditions as the Parliament thinks fit.

36.(1) Without altering the legislative authority of Parliament or of the provincial legislatures, or the rights of any of them with respect to the exercise of their legislative authority, Parliament and the legislatures, together with the government of Canada and the provincial governments, are committed to
(a) promoting equal opportunities for the well-being of Canadians;
(b) furthering economic development to reduce disparity in opportunities; and
(c) providing essential public services of reasonable quality to all Canadians.

(2) Parliament and the government of Canada are committed to the principle of making equalization payments to ensure that provincial governments have sufficient revenues to provide reasonably comparable levels of public services at reasonably comparable levels of taxation.

98. The power of the Parliament to make laws with respect to trade and commerce extends to navigation and shipping, and to railways the property of any State.

91.(10) Navigation and Shipping.

91.(13) Ferries between a Province and any British or Foreign Country or between Two Provinces.

92.(10) Local Works and Undertakings other than such as are of the following Classes:--

(a) Lines of Steam or other Ships, Railways, Canals, Telegraphs, and other Works and Undertakings connecting the Province with any other or others of the Provinces, or extending beyond the Limits of the Province;
(b) Lines of Steam Ships between the Province and any British or Foreign Country;

99. The Commonwealth shall not, by any law or regulation of trade, commerce, or revenue, give preference to one State or any part thereof over another State or any part thereof.

101. There shall be an Inter-State Commission, with such powers of adjudication and administration as the Parliament deems necessary for the execution and maintenance, within the Commonwealth, of the provisions of this Constitution relating to trade and commerce, and of all laws made thereunder.

102. The Parliament may by any law with respect to trade or commerce forbid, as to railways any preference or discrimination by any State, or by any authority constituted under a State, if such preference or discrimination is undue and unreasonable, or unjust to any State; due regard being had to the financial responsibilities incurred by any State in connection with the construction and maintenance of its railways. But no preference or discrimination shall, within the meaning of this section, be taken to be undue and unreasonable, or unjust to any State, unless so adjudged by the Inter-State Commission.

104. Nothing in this Constitution shall render unlawful any rate for the carriage of goods upon a railway, the property of a State, if the rate is deemed by the Inter-State Commission to be necessary for the development of the territory of the State, and if the rate applies equally to goods within the State and to goods passing into the State from other States.

105. The Parliament may take over from the states their public debts portion thereof according to the respective numbers of their people as shown by the latest statistics of the Commonwealth, and may convert, renew, or consolidate such debts, or any part thereof; and the States shall indemnify the Commonwealth in respect of the debts taken over, and thereafter the interest payable in respect of the debts shall be deducted and retained from the portions of the surplus

92A.(2) In each province, the legislature may make laws in relation to the export from the province to another part of Canada of the primary production from non-renewable natural resources and forestry resources in the province and the production from facilities in the province for the generation of electrical energy, but such laws may not authorize or provide for discrimination in prices or in supplies exported to another part of Canada.

92A.(3) Nothing in subjection (2) derogates from the authority of Parliament to enact laws in relation to the matters referred to in that subsection and, where such a law of Parliament and a law of a province conflict, the law of Parliament prevails to the extent of the conflict.

91.(1A) The Public Debt and Property.

revenue of the Commonwealth payable to the several States, or if such surplus is insufficient or if there is no surplus, then the deficiency or the whole amount shall be paid by the several States.

105A. -- **(1)** The Commonwealth may make agreements with the States with respect to the public debts of the States, including --

(a) the taking over of such debts by the Commonwealth;
(b) the management of such debts;
(c) the payment of interest and the provision and management of sinking funds in respect of such debts;
(d) the consolidation, renewal, conversion, and redemption of such debts;
(e) the indemnification of the Commonwealth by the States in respect of debts taken over by the Commonwealth; and
(f) the borrowing of money by the States or by the Commonwealth, or by the Commonwealth for the States.

(2) The Parliament may make laws for validating any such agreement made before the commencement of this section.

(3) The Parliament may make laws for the carrying out by the parties thereto of any such agreement.

(4) Any such agreement may be varied or rescinded by the parties thereto.

(5) Every such agreement and any such variation thereof shall be binding upon the Commonwealth and the States parties thereto notwithstanding anything contained in this Constitution or the Constitution of the several States or in any law of the Parliament of the Commonwealth or of any State.

(6) The powers conferred by this section shall not be construed as being limited in any way by the provisions of section one hundred and five of this Constitution.

CHAPTER V. THE STATES.

107. Every power of the Parliament of a Colony which has become or becomes a State, shall, unless it is by this Constitution exclusively vested in the Parliament of the Commonwealth or withdrawn from the Parliament of the State, continue as at the establishment of the Commonwealth, or as at the admission or establishment of the State, as the case may be.

Exclusive Powers of Provincial Legislatures.

92. In each Province the Legislature may exclusively make laws in relation to Matters coming within the Classes of Subject next hereinafter enumerated; that is to say,--

2. Direct Taxation within the Province in order to the raising of a Revenue for Provincial Purposes.

3. The borrowing of Money on the sole Credit of the Province.

5. The Management and Sale of the Public Lands belonging to the Province and of the Timber and Wood thereon.

7. The Establishment, Maintenance, and Management of Hospitals, Asylums, Charities, and Eleemosynary Institutions in and for the Province, other than Marine Hospitals.

8. Municipal Institutions in the Province.

9. Shop, Saloon, Tavern, Auctioneer, and other Licences in order to the raising of a Revenue for Provincial, Local, or Municipal Purposes.

10. Local Works and Undertakings other than such as are of the following Classes:--
(a) Lines of Steam or other Ships, Railways, Canals, Telegraphs, and other Works and Undertakings connecting the Province with any other or others of the Provinces, or extending beyond the Limits of the Province;
(b) Lines of Steam Ships between the Province and any British or Foreign Country;
(c) Such Works as, although wholly situate within the Province, are before or after their Execution declared by the Parliament of Canada to be for the general Advantage of Canada or for the Advantage of Two or more of the Provinces.

11. The Incorporation of Companies with Provincial Objects.

109. When a law of a State is inconsistent with a law of the Commonwealth, the latter shall prevail, and the former shall, to the extent of the inconsistency, be invalid.

111. Parliament of a State may surrender any part of the State to the Commonwealth; and upon such surrender, and the acceptance thereof by the Commonwealth, such part of the State shall become subject to the exclusive jurisdiction of the Commonwealth.

114. A State shall not, without the consent of the Parliament of the Commonwealth, raise or maintain any naval or military force, or impose any tax on property of any kind belonging to the Commonwealth, nor shall the Commonwealth impose any tax on property of any kind belonging to a State.

115. A State shall not coin money, nor make anything but gold and silver coin a legal tender in payment of debts.

13. Property and Civil Rights in the Province.

14. The Administration of Justice in the Province, including the Constitution, Maintenance, and Organization of Provincial Courts, both of Civil and of Criminal Jurisdiction, and including Procedure in Civil Matters in those Courts.

91.(29) Such Classes of Subjects as are expressly excepted in the Enumeration of the Classes of Subjects by this Act assigned exclusively to the Legislatures of the Provinces.

And any Matter coming within any of the Classes of Subjects enumerated in this Section shall not be deemed to come within the Class of Matters of a local or private Nature comprised in the Enumeration of the Classes of Subjects by this Act assigned exclusively to the Legislatures of the Provinces.

92.(16) Generally all Matters of a merely local or private Nature in the Province.

125. No Lands or Property belonging to Canada or any Province shall be liable to Taxation.

Part I

Canadian Charter Of Rights And Freedoms

Mobility Rights

117. A subject of the Queen, resident in any State, shall not be subject in any other State to any disability or discrimination which would not be equally applicable to him if he were a subject of the Queen resident in such other State.

6.(1) Every citizen of Canada has the right to enter, remain in and leave Canada.

(2) Every citizen of Canada and every person who has the status of a permanent resident of Canada has the right
(a) to move to and take up residence in any province; and
(b) to pursue the gaining of a livelihood in any province.

Endnotes

(1) Parliamentary Education Office, The Parliament of the Commonwealth of Australia, *The Australian Constitution as offered to 30 April 1991 together with Statute of Westminster Adoption Act 1986 and An Introduction and Outline*, Second Edition, Fyshwick, ACT: National Capital Printing for the Parliamentary Education Office.

(2) Department of Justice, Government of Canada, *A Consolidation Of The Constitution Acts 1867 to 1982, Consolidated as of April 17, 1982*. Ottawa: Queen's Printer, 1983.

(1) & (2) The idea for this comparative presentation of provisions of the Constitutions of federations, in this case those of Australia and Canada, of importance to matters involving taxation, fiscal institutions and structure, and fiscal federalism, was stimulated by a reading of Appendix 3 of *Intergovernmental Relations in Australia*, by Denis W. James, Australian Tax Research Foundation Information Series No. 3, Sydney, N.S.W.: Australian Tax Research Foundation, 1992, 112-16.

5

Tax Assignment and Fiscal Externalities in a Federal State

Bev Dahlby and
L.S. Wilson

The many similarities between Australia and Canada invite comparisons of public policies and the federal institutions of the two countries, including tax policy. One major difference in the tax systems of the two countries is the assignment of taxes between the central governments and the states/provinces. In Australia, most of the tax revenue is collected by the Commonwealth. The state governments have exclusive control of the payroll and property taxes, but they rely on grants from the central government to finance a major portion of their expenditures. (Walsh and Thomson, 1993) In Canada, the provinces also receive grants from the federal government, but they raise most of their revenue from their own tax sources, and the most important tax fields — personal and corporate income taxes, sales, and excise taxes — are co-occupied by the federal and provincial governments. Thus in Australia, the state governments collect a relatively small proportion of total tax revenue and the two levels of government rely on different tax bases, whereas in Canada, the provinces collect a relatively large share of total tax revenue and both levels of government utilize the same tax bases.

The assignment of tax fields has received public attention in Canada in recent years for three reasons. First, the on-going and seemingly never-ending efforts to amend the Canadian constitution to meet Quebec's aspiration for greater political and fiscal autonomy have placed the tax assignment on the public agenda for reform. The 1991 Allaire Report, which recommended a sweeping devolution of taxation and expenditure powers to the Quebec government, prompted public discussion on its proposed tax assignment and other options. (Mintz and Wilson, 1991 and Dahlby, 1992) Second, the federal government's introduction of a value-added tax (the GST) in 1991, despite strong opposition from the provincial governments which (except for Alberta) continued to levy retail sales taxes, has lead to a re-examination of the assignment of tax fields in Canada. (Boothe and Snoddon, 1994) Third, fiscal restraint by both levels of government and the reduction in federal transfers to the provinces has increased the province's interest in exercising more control over their largest source of tax revenue, the personal income tax.

In Australia, there is also interest in re-examining the assignment of taxes because the decline in Commonwealth grants to the states, as a share of Commonwealth outlays and as a share of GDP, has increased fiscal pressures on the states and highlighted their limited control over fiscal policy. (Walsh and Thomson, 1993)

In this paper, we try to make a preliminary assessment of whether the differences in the tax assignment in the two countries have had a significant effect on the fiscal policies of the two countries. Specifically, we examine two questions:

- Has the division of tax powers influenced the tax and expenditure mix in the two countries?
- Has the division of tax powers affected the overall level of taxation in the two countries?

There has been relatively little basic research on tax assignment in federations. The most thorough discussions of tax assignment issues are contained in a volume edited by McLure (1983a) based on a conference sponsored by the Federalism Research Centre and in McLure (1992, 1994). The recent resurgence of interest in tax assignment in federations has partly been motivated by attempts to modify the assignment of tax powers in the Russian Federation and other emerging market economies. (Shah, 1994; Boadway, Roberts, and Shah, 1994; and Wilson, 1994) While much of the literature on tax assignment has (justifiably) been concerned with attempting to maintain fiscal equity among individuals in a federal system, our focus will be on the fiscal externalities that arise with alternative tax assignments since these interactions are the most relevant for the issues — the tax/

expenditure mix and the overall level of taxation — that are the focus of our paper. The following sections describe the fiscal externalities that occur in a federal state.

Fiscal Externalities in a Federal State

We will refer to the central government as the federal government and to the provincial, state, or local governments as the state governments.[1] Interjurisdictional fiscal externalities occur when a government's tax and expenditure decisions affect the well-being of taxpayers in other jurisdictions either directly by changing their consumer or producer prices or their public good provisions or indirectly by altering the tax revenues or expenditures of other governments. What distinguishes the two types of fiscal externalities is that direct fiscal externalities affect the "utility functions" of non-residents whereas indirect fiscal externalities affect the budget constraints of other governments. Direct fiscal externalities are always horizontal (i.e., between state governments). Indirect fiscal externalities may be either horizontal or vertical (i.e., between the federal and state governments.) These fiscal externalities can arise through either taxation or expenditure decisions and may be either positive (beneficial) or negative (harmful).

Tax Externalities

In thinking about how tax externalities affect the fiscal behaviour of governments we will focus on the implications for the marginal cost of public funds which can be defined as the economic cost to taxpayers of raising an additional dollar of tax revenue. See Ballard and Fullerton (1992) for an introduction to the literature on the measurement and interpretation of the marginal cost of public funds. We assume that governments select their mix of taxes and the overall level of taxation to fund public expenditures based, in part, on their perceived marginal cost of public funds (MCF). Tax externalities can distort their fiscal decisions if the perceived MCF deviates from the total or social marginal cost of public funds which takes into account the effect of a tax change on all taxpayers and on all governments' budget constraints.

Table 5.1 gives examples of the three types of tax externalities. A direct horizontal tax externality occurs when part of the tax burden is borne by individuals who do not reside in the jurisdiction which imposed the tax. For example, a state hotel tax may be borne by visitors from other jurisdictions. Such tax exportation causes governments to underestimate the social

---

1. This section is based on Dahlby (1995).

Table 5.1
Tax Externalities

Types of Externality	Examples	Fiscal Implications	Relevance for Australia	Relevance for Canada
Direct Horizontal	*Tax Exporting:* A hotel tax which is borne by visitors from other states.	Increased reliance on taxes where at least part of the burden is borne in other jurisdictions.	Limited importance except perhaps for the pricing of state owned utilities.	Potential exporting of provincial excise and sales taxes.
Indirect Horizontal	*Tax Competition:* State death duties.	The potential mobility of the tax base leads to downward pressure on tax rates.	Reductions in state stamp duties on financial transactions.	Potentially significant with respect to provincial corporate income tax, sales and excise taxes, and personal income tax.
Indirect Vertical	*Tax Base Overlap:* Federal and state excise taxes on cigarettes.	Both levels of government will tend to impose high tax rates on the shared tax base, but the effect on total tax revenue is ambiguous because both levels of government could end up on the "wrong" side of the Laffer curve for total tax revenue.	The states' payroll tax base overlaps with the Commonwealth's personal income tax base.	Overlap is especially significant with respect to excise taxes on cigarettes, alcohol, and gasoline. Also significant in personal income tax, corporate income tax, and sales tax fields.

marginal cost of public funds (SMCF) if they ignore the tax burdens which are borne outside of their jurisdiction, and state governments will tend to rely on these taxes to a greater extent than a federal government which, presumably, takes into account the effect of such taxes on all taxpayers.[2]

An indirect horizontal tax externality can occur if a tax base is mobile between jurisdictions. A prime example is the "demise" of death duties in Australia and Canada. Grossman (1990) has shown that Queensland's abolition of death duties in 1976 increased in-migration to the state. Other states responded by lowering their death duties, and by 1983, all states had abolished death duties. A remarkably similar sequence of events occurred in Canada in the early 1970s when the federal government turned this tax field over to the provinces. Another example was the recent competition among Australian states resulting in reduction in stamp duties on financial transactions to half their previous level. Not all forms of tax competition are as extreme as these two examples, but state taxation of mobile tax bases can be expected to put downward pressure on state tax rates and tax revenues. Whether tax competition is a "good thing" or a "bad thing" depends on

---
2. See Arnott and Grieson (1981) and Wildasin (1987).

whether one views governments as basically benevolent institutions which reflect the population's preferences for publicly provided goods and services or as Leviathans which maximize total tax revenues. (Brennan and Buchanan, 1980) Under the benevolent government view, tax competition leads to under-provision of public services by state governments because they ignore the additional revenue that other jurisdictions obtain when they raises their tax rates, and thus they overestimate the SMCF.[3] The perceived deleterious effects of tax competition led Richard Musgrave (1983:11) to put at the top of his list of general principles for the assignment of tax powers in a federation that "middle and especially lower-level jurisdictions should tax those bases which have low inter-jurisdictional mobility." In a similar vein, Charles McLure (1983b:101) concluded that "severe conceptual faults, as well as troublesome administrative defects, render the corporate income tax not a proper source of revenue for jurisdictions as "open" as the American states." If governments are viewed as Leviathans, however, tax competition will help to constrain their rapacious appetites for tax revenues and improve citizens well-being. In this view, tax competition serves a valuable purpose in constraining "excessively high tax rates implied by policy-makers' pursuit of their own interests" (Edwards and Keen, 1994:2). As Brennan and Buchanan (1980) put it, "...the intergovernmental competition that a genuinely federal structure offers may be constitutionally 'efficient,' regardless of the more familiar considerations of interunit spillovers examined in the orthodox theory of fiscal federalism" (185) so that "...tax competition among separate units...is an objective to be sought in its own right" (186). In either of these views, then, the benevolent government view of Musgrave and McLure, or the government-as-leviathan view of Brennan and Buchanan, tax competition is presumed to reduce the size of the public sector.

Most of the literature on tax assignment has focussed on direct and indirect horizontal tax externalities. However, indirect vertical tax externalities can also occur in a federal system, and since these externalities have received relatively little attention, we will discuss them at somewhat greater length. An indirect vertical tax externality occurs when a tax rate change by one level of government affects the tax revenue of the other level of government. One example, which has received considerable attention in the United States, is the deductibility of state and local taxes from the federal income tax. Feldstein and Metcalf (1987:726) analyzed the impact of deductibility on the fiscal decisions of state and local governments in the United States in 1980 and found that "deductibility has a substantial effect on the amount of personal deductible taxes paid to the state and local

---

3. See Zodrow and Meiszkowski (1986) and Mintz and Tulkens (1986).

governments. The effect of deductibility on the amount of other revenue collected by state and local governments is more uncertain." Johnson (1988, 1991) has also recognized this concept of vertical externality in his discussion of the voter preferred level of government to undertake redistribution. In his model some of the costs of redistribution when done by lower levels of government are borne outside the jurisdiction, through the federal government budget constraint, thus voters prefer local redistribution to national.

Another example is tax base overlap which occurs when two governments tax the same base. The taxation of cigarettes by the Canadian federal and provincial governments is an example. Figure 5.1 shows how this tax externality occurs. The demand curve for cigarettes, D, is assumed to have a negative slope and the supply curve, S, is assumed to be perfectly elastic. Initially, the federal excise tax rate is t, a provincial government's excise tax rate is t, and the consumer price is P^0. The federal tax revenue is (area c + area e), and the provincial government's tax revenue is (area b + area d). The quantity of cigarettes consumed is x^0. If the provincial government raises its tax rate to t, the consumer price increases by the amount of the tax increase to P^1, and the provincial government's tax revenues (presumably) increase by (area a - area d). However, the federal government's tax revenues will decline by an amount equal to area e because the quantity consumed has declined to x^1.[4] Note that this situation is symmetric. An increase in the federal tax rate will reduce the provincial government's tax revenues.

The problem created by tax base overlap is that both levels of government will underestimate the social marginal cost of raising tax revenue if they neglect the revenue losses incurred by the other government.[5] It can be shown that the total downward bias in the governments' perceived marginal cost of public funds is a maximum when both levels of government collect equal amounts of tax revenue from the same tax base. The downward bias in the perceived marginal cost of public funds will lead both governments to levy a higher total tax rate on the shared tax base than they would if it was only taxed by one level of government. Indeed, it is possible to construct simple models of government behaviour where the governments wind up on the negatively sloped section of the Laffer curve for total revenue. See Keen (1995) .

---

4. This assumes that the reduction in demand does not reflect interprovincial smuggling which would lead to increased cigarette sales in other provinces and a offsetting increase in federal tax revenue.
5. See Boadway and Keen (1994) on the efficiency implications of tax base overlap.

Thus tax base overlap is equivalent to the common property resource problem that occurs in the private sector when property rights in a resource are not defined or enforceable. The over-exploitation of shared tax bases is the public sector equivalent of the over-exploitation of fishing grounds.

The potential problems created by tax base overlap are not widely appreciated. Hewitt and Mihaljek (1992:346) stated that "no economic justification exists for prohibiting overlapping tax assignments, and in many countries different levels of government indeed use the same taxes without negative consequences." However, calculations by Dahlby (1994) indicate that it may be a very significant problem in Canada. All of the provincial governments, except Quebec, levy their personal income tax as a proportion of the basic federal income. (Quebec collects its own provincial income tax.) In addition to this basic provincial income tax rate, all of the provinces, except Newfoundland, levy a surtax on high-income earners. The Dahlby study found that the perceived marginal cost of public funds for increases in the provincial governments' basic personal income tax rate ranged between 69 and 77 percent of the total social marginal cost of public funds. However, for an increase in the provinces' high-income surtax, the perceived marginal cost of public funds was at most 36 percent of the total social marginal cost of public funds, and in three provinces—Manitoba, Nova Scotia, and Prince Edward Island—an increase in the provincial surtax rate would actually reduce total federal and provincial tax revenues if the uncompensated labour supply elasticity is 0.1. The bias in the marginal cost of public funds caused by tax base overlap may explain why the Canadian provinces have introduced high-income surtaxes, and therefore impose more progressive income tax rate structures than the federal government, when the conventional wisdom holds that tax competition for mobile, high-income taxpayers will cause the provinces to have less progressive income tax rate structures.

Of course, these calculations do not mean that tax base overlap does in fact distort governments taxation decisions in a federal system. Tax base overlap may have contributed to the very high rates of taxation of cigarettes in Canada (relative to the U.S.), which lead to the recent coordinated reduction in the federal and provincial tax rates in Ontario, Quebec, and New Brunswick in an effort to stop cigarette smuggling from the United States, but this is just a conjecture. The only empirical study of the fiscal consequences of tax base overlap that we are aware of is by Locke and Tassonyi (1993). They analyzed the per capita expenditures of municipal governments in Ontario in 1986. These municipal governments share the property tax base with school boards. Locke and Tassonyi (1993:949) found that "a one percent increase in the size of the mill rate for school purposes relative to the local [municipal] mill rate causes local per capita expenditure to fall by approximately 0.2 percent." Their empirical results do not indicate whether a shared property tax base leads to a higher property tax burden than would occur if municipal and education spending decisions were made by the same government, but their results indicate that sharing the same tax base seems to affect governments' fiscal decisions. Obviously more empirical research on the fiscal consequences of tax base overlap would be very desirable.

Tax base overlap is only one example of a vertical tax externality. Deductibility of state taxes is another example which has already been discussed. Revenue sharing can also give rise to vertical fiscal externality. If a federal government shares the revenue from a tax base with state governments, which do not set their own tax rates, then increases in federal tax rates create a positive vertical tax externality. The fact that at least some of the revenue from a federal tax increase goes directly to the state governments may affect the federal government's perception of the marginal cost of public funds from that tax source.

To conclude, vertical tax externalities are a ubiquitous and inevitable characteristic of a federal system, especially where the states have independent taxing authority. While it is impossible to completely disentangle the federal and state tax fields because, for example, the sales tax base depends on disposable income which is affected by income tax rates, some allocations of tax fields between the levels of government probably cause less distortion than others. Giving each level of government its own tax base is probably superior in most circumstances to allowing both levels of government to utilize the same tax base.

Expenditure Externalities

We will also consider expenditure externalities because the assignment of taxes also affects these interactions among the governments in a federation. Table 5.2 shows examples of the three basic types of expenditure externality. The classic example of a direct horizontal expenditure externality is pollution abatement by one state which benefits the residents of another state by lowering cross-border emissions. An example of an indirect horizontal expenditure is a economic development grant provided by a state which attracts investment that would otherwise have occurred in other states, thereby reducing the tax base of the other states. An indirect vertical expenditure externality occurs when the expenditure decisions by one level of government affect the expenditures or revenues of the other level of government. An important Canadian example is the interdependence

Table 5.2
Tax Externalities

Types of Externality	Examples	Fiscal Implications	Relevance for Australia	Relevance for Canada
Direct Horizontal	*Benefit Spillovers:* Pollution abatement activity which benefits the downstream residents of other states.	Under-provision of activities which generate beneficial externalities.		Modest in the area of environmental activities. Potentially significant in higher education.
Indirect Horizontal	*Spending Competition:* Economic development grants which attract investment that would otherwise have occurred in other states.	Over-provision of activities which reduce the tax revenues of other state governments.		Potentially important in the area of economic development incentives.
Indirect Vertical	*Expenditure Interdependence:* State education expenditures which increase the federal government's income, payroll and sales tax revenues because of the increases in students' lifetime earnings.	Under-provision of activities which have a positive effect on the net revenues of the other level of government.	Possibly significant for education and infrastructure provided by states.	Provision of unemployment insurance benefits by the federal government and welfare payments by provinces. Possibly significant for provincial spending on education and infrastructure.

between the federal government's provision of unemployment insurance (UI) benefits and the provinces' welfare programs. If the federal government reduces the level or duration of UI benefits, more people will apply for welfare, thereby increasing the provinces' spending on social assistance. Estimates for British Columbia, for example, suggest welfare expenditures rise by approximately 30 cents for each dollar UI reduction. Conversely, short-term employment programs by the provinces, which allow unemployed welfare recipients to qualify for unemployment insurance benefits ultimately lead to higher UI spending by the federal government.

Vertical expenditure externalties can also occur through their effect on the revenues of the other level of government. For example, spending by a state government on education or physical infrastructure raises the potential earnings of its residents by making them more productive, and this will increase the federal government's income, payroll, and sales tax revenues. This may lead to under-provision of such activities by state governments.

The under-provision of a state activity which generates a vertical expenditure externality is illustrated in the following model which is described in more detail in Dahlby (1995). The federal and state governments are assumed to levy proportional taxes on labour income at the rates t_F and t_i, respectively. The state's public good, g_i, which can be provided at a constant marginal cost, c, increases the wage rate in state, $w = w(g_i)$ with $w'(g_i) > 0$ and $w''(g_i) < 0$. The additional labour income per dollar spent on g_i will be defined as:

$$\phi(g_i) = \frac{L}{c} \frac{dw}{dg_i} \quad (1)$$

where L is quantity of labour supplied. It is assumed that the uncompensated labour supply, η, is positive. If g_i were financed with lump-sum taxes, the optimal g_i occurs where an additional dollar spent on g_i generates an additional dollar of income, i.e. $\phi(g_i^o) = 1$.

If the state government uses a tax on labour income to finance its expenditures, and chooses g_i to maximize the representative individual's indirect utility function, subject to the revenue constraint the $cg_i = R_i = t_i wL$, then g_i will be determined according to the following version of the Atkinson and Stern (1974) condition for optimal public expenditures:

$$(1 - t_i - t_F) \phi(g_i) = MCF_i (1 - \rho_i) \quad (2)$$

where MCF_i is the state's perceived marginal cost of public funds and ρ_i is the additional revenue obtained by state i for each additional dollar spent on g_i:

$$\rho_i = \frac{1}{c} \frac{dR_i}{dg_i} = t_i \phi(g_i)(1 + \eta) \quad (3)$$

Note that ρ_i includes the effect of the increase in the wage rate on the amount of labour supplied. The left-hand side of (2) shows the private after-tax benefit of an additional dollar of expenditure on the public good, and the right-hand side shows the perceived cost to the state in providing an additional dollar of expenditure on the public good.

Note that there are two potential sources of bias in the state's choice of g_i. The first arises from the overlapping federal and state tax bases. It is assumed that state i underestimates its marginal cost of public funds because it does not take into account the reduction in the federal government's revenue that occurs when it raises its tax rate. On the other hand, the state government also underestimates the social marginal benefit of spending on g_i because it is assumed to ignore the increase in the federal government's revenues when g_i increases. It can be shown that the optimal g_i from the state's perspective satisfies the following condition:

$$\phi(g_i^*) = \frac{1}{1 - t_F} \qquad (4)$$

This model is illustrated in Figure 5.2. Since $0 < t_F < 1$, the state will provide less than the optimal amount of g_i. Note that the under-provision of g_i is greater the larger the federal income tax rate. If only the state government levied the income tax, the optimal amount g_i would be provided. Since it is unlikely that a federal government is willing to withdraw from the income tax field, optimal provision of g_i can also be achieved if the federal government provides a matching grant to the state government where the matching rate is the additional revenue received by the federal government for each additional dollar spent by the state government. Note that the vertical expenditure externality provides a rationale for matching grants to state governments for productivity improving expenditures, such as education, which does not depend on horizontal benefit spillovers or interjurisdictional mobility.

This model has illustrated the potential for fiscal problems that can arise in a federation as a result of vertical expenditure externalities, and obviously more research is required to determine the significance of these externalities for the fiscal behaviour of federal and state governments. One implication of the analysis for the tax assignment problem is that if state governments provide significant productivity-enhancing public services, then they should collect income taxes so that they can capture at least some of the tax revenue generated by their activities.

Applications to Australia and Canada

Having described our theoretical framework, we will now return to Table 5.1 which contains a preliminary assessment of the fiscal implications of the tax assignments in Australia and Canada. Given the limited taxing powers of the Australian states, direct horizontal tax externalities are of limited importance in Australia, except perhaps for the pricing of state-owned utilities which Walsh and Thomson (1993) argue is a disguised form of state taxation. To the extent that higher utility prices lead to higher prices for goods that are exported to other states, some of the "tax" burden may be shifted to the residents of other states. In Canada, the potential for tax exporting is more significant especially with respect to provincial excise taxes and sales taxes. Differential rates of sales and excise taxes may lead to interprovincial cross-border shopping in some areas (Dahlby, 1995). Furthermore, it has been estimated that about one third of the provincial retail sales tax base is business inputs. To the extent that the retail sales taxes increase the price of goods that are sold in other provinces, some tax exporting may occur.

Tax base mobility and the resulting tax competition is also probably less important in Australia than in Canada because of the provinces' presence in the corporate and personal income tax fields and the potential for cross-border shopping due to differentials in retail sales taxes and excise taxes noted above.

A form of vertical tax base overlap occurs in Australia because the states' payroll tax base is wage income which is also taxed under the Commonwealth's personal income tax. In Canada, tax base overlap is especially significant in the excise tax field where both the federal and provincial governments levy taxes on gasoline, tobacco, and alcohol. Overlap in the corporate and personal income tax fields and the sales tax fields are also important as the calculations of the provincial MCFs in Dahlby (1994) have indicated. Limitations on the deductibility of provincial payroll taxes under the federal corporate income tax have been introduced because of the federal government's concern that deductibility was distorting the provinces' tax mix in favour of these taxes.

With regard to the expenditure externalities, we will focus on the vertical externalities, see Table 5.2. In Australia, this may be potentially important because of the states' responsibility for education and infrastructure and their absence from the personal income tax field. In Canada, the interdependence of the federal UI and the provincial welfare programs has already been mentioned. In the past, the effects of UI changes on provincial welfare spending was moderated by the 50 percent matching grant that the "have not" provinces received under the Canada Assistance Plan. The move to block funding will probably exacerbate the problem. Provincial spending on education and infrastructure may give rise to a vertical expenditure externality, although the provinces' presence in the personal and corporate income tax fields would have ameliorated this effect, at least in comparison with Australia.

Has the division of tax powers influenced the tax mix in Australia and Canada? Table 5.3 presents some evidence for this. It shows OECD and Canadian Tax Foundation revenue data to compare the percentage of taxes collected at the state/provincial-local level and shares of the main taxes in total tax revenues. As previously noted, the states in Australia do not levy personal or corporate income taxes, whereas the Canadian provinces collect just over a third of all taxes from these sources. The potential for tax competition among the provinces might make personal and corporate income taxes less important in Canada than in Australia, but the tax base overlap could work in the opposite direction. Which of two efforts is most important depends on the nature of the response to provincial tax changes. A given decline in a province's tax base in response to a tax increase may be due to an overall decline in the base or to a migration of that base elsewhere, to

Table 5.3
Sources of Tax Revenue in Australia and Canada, 1991

	Percentage Collected at the State/Provincial-Local Level		Percentage of Total Tax Revenue	
	Australia	Canada	Australia	Canada
Income and Profits	0	36.76	56.0	50.3
- Individuals			41.1	42.0
- Corporate			14.5	8.3
Social Security and Payroll	78.95	42.52	6.5	9.2
General Consumption	0	53.40	8.1	15.0
Specific Goods and Services	18.60	43.60	14.6	8.3
Property	100.00	100.00	9.8	9.6
- Percent collected by local government	41.38	83.33		

Source: OECD, *Revenue Statistics of OECD Member Countries*, Paris, 1993, Tables 38, 41, 123, and 125

another province. Capital is more mobile than labour, and smuggling may make some specific sales tax bases mobile. The OECD revenue data indicate that personal and corporate income taxes represent a larger share of revenue in Australia than in Canada, but this is entirely due to the relatively large share of revenue contributed by corporate income taxes in Australia. Tax competition among the provinces or vis-à-vis the United States, given the mobility of capital, might explain the relatively low share of corporate income taxes in total tax revenues in Canada. There are other possible explanations however. Corporate income taxes as a percentage of total taxation in Canada has been steadily declining over the last three decades, whereas they have been relatively constant in Australia. An analysis of the downward trend in corporate income taxes in Canada by Douglas (1990) has revealed that approximately two-thirds of the relative decline in corporate tax revenues was due to a long-term decline in the corporate profit rate and that reductions in the average rate of taxation on corporate profits was of secondary importance in explaining the decline. Why the trend in corporate taxation is different in Australia and Canada certainly warrants further investigation.

Income and general consumption taxes fall more directly on labour which is less mobile but responsive in overall supply. The externality is thus more likely to be the vertical one arising from tax base overlap implying higher use in Canada than Australia. From Table 5.3 we see that this is the case, particularly for general consumption taxes which are shared, in Canada, almost equally between federal and provincial governments.

Social security and payroll taxes also fall on the mobile labour income base but, unlike for income and consumption taxes, this base is shared between levels of government in both countries. These taxes are more evenly split between levels of government in Canada than in Australia. As discussed earlier the more evenly split is the burden the greater will be the downwards bias in the individual government's perception of the marginal cost of public funds they face. This is consistent, then, with the results in Table 5.3 where a greater portion of revenue is collected using these taxes in Canada.

Taxes on specific goods and services are a larger share of total revenue in Australia than in Canada. This is consistent with our view that there is significant mobility of this base and thus large indirect externalities between provinces in Canada. Thus the fact that these taxes are made greater use of at the provincial level in Canada, than at the state level in Australia, leads to them being of less overall importance as a revenue source.

Property taxes in both countries are collected exclusively by the state/provincial-local governments. In Australia, local governments collect less than half of the property tax revenue whereas they collect over 80 percent in Canada. Property tax revenue as a percentage of total revenue is about the same in both countries.

Overall, the differences in the tax mix in the two countries cannot be completely explained in terms of the differences in tax assignment, but our analysis suggests the differences in the mix are broadly consistent with our theory. At the same time, for each tax, there are other possible explanations for the differences in the tax mix, including differences in tastes for progressivity.

Has the division of tax powers affected the overall level of taxation in the two countries? Figure 5.3 shows taxes as a percentage of GDP in the two countries over the period 1965 to 1991. At the beginning of this period, taxation as a percentage of GDP was 2.7 percentage points higher in Canada. By 1991, it was 8.1 percentage points higher, suggesting that the Canadian tax burden has grown much more rapidly than in Australia. However, as Figure 5.4 shows, the differences in taxation as percentage of GDP between the two countries has not steadily widened over the period. In the early 1970s it was about 7.5 percentage points, and as recently as 1986, the difference was only 2.8 percentage points. The current gap between in the tax to GDP ratio is largely due to the fact that the tax ratio in Australia has declined by 1.6 percentage points since 1986, whereas it has increased by 3.6 percentage points in Canada. It is extremely unlikely that the different trends in the tax to GDP ratio are attributable to differences in the tax assignments in the two countries because there were no major changes in the tax assignments in the two countries over this period. Other factors, such as economic performance, demographic or geographic variables, or other fiscal institutions such as intergovernmental grants, may be responsible for the recent divergence in the level of taxation in Australia and Canada.

Conclusions

This paper provides preliminary evidence aimed at understanding how differences in tax assignments in Australia and Canada may affect the tax policy in the two countries. Our theory shows the impact of both horizontal and vertical tax and expenditure externalities on optimal policy choice. The impact of horizontal competition is well known; states will collectively under-utilize taxes on those bases which are mobile between states. Similarly, states will under-invest in projects where some of the benefits fall on residents in other jurisdictions.

Less well known are the problems arising from vertical externalities. Where a tax base is shared by more than one level of government, the impact of taxation by one level on the revenues of the others, through changes in the size of the base, will be neglected, resulting in overuse of the tax. Parallel to this, if the benefits of expenditure are partially captured by the other level of government, there will be under-expenditure. Generally then, where lower levels of government share bases with higher levels, the overall mix of taxation will not be optimal. Whether there is too much or too little taxation of a particular base depends on the nature of the externality. If it is mainly horizontal, through migration of the base, then the base will be underused. If it is mainly vertical, through shrinking of the base resulting in revenue reduction to other levels of government, then the base will be overused.

Evidence from comparison of the tax systems in Australia and Canada confirms these problems. Australian states do not utilize several of the large tax bases which are shared between levels of government in Canada. In Australia all personal, income and general consumption taxes are collected exclusively by the central government. As the theory predicts corporate taxes, where the base is mobile between states, are relatively under used in Canada while consumption taxes, where the response is in the size of the base, are overused. Government spending in Canada also makes up a larger portion of the GDP than in Australia.

This analysis suggests that the Canadian tax system could be improved if taxing authorities took these vertical and horizontal externalities into account. There are several alternative ways this could be done. One is to assign the major tax collection responsibilities to the federal government as is done in Australia. Secondly, tax bases should, as much as possible, not be shared. If possible, different levels of government should be assigned sole access to particular bases. Finally, the equalization and intergovernmental transfer system could be improved to correct for these externalities.

Figure 5.1
Tax Base Overlap

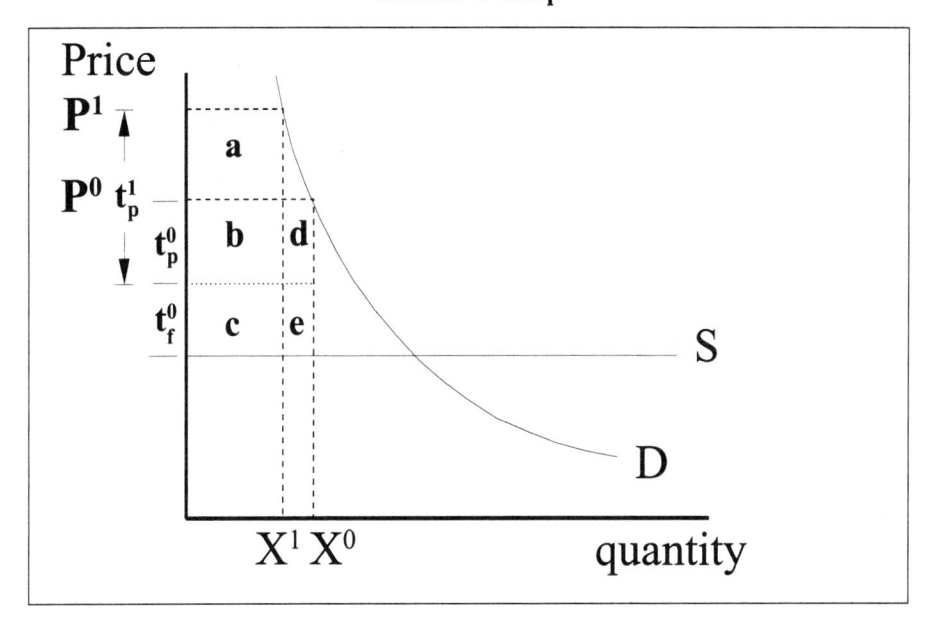

Figure 5.2
A Vertical Expenditure Externality

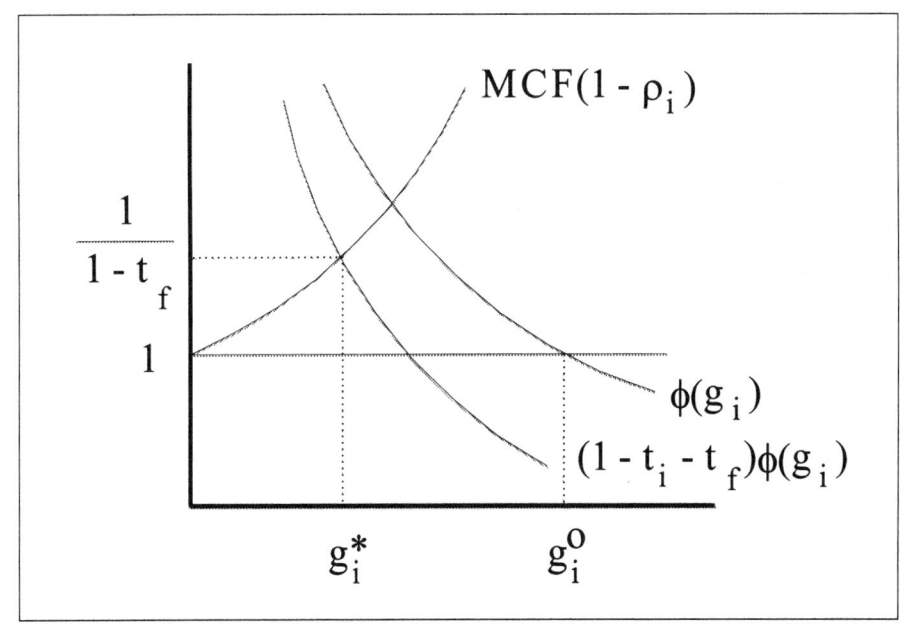

Figure 5.3
Tax Revenue as a Percentage of GDP

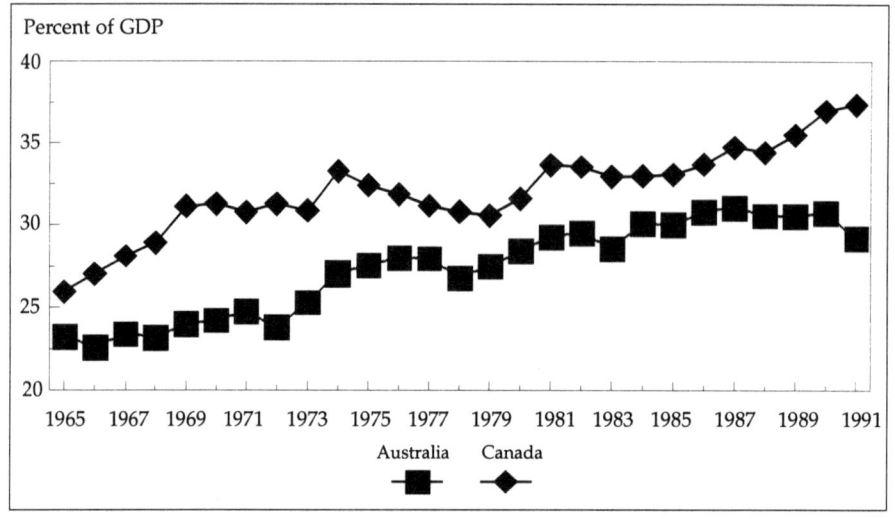

Source: OECD Revenue Statistics, Table 3.

Figure 5.4
The Difference in the Canada-Australia Tax Ratio

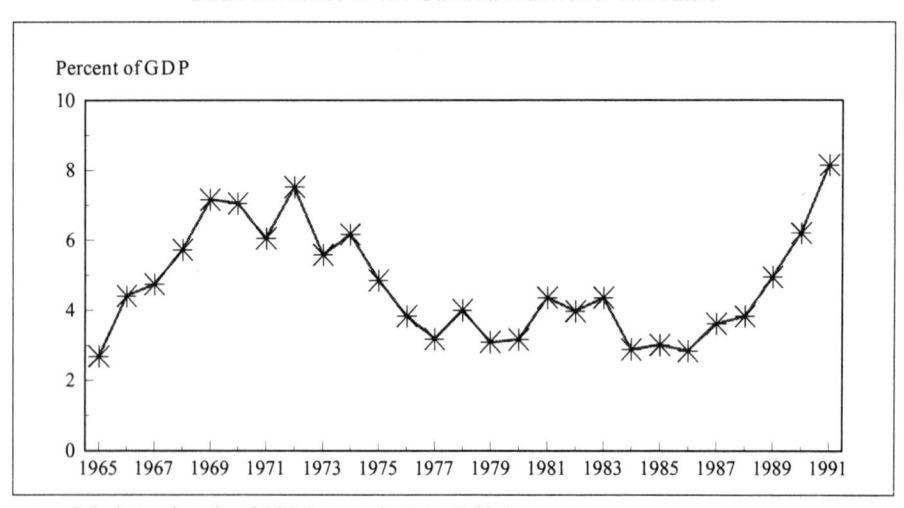

Calculations based on OECD Revenue Statistics, Table 3.

References

Allaire, J. et al. 1991. "A Quebec Free to Choose," *Report of the Constitutional Committee of the Quebec Liberal Party*, submitted to the 25th Party Convention.

Arnott, R. and R.E. Grieson. 1981. "Optimal Fiscal Policy for a State or Local Government," *Journal of Urban Economics* 9, 23-48.

Atkinson, A.B. and N. Stern. 1974 "Pigou, Taxation and Public Goods," *Review of Economic Studies* 41, 119-28.

Auerbach, A.J. and J.M. Poterba. 1987. "Why Have Corporate Tax Revenues Declined?" *Tax Policy and the Economy*, L. Summers (ed.), MIT Press.

Ballard, C. and D. Fullerton. 1992. "Distortionary Taxes and the Provision of Public Goods," *Journal of Economic Perspectives* Vol. 6 No. 3 (Summer), 117-131.

Boadway, R. and M. Keen. 1994. *Efficiency and the Fiscal Gap in Federal Systems*.

Boadway, R., S. Roberts, and A. Shah. 1994. *The Reform of Fiscal Systems in Developing and Emerging Market Economies*, Washington, D.C.: Policy Research Department, The World Bank.

Boothe, P. and T. Snoddon. 1994. "Tax Collection in Canada: Prospects for Reform," *Commentary* No. 63 (October), Toronto: The C.D. Howe Institute.

Brennan, G. and J. Buchanan. 1980. *The Power to Tax: Analytical Foundations of A Fiscal Constitution*, Cambridge: Cambridge University Press.

Canadian Tax Foundation. 1993. *The National Finances, 1993*, Toronto: Canadian Tax Foundation.

Dahlby, B. 1992. "Taxation Under Alternative Constitutional Arrangements," P. Boothe (ed.), *Alberta and the Economics of Constitutional Change*, Edmonton: Western Centre for Economic Research, University of Alberta, 111-155.

Dahlby, B. 1994. "The Distortionary Effect of Rising Taxes," *Deficit Reduction: What Pain; What Gain?* R. Robson and W. Scarth (eds.), Toronto: The C.D. Howe Institute.

Dahlby, B. 1995. *Distortionary Taxation and the Design of Intergovernmental Grants*, Washington, D.C.: Policy Research Department, The World Bank.

Douglas, A. 1990. "Changes in Corporate Tax Revenue," *Canadian Tax Journal* 38 (January/February), 66-81.

Edwards, J. and M. Keen. 1994. "Tax Competition and Leviathan," *Working Paper W94/7*, London: The Institute for Fiscal Studies.

Feldstein, M. and G. Metcalf. 1987. "The Effect of Federal Tax Deductibility on State and Local Taxes and Spending," *Journal of Political Economy* 95: 710-736.

Grossman, P. 1990. "Fiscal Competition Among States in Australia: The Demise of Death Duties," *Publius* 20 (Fall), 145-160.

Hewitt, D. and D. Mihaljek. 1992. "Fiscal Federalism," *Fiscal Federalism in Economies in Transition*, V. Taints (ed.), International Monetary Fund, Washington, D.C., 330-349.

Johnson, William R. 1988. "Income Redistribution in a Federal System," *American Economic Review*, 78, 3, 570-573.

Johnson, William R. 1991. "Decentralized Income Redistribution Reconsidered," *Economic Inquiry*, 29, Jan., 69-78.

Keen, M. 1995. "Pursuing Leviathan: Fiscal Federalism and International Tax Competition," University of Essex.

Locke, W. and A. Tassonyi. 1993. "Shared Tax Bases and Local Public Sector Expenditure Decisions," *Canadian Tax Journal*, 41, 5, 941-957.

McLure, C.E. 1983a. *Tax Assignment in Federal Countries*, Canberra: Centre for Research on Federal Financial Relations, Australian National University.

McLure, C.E. 1983b. "Assignment of Corporate Income Taxes in a Federal System," *Tax Assignment in Federal Countries*, C.E. McLure (ed.), Canberra: Centre for Research on Federal Financial Relations, Australian National University, 101-124.

McLure, C.E. 1992. "A North American View of Vertical Imbalance and the Assignment of Taxing Powers," *Vertical Fiscal Imbalance*, D.J. Collins (ed.), Sydney: Australian Tax Research Foundation.

McLure, C.E. 1994. "The Tax Assignment Problem: Ends, Means and Constraints," *Australian Tax Forum*, 11, 153-183.

Mintz, J. and H. Tulkens. 1986. "Commodity Tax Competition Between Member States of a Federation: Equilibrium and Efficiency," *Journal of Public Economics* 29, 133-172.

Mintz, J.M. and T.A. Wilson. 1991. "The Allocation of Tax Authority in the Canadian Federation," Institute for Policy Analysis, University of Toronto, Policy Study 91-7.

Musgrave, R.A. 1983. "Who Should Tax, Where, and What?" *Tax Assignment in Federal Countries*, C.E. McLure (ed.), Canberra: Centre for Research on Federal Financial Relations, Australian National University, 2-19.

Shah, A. 1994. *The Reform of Intergovernmental Fiscal Relations in Developing and Emerging Market Economies, No. 23 Policy and Research Series*, Washington, D.C.: Policy Research Department, The World Bank.

Walsh, C. and N. Thomson. 1993. *Federal Fiscal Arrangements in Australia: Their Potential Impact on Urban Settlement*, Canberra: Federalism Research Centre in association with the South Australian Centre for Economic Studies.

Wildasin, D. 1987. "The Demand for Public Goods in the Presence of Tax Exporting," *National Tax Journal* 40(4) (December), 591-601.

Wilson, L. S. 1994. "Federal-State Fiscal Arrangements in Malaysia," The University of Alberta.

Zodrow, G.R. and P. M. Meiszkowski. 1986. "Pigou, Property Taxation, and the Under-Provision of Local Public Goods," *Journal of Urban Economics* 19, 356-370.

Making a Mess of Tax Assignment: Australia as a Case Study

6

Cliff Walsh

The Assignment of Taxing Powers

An attempt to use casual observation of current practices in federal systems as the basis for deducing something about the appropriate principles for assignment of tax bases between spheres of government would be confounded by the fact that virtually every sort of tax is used by each sphere of government somewhere. There are, nonetheless, some regularities (over and above the fact that customs duties invariably are allocated to the centre). For example, the more progressive elements of tax systems tend to reside predominantly at central or federal level; and, at local government level, property taxation and user charges are the most common forms of revenue raising. On the other hand, in some countries (for example, Germany) revenue sharing (as opposed to tax base sharing) is a distinctive feature. In others, very clear separation of access to tax bases occurs (for example, in Australia, where the income tax currently is exclusively in the hands of the central government). In yet others, extensive tax base sharing is prevalent, with two or more spheres of government having either independent (e.g., US) or harmonised (e.g., Canada for income taxes) access to one or more of the major tax bases.

Constitutional provisions, judicial interpretations of those provisions, and political deals all intersect to explain the different ways in which access to tax bases is arranged and/or shared in various federal countries. Clearly, no one set of principles would be capable of capturing all of the relevant influences.

The fiscal federalism literature, nonetheless, has established a broad set of principles for what it regards as the appropriate assignment of taxing powers in multi-level government systems. Two factors which feature significantly in this literature are mobility of taxpayers, or tax bases, on the one hand and, on the other, especially in more recent literature, the possibility of tax exporting by jurisdictions.

So far as mobility is concerned, the principal issues revolve around the consequences for location of individuals when jurisdictions use the tax structure to achieve redistributional purposes, for the location of businesses where jurisdictions tax income from capital, or more generally, for the location of transactions when transations-based taxes are applied. As a general principle, it is suggested, taxation of highly mobile tax bases and the use of relatively progressive taxes, should reside with higher rather than lower levels of government in order to avoid distortions of locational decisions. Tax exporting, on the other hand, occurs when, through its market power in relation to the production and pricing of particular commodities, a jurisdiction can raise a substantial part of the revenue for expenditure on local goods and services from taxes which are effectively paid by residents of other jurisdictions. Some literature (e.g., Mieszkowski and Toder 1983; Wildasin 1984; Gerking 1981), however, suggests that even where tax exporting is possible, it may be less a source of distortion than traditionally had been assumed, either because it affects only average tax prices or it has offsetting general equilibrium ramifications.

Both of these problems, mobility and tax exporting, could be avoided if governments were able and willing to rely predominantly on benefit taxes and user charges. Indeed, throughout the public finance literature, the preferred tax arrangement is one in which benefit taxes or user charges are applied as extensively as possible. Because of preference revelation problems, however, benefit taxation (other than in proxy form) is unlikely to be applicable to those goods which have characteristics of being, broadly speaking, national public goods. By the same token, however, neither tax exporting nor mobility is likely to be such a significant problem the higher the level of government at which taxes are applied: the greater capacity of lower levels of government to rely more on user charges turns out to correspond to the principles of tax assignment in federal systems.

A useful summary of the principles established in the traditional literature relating to tax assignment in multi-level government systems is provided by Richard Musgrave (1983). Broadly speaking, they imply:

1. Because of the incentives they potentially create for migration among jurisdictions by the poor and by the relatively rich, highly progressive taxes are best allocated to higher levels of government.
2. Because of their capacity to distort the location of economic activity, highly mobile tax bases, such as taxes on company incomes or on financial transactions, generally also should be allocated to higher rather than lower levels of government.
3. Lower levels of government most appropriately should use taxes on relatively immobile bases (e.g., land) and user taxes and fees, because they create, in principle, no distorting incentives.
4. Tax bases that are distributed across jurisdictions in highly unequal fashion (e.g., on natural resources) in principle should be centralised to avoid both inequities and allocative distortions that arise from local or regional taxation.

Clearly, not all of these principles have always and everywhere been applied in the development of tax systems. However, harmonisation of tax bases between constituent units and agreements, where necessary, to share revenues from centrally administered tax bases can act as alternatives to assignment on Musgravian principles. Furthermore, higher level subnational spheres of government would have relatively higher freedom of choice among tax bases even under strict application of the principles.

Other considerations, moreover, suggest alternative assignment principles. Competition between jurisdictions for access to tax bases, in particular, can have a useful effect in constraining the potential exercise of exploitative power (Brennan and Buchanan 1980; McLure 1986); and harmonisation of tax bases is not an unambiguously good thing in all circumstances: the other side of the harmonisation coin is, in effect, the formation of a revenue-raising cartel that can, artificially, reduce the political costs to its members of raising revenues.

Ultimately, of course, the question to be posed is, how large are the welfare losses which might arise from an "inappropriate" allocation of tax bases? How large, in other words, are tax-induced distortions?

Empirical studies of this issue, as yet, are limited in availability. One important study, by Mieszkowski and Toder (1983), of the distortions which arise from decentralised taxation of energy resources in the United States suggests that the efficiency losses amount to about 4 percent of energy revenue. Although their analysis and the estimates contained in it are surrounded with provisos, they do not suggest distortions of particularly great significance.

In a more recent analysis, Goodspeed (1989) has examined the use of redistributive taxes at the local level in the context of a general equilibrium model of a metropolitan region. Comparing the efficiency and redistributive consequences of local income taxation with the alternative of local "head taxes," he suggests that local governments can employ progressive income taxes with relatively small efficiency costs, implying that the constraint on local use of progressive taxation claimed by supporters of the traditional Musgravian principles of tax assignment may be somewhat overstated.

Overall, without discounting entirely the value of the discussion of tax assignment principles that has occurred in the traditional public finance literature, it would have to be said that the practical guidance offered to reform or design of tax assignment in federal or multi-level government systems is limited. From an efficiency perspective, it may be relatively more important that the bases which governments use, however they may be assigned between them, should be as broad-based as possible, than that they should be assigned according to "traditional" fiscal federalism principles. Even this conclusion, however, would be subject to challenge by those who consider governments to be, actually or potentially, revenue-maximising leviathans: for them, tax bases full of loopholes and subject to erosion through mobility would be more appropriate in constraining the capacity of government to coercively extract revenue from the system.

One conclusion which would be common both to models of optimal taxation and to revenue-maximising models would be that, to the greatest extent possible, earmarked taxes based on benefit principles would be most likely to induce efficient decision making by taxpayers and governments about the appropriate levels of public service provision.

With this discussion of "general principles" as background, the thesis advanced in this paper, by implication if not by formal empirical testing and full comparative analysis, is that whether a federal nation has an optimal assignment of taxes cannot be determined *a priori*, and certainly cannot be assessed without examining both the total national tax system and the public expenditure system, and their impacts and consequences, simultaneously and as a whole; and Australia has probably got its tax assignment substantially more "wrong" than Canada — reflected in, and reflecting, the extremely high degree of vertical fiscal imbalance in Australia. My focus is essentially on Australia and the lessons to be learned from its tax system and tax assignment in federal context, as an illustration or case study of what needs to be avoided. However, I offer some remarks on Canada's federal fiscal system, based on my analysis of Australian reform options, in the concluding section.

Australia's Fiscal and Federal System in Broad Perspective

A full analysis of the nature and consequences of Australia's federal fiscal arrangements, and of the constitutional and politico-economic forces that have shaped them, obviously is beyond the scope of this paper. The basic points, however, are not difficult to articulate.

In Australia, as illustrated in Table 6.1, state and local governments are responsible for about 48 percent of total annual public sector spending and about 88 percent of public sector annual capital outlays. They also are responsible for managing and controlling about 84 percent of essential economic and social infrastructure, and they employ about 78 percent of the public sector workforce and manage about 49 percent of public sector debt.

The dominant state/local shares in capital spending, asset management and employment, of course, reflect the fact that the state/local sector is responsible for providing the vast majority of economic and social services to

Table 6.1
Structure of Australian Public Sector, 1993-94

	Share of Total Public Sector			Total Public Sector as a share of national aggregate
	Commonwealth %	State %	Local %	%
Outlays				
Current	56	41	4	
Capital*	12	67	21	
Total	52	43	5	39[a]
Own-source revenue				
Taxation	74	21	4	30[a]
Total	69	27	4	35[a]
Net debt[b]	52	47	2	38[a]
Capital stock[d]	16	—84—		29[c]
Employment[b]	22	68	10	20[e]

Sources: ABS, *Government Financial Statistics, Australia* (Cat 5512.0).
ABS, *Estimates of Capital Stock* (Cat 5221.0) unpublished.
ABS, *Employed Wage and Salary Earners, Australia*, (Cat 6248.0) at June 1994.
ABS, *Labour Force* (Cat 6202.0).
ABS, *Public Sector Financial Assets and Liabilities, Australia*, (Cat 5513.0) at 30 June 1994.

Notes:
(a) Ratio to GDP.
(b) As at 30 June 1994.
(c) Share of total net capital stock (excluding public financial enterprises).
(d) For 1993–94.
(e) Share of total employment.
* Measured net of assets sales, which bulk particularly large at Commonwealth level.

people and to businesses — education, health and hospitals, public housing, law and order, electricity, roads, public transport, water and sewerage, and so on. The bulk of state/local annual expenditures are on the purchase of goods and services — on wages and salaries paid to employees and contractors and on materials required to manage and deliver government services and to complete capital works programs.

The Commonwealth, by contrast, principally spends for its own purposes on transfer payments — cash benefits to persons for social security and health and the like — although it also has important principal roles in defence and foreign affairs and in telecommunications and aviation.

Despite the roughly fifty-fifty split between the Commonwealth and the state/local sector in annual outlays for their own purposes, the state/local sector is responsible for raising only about 25 percent of taxation revenues. It is precluded from the major broad-based sources of tax revenue (incomes and sales of goods) and depends on payments of various sorts from the Commonwealth for, on average, about 40 percent of its total revenues. It is this juxtaposition of facts — a large share of the state/local sector in expenditure responsibilities relative to their share in revenue sources — that is referred to as a situation of "vertical fiscal imbalance (VFI)." Table 6.2 puts VFI in Australia into sharp statistical perspective.

Table 6.2
Vertical Fiscal Imbalance: 1993-94

	Percent of own-source revenue		Percent of own-purpose expenditures	ratios of revenue/ expenditure shares	
	Taxation Revenue	Total Revenue		Tax expenditure	Revenue expenditure
Commonwealth	74	69	52	1.42	1.33
State	21	27	43	0.49	0.63
Local	4	4	5	0.80	0.80
Total	100	100	100		

Source: ABS, *Government Financial Statistics*, (Cat 5512.0).

Particularly because of the remarkably low share of the *state* sector in tax revenues — about 21 percent of the total, lower even than local governments' share in many so-called unitary systems — Australia has by far the highest degree of vertical fiscal imbalance among the major federations in the industrialised world (see Table 6.3). It is high even by the standards of most unitary countries.

Table 6.3
International Comparison of Vertical Fiscal Imbalance (1986)

	Federal	'State'	Local
Australia	1.3	0.4	0.8
Canada	1.0	0.9	0.5
Germany	1.0	0.9	0.8
United States	0.9	1.3	0.7

(Level of Government)

Source: *Report of the Working Party on Tax Powers*, October 1991, p. 8.

If you were told of a major business enterprise which persistently had relied on grants or subsidies to fund at least 40 percent of its revenues — which financed only about 60 percent of its activities from charges on its customers — you probably would conclude that it was likely to be unduly sheltered from market forces. You would expect to find that it was relatively unresponsive to the preferences of its clients, that it was not highly innovative in its delivery of services, and that a great deal of its entrepreneurial energy was directed towards protecting — and, if possible, increasing — its income from grants and subsidies.

Notwithstanding some spectacular examples in the last decade of state policy and management failures in Australia, it would be grossly unfair to state and local governments to suggest that they are hopelessly inefficient and totally lacking in innovative spirit. Indeed, at least since the mid 1970s, the states have undergone something of a renaissance. They have established a high degree of professionalism in administration and, for the most part, in policy formulation — and (with some spectacular exceptions) in financial management — and they sometimes have proved themselves to be highly innovative in policy development.

However, the Australian states are unquestionably hamstrung and frustrated by the fiscal dominance of the Commonwealth. As a consequence, some of what would be widely acknowledged to be the worst features of state policies — including hidden, distorting and wasteful competition to attract new business development, the recent remarkably unsuccessful experiences of states becoming venture capital partners with the private sector, and other instances of regulatory and policy failure — almost certainly have been induced or exaggerated by the degree of imbalance in fiscal powers which characterises the Australian federal system and by the associated lack of breadth and flexibility in the sources of revenues available to the states.

Federal systems of government inevitably involve a degree of complexity that might be avoided in unitary systems which have a high degree of centralisation of decision making and, correspondingly, a high degree of uniformity in outcomes. This is the "price" we pay for the fact that federal systems share powers between spheres of government in order to limit the potential coercive use of those powers by governments and that they allow for greater citizen access to governments and facilitate diverse, flexible and innovative responses to citizens' needs. That said, two important observations follow.

First, if federal systems are to be successful, relative to unitary alternatives, in protecting citizens against excessive coercion and in increasing democratic participation through multiple access to governments, it would seem to be essential that, to the greatest extent possible, all governments should have *independent* access to revenues to enable them to respond to citizen preferences *and* that they be capable of being held appropriately responsible and accountable for their use of those revenue sources. I have previously suggested that this might be described, somewhat loosely speaking, as the principle that *there should be no representation without taxation* (Walsh 1991)— the reverse of the familiar old adage, but no less pertinent.

Second, as a more practical matter, the achievement of mature intergovernmental interactions in which conflict is mediated rather than magnified, in which unnecessary administrative duplication and complexity is avoided, and in which cooperative approaches to microeconomic (structural) reform and to reform of public sector service delivery are encouraged, would seem likely to depend on participants approaching the issues knowing that their interests, fiscal as well as political, are equally promoted or protected in the process. In a manner of speaking, *federal balance would appear most likely to be promoted where there is fiscal balance*.

On both counts, Australia's current federal fiscal arrangements fail the test — and not just by a bit, but by a long way.

The Consequences of Fiscal Imbalance

Those who seek to defend the current arrangements include some who are fundamentally opposed to change — the committed majoritarian centralists, who believe that the Commonwealth has the right, and should have the power, to *control* all policy levers to promote Commonwealth-defined "national" goals. Others — who might be termed pragmatic or opportunistic centralists — see the current Commonwealth emphasis on fiscal restraint (at least as applied by the Commonwealth to the states) and its commitment to microeconomic reforms, as an opportunity to achieve a re-orientation of state policies towards lower spending and greater emphasis on strategies to achieve efficiencies in state agencies and utilities that is worth preserving, while acknowledging that, in future, the case for rebalancing fiscal powers may be desirable.

In effect, both camps attribute the undesirable and dysfunctional outcomes of present federal fiscal arrangements principally to failings of the states rather than acknowledging the possibility that the arrangements themselves — the Commonwealth dominance they seek to preserve or even extend, and the leader-follower model that the Commonwealth constantly demands should be applied — might be a root cause of the problems which needs to be fixed if the perceived failings are to be overcome.

Increasingly, however, and in parallel with changes both in thinking about the virtues of federal systems and in assessments and understanding of the requirements for successful macroeconomic management, there has been substantially more emphasis on, and concern about, the consequences of the Commonwealth's revenue dominance and of the extensive system of grants which is its counterpart, in terms of their impact on public sector efficiency, responsiveness and flexibility, and accountability. A full analysis and explanation can be found elsewhere (for example, Walsh, 1990, 1992 and 1993, and Report of the Working Party on Tax Powers, 1991), the following offers a brief encapsulation.

First, the centralised control of the major revenue raising sources by the Commonwealth creates the threat of increasing centralisation of decision-making power in relation to policy areas where the states are acknowledged to have the principal role. The rapid shift in the balance of Commonwealth grants towards tied (specific purpose) grants and an increased demand by the Commonwealth for joint — but Commonwealth dominated — decision-making procedures (e.g., housing, vocational education and training, competition policy) in recent years illustrates this threat of attempted centralisation of power in action. Commonwealth interests, however, should *not* be equated with "the national interest" which rather encompasses the interests of *all* political jurisdictions.

Second, the capacity of the different spheres of government in the federal system to be responsive to their voters, community groups and other interests is prejudiced by the imbalance in their access to financial resources. The financial dominance of the Commonwealth has given it greater overall capacity to respond to groups seeking an avenue to achievement of their objectives among various spheres of government — to the point where some groups now concentrate virtually their entire attention and lobbying resources on "national" pressure to achieve local and regional objectives (for example, in relation to housing, urban and regional development, and regional environmental issues). "Three stop shopping" by lobby groups, community groups and individuals, to be sure, may have dangers, too, but competition between and within spheres of government should help to limit the capacity of inefficient policy proposals winning too often.

Third, the extreme dependence of Australia's state/local sector on Commonwealth grants — and the annual ritual of the Commonwealth unilaterally determining grant funding levels — has institutionalised and ritualised conflict in the peak institutions of intergovernmental relations — Premiers' Conferences and Council of Australian Government (COAG) meetings — and in Ministerial Councils. This hinders their capacity both to successfully identify and isolate essential from inconsequential differences of views and values, and to promote cooperation, coordination and harmonisation where this is possible and desirable.

Fourth, the extensive system of grants to the states leads to a substantial blurring of responsibility and accountability for political decisions. Where spending and taxing decisions are unnecessarily divorced, even sophisticated citizen/voters have difficulty in attributing responsibility for a lack of responsiveness among the various spheres of government. Buck-passing becomes an intrinsic element of the system, and one in which the states have a comparative advantage: it is difficult to attribute blame to them when their revenue sources are small (own-taxes) and uncertain (grants).

Fifth, by breaking the nexus between the capacity of governments to make decisions about public sector activity levels and the responsibility for raising the revenue necessary to do so, the intergovernmental grants system creates distortions — *fiscal illusions* — in perceptions of citizen/voters, bureaucrats and politicians about the true tax costs of public sector decisions. Although, once Commonwealth grants are determined, a decision by a state to spend an extra dollar requires it to raise the extra revenue entirely from its own sources, given the fact that on average state revenues fund only about 60 percent of state activities, it is not difficult to see that an impression can be created in the minds of voters and decision makers that the states spend "60 cent dollars." The converse implications are relevant, too. Because the

Commonwealth pays out over 30 percent of its revenues in grants to the states it, in effect, raises nearly $1.50 for every $1.00 it spends on its own purposes: *resistance to desirable spending on the Commonwealth's own core functions — including welfare and health benefits — may be increased compared with a more balanced system of own-purpose revenue raising.*

Sixth, the lack of certainty which exists in relation to the grants the states are likely to receive in future years — the capacity of the Commonwealth to unilaterally and arbitrarily set the totals and to alter pre-announced formulae, and its tendency often to regard grants to the states as more of a balancing item than its expenditures on other purposes — damages the capacity of the states to engage in rational medium-term budget planning.

Seventh, the limited buoyancy and flexibility of State revenues, combined with uncertainties about Commonwealth determined revenues, offers inducements to the states to seek "creative" ways of generating potential future revenues (exemplified in the venture capitalist roles attempted in Western Australia and Victoria in the 1980s and encouragement of the entrepreneurial State Banks in South Australia and Victoria) and to seek off-budget financing for state capital projects in circumstances where it is not always appropriate.

Eighth, notwithstanding the potential for Australia's federal fiscal arrangements to encourage and sustain inefficient state decision making, the size of the Commonwealth's share in funding the states' budgets almost certainly results in the states, collectively and individually, receiving "ratings" from the international agencies consistently higher than their less "dependent" counterparts in other federations. That is, the role of the ratings agencies in disciplining state decision making, increased in significance though it may have become, is moderated by an "understanding" (or presumption) that the capacity of the Australian states to meet their future obligations is implicitly underwritten by the Commonwealth.

State Taxes, Microeconomic Reform and Perverse Incentives

Consideration of such issues have contributed to increasing calls from across the academic, bureaucratic and political spectrum in Australia for at least some form of revenue sharing deal for the states and possibly access to additional independent, broad-based, revenue-raising powers. (See for example, Walsh 1993, Report of the Working Party on Tax Powers 1991, Premiers and Chief Ministers 1991, and even the union movement-funded Evatt Research Foundation 1989.)

However, there are yet further considerations which have received much less attention than they deserve. These arguments more directly concern characteristics of the states' own-source taxes and/or the consequences for state and Commonwealth revenues of microeconomic reforms.

As Table 6.4 illustrates, the system of tax collection in Australia has the appearance of being highly stratified: the Commonwealth alone collects taxes on personal and company incomes and on sales of goods, and it collects virtually all excise duty revenues as defined by the ABS (the exception is state government levies on sales by their business enterprises).

Table 6.4

Sources of Revenue for Each Sphere of Government, 1993-94
(Percent of Total Revenues)

	Commonwealth	State	Local
Own-source revenues			
Taxes, fees and fines:			
Personal income tax	47	—	—
Company income tax	12	—	—
Excises	11	1	—
Sales tax	10	—	—
Customs duty	3	—	—
Payroll tax[a]	1	8	—
Stamp duties[b]	—	8	—
Motor vehicle taxes	—	4	—
Franchise taxes	—	6	—
Municipal rates[c]	—	—	59
Other	5	10	4
Total Taxes Fees and Fines	90	37	64
Net operating surplus of GBE's[d]	5	10	10
Other[e]	5	10	3
Total Own-source revenues	100	57	77
Payments from other governments			
from Commonwealth[f]	n.a.	43	13
from State	n.a.	n.a.	10
Total revenue	100	100	100

Source: ABS, *Government Financial Estimates, Australia* (5501.0), *Taxation Revenue, Australia* (5506.0) and *Government Financial Statistics, Australia*, (5512.0). Some data preliminary.

Notes:
(a) Includes fringe benefits tax, for Commonwealth.
(b) Includes financial institutions duties.
(c) Includes other local government property taxes.
(d) Net operating surplus of GBE's is included as revenue in the ABS Government Financial Estimates.
(e) Includes mining royalties, interest receipts and other property income.
(f) Payments from the Commonwealth to States for on-passing to local government recorded under local.

The bulk of state own-source tax revenues are derived from payroll taxes, stamp duties and related taxes on financial transactions, taxes and fees on motor vehicles, and franchise taxes (i.e., business licence fees) on alcohol, tobacco and petroleum products. About one quarter of their revenues derive from a host of smaller revenue sources, including land, gambling, insurance and "levies" on public sector business enterprises. Local governments, on the other hand, derive their own-source revenues almost entirely from property rates and other property-based levies.

It should be noted, however, that this stratification of revenue across spheres of government is, to an extent, more apparent than real. For example, payroll tax (PRT) clearly is a close relative of pay-as-you-earn (PAYE) income tax collections on wages and salaries and an even closer relative to fringe benefits taxes (FBT — paid by companies in Australia); and state "franchise" (business licence) fees on liquor, tobacco and petroleum products are, in effect, state sales taxes, on these products only, under an assumed name. Table 6.5 expands the picture so far as state taxation is concerned.

Table 6.5
Relative Importance of State Taxes, 1993-94
(Percent)

Tax Type	NSW	VIC	QLD	WA	SA	TAS	NT	ACT	Total
Payroll	25.0	23.5	20.3	23.9	22.1	23.5	24.5	19.5	23.5
Property	6.1	9.0	9.0	6.1	4.6	8.1	0.0	23.8	7.5
Financial	25.4	21.6	21.4	25.0	20.4	16.5	22.1	18.2	23.1
Excises & Levies	0.2	4.2	0.7	4.7	2.4	2.3	0.0	0.0	2.0
Gambling	10.2	10.5	12.7	6.4	7.9	8.1	7.8	9.6	10.0
Insurance	7.0	6.3	3.5	4.3	7.4	4.5	2.5	2.3	5.9
Motor Vehicles	11.4	10.2	18.1	11.4	13.0	12.4	9.8	12.3	12.1
Franchise Fees	14.4	14.7	14.0	18.1	22.0	22.8	30.9	14.3	15.6
Other Goods	0.3	0.1	0.2	0.0	0.2	1.8	2.5	0.0	0.3
TOTAL	100.0	100.0	100.0	100.0	100.0	100.0	100.0	100.0	100.0

Source: ABS, *Taxation Revenue, Australia 1993-94* (5506.0).
Note: Financial and Total *excludes* Government borrowing guarantees levies.

What does seem clear, first of all, is that state tax bases are relatively narrower, on the whole, than those available to the Commonwealth — some by nature (e.g., taxes on gambling, insurance and motor vehicles) and some, at least in part, by political design (e.g., PRT because of small business exemptions and land tax because of exemptions for owner-occupied residential land and rural land). While removing or reducing exemptions and concessions might be partial remedies, the point remains that State taxes, on balance, probably impose greater distortions (higher marginal social costs, technically speaking) compared with revenues raised from the broader-based Commonwealth taxes — a situation which has been worsened as the Commonwealth has propelled the states toward greater reliance on their own revenue sources by earlier arbitrarily cutting, and now limiting growth of, its grants.

Second, additional distortions arise from the nature of many of the tax bases available to and utilised by the states. In particular, a substantial proportion (probably over 60 percent) of state taxes fall on business *inputs* (rather than on profits or even outputs/revenues), distorting input decisions and reducing business efficiency. Among the culprits are PRT, petroleum franchise fees and financial transactions taxes (including stamp duties). Just how badly distorting these taxes are has not been fully analysed — an interesting observation in itself, given the increasingly large impact some of them have had as Commonwealth grants have been squeezed.

Be that as it may, it would seem clear, *a priori*, that a switch to taxes on incomes (company or personal), or on goods and services, would be significantly less distorting than business-input taxes. The benefits of such a switch, moreover, would be highest for the traded-goods sector, since PRT is a tax which generally is not rebated on exports and not paid by importers (unlike, for example, a VAT or GST).

Third, providing the states with a basis for raising a greater part of their revenues from taxes which fall on *individuals* (incomes or sales of goods and services) would help to reduce the capacity of the states to seek to attract industry through the relatively hidden form of negotiated concessions on business input taxes. This would not prevent negotiated, competitive bidding to attract new business investment, but it would help to ensure it occurred in more explicit, more transparent forms.

Fourth, the distorting effects of state taxes are likely to be further compounded by the fact that state taxes and some of those applied by the Commonwealth and local governments are overlapping (competitive). This is not an unambiguously damaging fact: much depends on how well harmonised the tax bases are and how high the combined effective tax rates are on those bases relative to the size of the base and its elasticity. Nonetheless, this is an issue of concern which has had little attention paid to it. Thus, for example, PRT and FBT clearly are interrelated, with most states also applying PRT to fringe benefits at least for anti-avoidance purposes. Some, if not all, also apply PRT to employer superannuation contributions, interacting with changes to Commonwealth tax treatment of superannuation.

State franchise fees apply in addition to already high rates of Commonwealth excise duty on alcohol, tobacco and petroleum products; state land taxes (thought usually only applied on commercial land use) apply to the same base as municipal rates; and so on.

Fifth, a number of the already limited and inadequate tax bases available to the states, moreover, are likely to become eroded and/or unstainable over time as a result of increasing global competitiveness. The recent cuts in stamp duties on marketable securities by all states, triggered by a decision by Queensland to cut its rates by 50 percent, is only the first sign of pressures that will increase to reduce all taxes which fall on highly mobile factors, transactions, goods and services. Other taxes on financial transactions, and eventually probably payroll tax on domestic production of traded goods, will face increasing pressures. Without access to alternative broad-based revenue sources, at least part of the burden of adjustment will involve increases in other (narrow-based) state taxes and yet higher efficiency costs of state taxation.

In addition to the characteristics of specific elements of state tax systems, the general lack of broad-based taxes on individuals available to the states creates further distortions which act as disincentives to microeconomic reform activities by the states.

For one thing, the fact that the states' taxes impact largely on businesses, or on narrow classes of consumption, has encouraged state governments to regard public utility prices as the closest thing they have to broad-based taxes on individuals ("consumers/voters"). They have interfered in public utility pricing — for example, through imposing unwarranted CPI-related price ceilings, offering targeted concessions, and providing disguised cross-subsidies — to bolster political support and/or to deliver income-related concessions which otherwise might be delivered through general taxation measures. By the same token, the difficulties of getting state governments to allow their authorities to adopt appropriately commercial pricing policies is linked to the fact that the states do not have direct access to a broad-based source of tax revenue through which they can offer compensation for the loss of concessions and/or for the across-the-board effects of more commercial pricing.

Equally importantly, full-bodied national competition policy reforms and other microeconomic reforms do appear likely, in the long-run, often to be revenue-reducing (or at least revenue-limiting) in relation to tax and dividend revenues available to the states from their business enterprises. The fact that the Industry Commission report on Hilmer and related reforms suggested large, economy-wide, net revenue benefits to all governments from the package as a result of the stimulus to economic activity from efficiency improvements ignores the fact that, in practice, the states have to implement Hilmer reforms, in effect, one-by-one, with directly obvious potential revenue reduction consequences compared to the dispersed and longer-run nature of the economy-wide revenue benefits, and is of less comfort to the states when their efforts directly reward the Commonwealth to a disproportionate extent. A broader-based source of state revenue would see them obtain revenue benefits more closely in proportion with their expenditure responsibilities and provide them with greater confidence that the revenue rewards will actually flow to them (given that existing state revenues are very inelastic with respect to GSP changes).

It also seems plausible to argue that the lack of rapid progress by many state governments in reforming and reducing expenditures on service delivery may stem, in part, from the fact that they lack an effective broad-based tax through which they can deliver to voters/taxpayers at least part of the fiscal dividend which can flow from (often politically painful) efficiency-oriented reforms.

Overall, it seems to me to be a plausible hypothesis — although I stress that, at this stage of our empirical ignorance in Australia, it is only a tentative hypothesis — that the total efficiency costs of the 21 percent of total national tax revenues raised from the states' own-sources might not fall far short of the efficiency costs of the 74 percent of tax revenues raised by the Commonwealth — given that 65 percent of Commonwealth revenues are raised from relatively efficient (and integrated) personal and company income taxes and a further 12 percent from excises on goods with relatively inelastic demand. Add to that the likely efficiency costs of the degree of vertical fiscal imbalance embedded in Australia's fiscal arrangements and the case for a major overhaul of the federal fiscal system as a key element of the microeconomic reform agenda appears overwhelming. *The likelihood that reform also would lead to a less regressive tax system overall adds a further important argument to the case for action.*

The Causes of Fiscal Imbalance

If the consequences of the grants system and of the underlying division of access to revenue sources are potentially as adverse as I have suggested, the question naturally arises: why has the current structure of financial arrangements been allowed to be established and to persist?

Although financial arrangements were a recurring source of debate in the initial decades following federation, by the late 1930s Commonwealth grants represented only about 11 percent of Australian state revenues, compared with around 40 percent today (and even more in earlier years). In 1938-39, state taxation represented about 46 percent of total taxation. Income tax revenues generated the majority — 60 percent — of state revenues, while the Commonwealth relied on indirect taxes for 75 percent of its revenue (mainly customs and excise duties, but also from sales taxes introduced in the 1930s). Commonwealth income tax collections were only about 30 percent of total income tax collections.

What has changed since then, principally, has been the acquisition of monopoly control over income taxation by the Commonwealth. Initially this occurred as a wartime measure, intended to last only as long as the emergency plus one year, with the states compensated through the payment of "reimbursement grants" for income tax revenues foregone by them. But when the war ended, the Commonwealth decided that it wished to retain monopoly control over the personal and company income tax in the interests of coping with repayment of wartime debt and financing post-war reconstruction, as well as to promote equity and simplicity in taxation, to fund new welfare measures, and to facilitate implementation of (the newly discovered) Keynesian macroeconomic management of the economy. The High Court facilitated this move by agreeing that the Commonwealth could make its payment of grants to any or all states conditional upon them not re-entering the income tax field.

The High Court's refusal to allow the states to impose a broad-based indirect sales tax on goods has played a part, too. Its ridiculously broad, and sometimes inconsistent, definitions of the meaning of "duties of excise," which are constitutionally the exclusive province of the Commonwealth, as involving any impost not just on manufacture or production but also on the distribution and sale of goods, have confined the states to narrow tax bases. It is clear, nonetheless, that the states' continued acquiescence in the Commonwealth's exercise of monopoly control over income tax revenue is the principal cause of the high degree of vertical fiscal imbalance which characterises Australia's federal fiscal arrangements.

There is nothing legally or constitutionally preventing the states from, individually or collectively, re-entering the income tax field. The obstacles to their doing so, rather, are a combination of political convenience and political threat.

A former Queensland premier is reputed to have once said "the only good tax is a Commonwealth tax." In this simple phrase, he captured the essence of the attitude of state Premiers throughout the post-war period — at least until recently: as long as the Commonwealth was willing to accept the political cost of raising the bulk of tax revenues, and to pass a reasonable share on to the states, why complain?

In any event, although the time has long passed when the Commonwealth made it an explicit condition for the payment of financial assistance grants that the states refrain from re-entering the income tax field, the threat that grants would be cut remains, at least implicitly. Certainly, if any one state were to attempt to "go it alone" in reintroducing an income tax, it could reasonably expect to have its financial assistance grants cut without the offsetting benefit of a cut in Commonwealth income tax rates: its residents would, in a meaningful sense, face double taxation. Even a concerted move by all states would likely ignite a damaging "tax rates" battle with the Commonwealth.

A Scheme for Returning Taxing Powers to the States

It will be clear from my earlier discussion that, in my view, a strong case exists for reducing the degree of VFI — the dependence of the Australian states on Commonwealth transfers — essentially by giving the states independent access to broad-based sources of revenue in place of a substantial part of the nearly $15 billion of Financial Assistance (general revenue) Grants they currently receive. I also see those broad-based revenue sources offering the potential to achieve reforms within existing state tax systems, although this is a separate issue.

Before fully explaining why, let me set out briefly a possible scheme for having the states gain a substantial increase in their independent revenue raising capacity. As will become clear, my preference is for the states to be free, within otherwise carefully negotiated and controlled circumstances, to independently vary a *flat rate* of personal income tax on their residents. Other options exist — including the possibility that access to a broad-based tax on goods and services might be given to the states — none of which can be considered totally irrelevant. One advantage of the option I prefer, however, is that it could be implemented fairly quickly and easily. Among other things, it would *not* require constitutional amendment.

The essential elements of the scheme for reducing VFI that I first proposed in 1987 (Walsh 1987b) are:

1. There would be a negotiated agreement that the Commonwealth would cut its *personal* income tax rates across the board and make corresponding cuts in its grants to the states, thereby making space for the states to re-enter the personal income tax field. The states would agree *not* to re-enter the company income tax field.
2. The states and the Commonwealth would agree to adopt a common Income Tax Assessment Act (i.e., definition of the income tax base) and to retain a single income tax revenue collection system through the Australian Tax Office.

3. Each state would be free (or free within agreed upper limits) to determine the *flat rate* of personal income tax it wished to apply to individuals *resident* in its state on incomes above the (jointly agreed) tax free threshold. That is, different states could choose different "state income tax rates," but *each would be limited to applying a single rate of personal income tax to its residents*. Revenues would be collected for the states, as well as for the Commonwealth, by the ATO through the PAYE and provisional tax systems, with final adjustments made, where necessary, through annual assessments of joint Commonwealth-state income tax returns.

Although I envisage a number of differences in the details, in essence, this scheme is a close relative of the Canadian arrangements, where the provinces (except Quebec) "piggy-back" on the federal income tax. A key difference is that, in my preferred scheme, the states would apply a flat rate to the taxable *incomes* of individuals (a tax on base) while, in Canada, the provinces apply a flat rate to the federal *income tax liabilities* of their residents (a tax on tax).

How large a cut in Commonwealth personal income tax rates and grants to the states might be made under this scheme is, ultimately, a matter of judgement. In the interests of achieving the greatest feasible degree of vertical fiscal *balance*, a case could be made for the Commonwealth to cut its personal income tax collections to the point where the only revenue it receives in excess of that required to fund its own-purpose outlays would be that needed to ensure fiscal equalisation payments are fully funded *and* to fund the minimum specific purpose payments agreed to be necessary to secure harmonisation or coordination in relation to programs that are essentially state responsibilities. But even a less ambitious first step would serve to at least partially rebalance fiscal powers and to require the States to accept greater responsibility for financing their spending programs.

On the latest data currently available on taxable incomes by state of residence (1992-93), the $14.9 billion of Financial Assistance Grants included in the pool for fiscal equalisation in 1995-96 could be reduced to, at most, $6.6 billion without any state or territory having to face a negative fiscal equalisation transfer. The balance ($8.3 billion) would be raised by all states and territories applying a flat rate of tax on the taxable incomes of their residents of about 5 percent (calculated to the highest feasible whole number), with the Commonwealth reducing its rates across-the-board by 5 percentage points and reducing its grants by $8.3 billion in total. The ACT (with the highest taxable incomes per capita) would almost completely replace its scheduled grant with its income tax revenues, while the other states and territories would receive a share of the $6.6 billion equalisation pool to ensure they were no worse off. This is illustrated in Table 6.6.

Table 6.6
Estimated Effect of a State Income Tax Rate of 5 per cent on Taxable Incomes of Residents

	Financial Assistance Grants 1995-96 [a] $ million (1)	State Revenue at 5 Percent PIT Rate on Residents [b] $ million (2)	Equalization Grant $ million (3) = (1) - (2)
NSW	4,209	2,923	1,285
Vic	2,986	2,124	862
Qld	2,868	1,318	1,550
WA	1,540	787	753
SA	1,500	634	866
Tas	650	194	455
NT	877	77	800
ACT	228	197[c]	30[c]
Total	14,858	8,255	6,602

Notes:
[a] FAGs as estimated at 1995 Premiers' Conference: subject to change in line with updates of or outcomes for population totals and shares and CPI changes.
[b] Based on 1992-93 data on Taxable Incomes by State of residence. PIT = Personal Income Tax.
[c] The ACT receives a small equalisation grant at a 5 percent rate but would have to hand-back revenue at 6 percent rate.

This scheme, and this outcome, would be essentially equivalent to that proposed by all state premiers and territory chief ministers in 1991 (Premiers and Chief Ministers, 1991) in a remarkable break with the previous post-war history of political opportunism in relation to the grants arrangements. The major additional element in the states' proposal was that the state component of what they called the "*shared national personal income tax*" (then estimated at 6 percent) would be held fixed for an initial three year period. This not only ensured revenue neutrality, overall, budget neutrality for the Commonwealth and the states, and tax liability neutrality for individual taxpayers in all states and territories in the first year of the scheme; it also meant that none of the Premiers could credibly be charged with double taxation: the possibility of income tax rates being increased (or even decreased) in some states relative to others was deferred beyond the next election in all jurisdictions. Moreover, the nature of the scheme, and the name appropriately given to it as a shared tax scheme, made clear that there was not a new tax being introduced — i.e., it was *not* a states' income tax *on top of* the existing taxes.

As indicated previously, variants on the scheme could include a negotiated (and, over time, renegotiable) upper bound on state income tax rates, possibly also packaged with agreements about eliminating or reducing some existing state taxes. To illustrate the orders of magnitude involved, the replacement of payroll taxes with state personal income taxes would require approximately an additional 3 percentage points added to the states' income tax rates and similarly for replacing all financial transactions taxes (including stamp duties on conveyances). State tax replacements of this size obviously would be assisted by the Commonwealth making additional space for state income taxes — for example, by substituting a broad-based consumption tax for part of its income tax collections and lowering its income tax rates accordingly.

The rejection by the Commonwealth of the states' 1991 proposal, while probably predictable in the circumstances of the time (Paul Keating's eventually successful challenge to Bob Hawke's Prime Ministership was approaching its peak), represented a sadly missed opportunity not only to grasp the key element of federal fiscal reform, but also to further accelerate state level microeconomic reforms in Australia and to improve the whole climate and conduct of intergovernmental relations. Nonetheless, the fact that the proposal was founded on an officials' report signed off by Commonwealth Treasury (Report of the Working Party on Tax Powers, 1991) and was firmly backed by all state and territory political leaders may come to be seen as a moment of historical significance in the evolution of fiscal reform.

Unlike the "New Federalism" arrangements introduced by the former Fraser government (1975-1983), which had formal *tax revenue sharing* as their centrepiece and gave the states the right to apply an income tax surcharge *on top of existing income taxes* (or to give a rebate), my proposed scheme (tax *base* sharing) would propel the states into directly accepting responsibility for explicitly setting income tax rates on their residents, and it would give them the space to do so without having to increase the overall burden of taxation. By contrast, the Fraser government legislation permitting state income tax surcharges and rebates was never utilised by the states, in large measure because the Commonwealth made no "tax space" for the states. The relevant Commonwealth legislation was only removed from the statute books in 1989 — its removal at that time apparently having been in anticipation of the possibility that one state (NSW) might be planning to use it to give *rebates* to its residents (and that others, apparently, were contemplating modest surcharges).

A return to tax revenue sharing — that is, giving the states a "guarantee" of a specified share of Commonwealth tax collections — would not be a fully adequate alternative. It would temporarily give the states greater certainty about a major component of their revenues, but it would be Commonwealth legislation which achieved this, and it always would be open to the Commonwealth to scrap the scheme unilaterally, as it did in the early 1980s. Moreover, the attribution of responsibility to the states for revenue raising under tax revenue sharing would, at best, be purely notional. It might be better than what we currently have, but the gains — compared to feasible alternatives — would be very limited.

Alternatives and Objections: Is Commonwealth Policy-Making Really Threatened?

I realise that the particular scheme I am proposing for re-establishing access by the states to a broad-based source of revenue faces potential objections from several different directions.

Among those who have been bold enough to support the view that a rebalancing of fiscal powers *is* a desirable objective, some have suggested that a broad-based tax on goods and services would be the preferable new state tax base. While I have been (and remain) a supporter of reforms designed to broaden the indirect taxation base in Australia to include a retail sales tax or a goods and services rax — which would have to be a component of the implementation of *this* option — I am not convinced that giving the states access to a broad-based consumption tax is the best option.

For one thing, under present High Court interpretations of section 90 of the Constitution, the states could not themselves impose broad-based taxes *on goods*, and the prospects of achieving constitutional change to allow them to do so are, at best, uncertain. The alternative of having the Commonwealth impose a broad-based goods and services tax, with the states nominating surcharges to be applied to sales within their jurisdictions, could not involve independent determination and adjustment of sales tax rate surcharges by individual states because Commonwealth taxation legislation cannot discriminate among the states.

Even if a way could be found through these difficulties (and through the fact that a GST cannot even be discussed at a political level in Australia), national economic management considerations favour the states' income tax option over the sales tax (VAT or GST) option. Among the arguments in support of a greater weight for sales taxation in the overall tax mix are the claims that sales taxes have a more direct impact on aggregate demand and offer more favourable incentives (possibly) to saving and (certainly) to exporting, than the current tax regime. Since these effects are at the heart of macroeconomic policy concerns, there is a strong argument that the Commonwealth should be the dominant player in indirect taxation. The fact that differential sales tax rates between states appear likely to be more distorting than would differential income tax rates adds further weight to the argument.

For these and a variety of other practical reasons, I am inclined to the view that the introduction of a broad-based consumption tax in Australia, if it were to occur, would best not be complicated by also trying to make it directly accessible to the states. Indeed, if anything, the introduction of a broad-based indirect tax *by the Commonwealth* would increase the scope for successfully allowing the states to re-enter the personal income tax field. The Commonwealth could make space for the states to substitute income taxes not only for the general revenue grants they now receive, but also for their least desirable state taxes (especially those on business inputs) by using its broad-based sales tax revenues to lower Commonwealth income tax rates.

The major line of attack on a scheme for state personal income taxes will come from those who view the equity of the tax system and the capacity of the Commonwealth to successfully pursue its macroeconomic management and other "national" objectives as threatened by giving the states independent access to the income tax base — or, for that matter, any other broad tax base.

So far as the equity of the tax system is concerned, under my proposed arrangement, with the states imposing *flat* rates of income tax on a commonly agreed base, the Commonwealth would still effectively determine the overall degree of *progression* in the personal income tax system. Moreover, giving the states access to the personal income tax could prompt a wider reassessment of existing state taxation: if some of the least efficient and least equitable state taxes were replaced by state income tax revenues, the objective of promoting equity through the tax system would actually be enhanced by a state income tax scheme of the sort I propose.

It also is the case that there is *no* necessary implication that the capacity of the Commonwealth to influence state spending priorities to meet what the Commonwealth sees as national objectives in relation to public services, such as education and health, would be reduced. The scheme, as illustrated earlier, could be limited to reducing only the Commonwealth's *untied* (general revenue) transfers. (Even going further and absorbing some or all of the current tied grant transfers into the state tax component would still leave the Commonwealth free, from within its still substantial budget resources, to offer incentives to the states to modify their policies and priorities).

In the end, however, the battle lines can be expected to be drawn around the question of effective macroeconomic management. It will be argued that giving the states greater revenue-raising freedom, and at the same time reducing the magnitude of the Financial Assistance Grants which have given the Commonwealth a capacity to influence the level of state spending, increases the risk of the states undermining Commonwealth macroeconomic management objectives and/or reduces the Commonwealth's budgetary flexibility.

Without entering into the debates about the efficacy of different forms of macroeconomic management policy, the outlines of a rebuttal to this argument would run broadly as follows.

At the broadest level, the claims usually made that the economic theory of federalism establishes that control of fiscal policy for macroeconomic management purposes is appropriately, *and essentially exclusively*, a function of central government never was strictly true (see Walsh, 1993, for a fuller explanation). What, strictly speaking, is required is *fiscal policy coordination* between national and sub-national jurisdictions to ensure that "stability" is secured both at the overall national level and among individual economic regions, to the greatest extent possible.

As in other contexts, the need for coordination in fiscal policy arises from interdependencies between the decisions of individual governments. Fiscal decisions of sub-national governments, even those required to balance budgets, spill over to affect demand in other jurisdictions and hence affect national stability. (Conversely, of course, uniform decisions by central governments can have differential effects on regional stability, but, curiously, no-one seems to worry about this fact or to examine its possible ramifications for the appropriate role of regional fiscal policy.)

In Australia, over most of the post-war period, "coordination" has been equated in the Commonwealth's mind, and that of many commentators, with something approaching complete Commonwealth determination of fiscal outcomes, achieved through both Loan Council control of borrowings and Commonwealth control of a large proportion of state revenues and hence their capacity to spend.

For what it is worth, "armchair" empiricism does not suggest that Australia's unusually high degree of vertical fiscal imbalance, and associated high degree of centralisation of fiscal power, has resulted in a superior macroeconomic management performance compared to that of all other mature federations in North America and Europe (USA, Canada, Germany and Switzerland in particular) which exhibit a greater degree of balance in the distribution of fiscal powers. Ted Evans and Ian McKenzie (1989) offer a brief outline of some views by (then) Commonwealth Treasury officials on macroeconomic management and federalism, and cast doubt on the need for the current degree of Commonwealth dominance. Moreover, a preliminary and tentative empirical analysis of the relationship between economic performance and revenue-raising centralisation in OECD countries undertaken by Kerry Barwise and Frank Castles (1991) suggested little or no difference in growth or unemployment performance and a worsening of inflation performance as revenue centralisation increases.

For short-run macroeconomic management purposes, the impact on state spending of changes to state grants *which lie within the range of political feasibility* are likely to be too slight and too uncertain to be a decisive consideration. In any event, it is difficult to see why controlling 40 percent of the funding of state outlays gives the Commonwealth greater purchase on state decision making than if it applied the same cuts in real terms to grants that represented only 20 percent or only 10 percent of state outlays. Moreover, with over 50 percent of own-purpose outlays and revenues spent on its own account, the Commonwealth has substantial fiscal clout within its own-purpose budget. By comparison, the largest state has own-purpose expenditures less than one-third as large as those of the Commonwealth.

In the end, in the short run, the Commonwealth relies as much on the goodwill of the states — and on the judgements of state voters and of ratings agencies and financial markets about state policies — as on its direct influence on their revenues, and it is at least arguable that it will better secure that goodwill where it is sought through negotiation among "fiscal equals" than where it is persistently pursued through the exercise of brute fiscal force.

In the longer run, moreover, the critical issue is not likely to be so much the size of public sector demand *per se* as its efficiency and its contribution to national productivity and social justice. While Commonwealth influences on the spending capacity of the states may have helped to reinforce this message, a system which forces the states to accept greater responsibility for funding their spending from adequate, independent revenue sources arguably could have achieved at least as much. For one thing, voters, financial markets, ratings agencies and media commentators would have concentrated more attention on the performance of the states more quickly than they have until recently. For another, access to a broad-based tax, through which citizens can be offered a "productivity dividend" in the form of tax cuts, would give the states a stronger basis for winning political support for the pain associated with microeconomic reforms. Equally importantly, the states would be less inclined to use concessions and public utility prices as ways of giving "tax cuts" to residents if they had their own broad-based tax revenue source, hence allowing greater scope for reforms to the pricing of public services.

None of this is to deny that the Commonwealth should have the lead role in relation to coordinating counter-cyclical stabilisation policy. Along with this goes a presumption that the federal government ought to have "automatic stabilisers" under its control. In terms of the tax system, this principally implies that the progressive part of the income tax system, which generates disproportionately large revenues in a boom and contrariwise in a slump, ought to be in the hands of the federal government. This can be attained, however, without denying the states some share of the income tax base on some agreed basis, especially if they are restricted to flat (proportional) tax rates. (There may be a risk of the states stepping in if the federal government were to cut tax rates for demand management purposes, but it seems to me that, quite apart from the fact that tax rate variations are infrequently used nowadays for these purposes, this would best be avoided by negotiation and consultation.)

Moreover, there is no direct implication that, on average, federal governments need revenue bases greater than those required to fund their own purpose expenditure responsibilities in order to effectively manage macroeconomic policy. Indeed, *a priori*, with around 50 percent of total public sector own-purpose expenditure responsibilities and the capacity to run larger budget deficits than the states without risking its ratings, the federal government in Australia arguably has as much fiscal clout as it really requires without needing virtual monopoly control of major tax bases. In fact, it already has *additional* control compared to other federal countries because, through the Australian Loan Council, the federal government is able to exert substantial influence over, if not control of, state and public trading enterprise borrowing, as well as having control of monetary policy.

Making Fiscal Coordination a Reality

To bring all these points together, *fiscal policy coordination through a process of negotiation*, rather than through *control* by the Commonwealth, has the capacity to deliver superior outcomes, especially in a world where ratings agencies, financial markets and public opinion hold greater sway than ever before. The mechanisms for achieving this form of coordination, capable of working within and supporting a more balanced system of access to revenues by the states, have already begun to be developed in Australia. The annual preparation of a *National Fiscal Outlook* and its use as a basis for establishing, monitoring and requiring public reports against Loan Council Allocations, is precisely the sort of medium-term framework required to underpin a more active, cooperative fiscal coordination process. A renaming of the Loan Council to refer to it as the *National Fiscal Coordination Council*, in which the Commonwealth, states and territories would jointly seek to promote short and medium term fiscal objectives, and decide how they each should contribute, would help to recast official and political thinking.

There would, of course, be a need to develop procedures and agreements to ensure that the coordination process is workable and sustainable. As I have already indicated, I believe *greater revenue raising independence and predicability given to the states would contribute greatly to their cooperative participation* — that greater independence, indeed, could be made part of a package of measures constituting an agreement about how a Coordination Council would work and what its scope would include.

Part of the package valuably might include making the Council one in which treasurers and/or finance ministers meet regularly (i.e., more than once a year *and invariably in advance of the annual Premiers' Conference*) — at least to ensure that much of the detail about, and the element of surprise and conflict over, budgetary and economic matters is taken away from annual Premiers' Conferences and made part of a continuing process of information exchange, consultation and negotiation.

The role of the Coordination Council might also encompass reviews of other aspects of the national tax system, the role and design of tied grants, progress on microeconomic reform and so on — helping to sustain and further drive valuable fiscal and economic reforms, including by more deeply involving state and territory treasurers and finance ministers in the process.

The deliberations of the Council and its associated treasury officials' meetings might also be assisted by the establishment of a reference group (or advisory commission) comprised *largely* of independent economic and fiscal experts. This would contribute to scrutiny and transparency and to providing a context in which agreements about fiscal coordination are encouraged and self-enforced.

Conclusions:
Towards a New Approach to Promoting National Objectives

If the establishment of such an approach to macroeconomic management in Australia were to enable the states to be given access to the personal income tax base on an agreed basis, the fiscal mess — the welfare costs and inequities that I referred to earlier — that Australia's current federal fiscal arrangements have promoted could be reduced or eliminated. The efficiency costs associated with divorcing revenue-raising responsibilities from expenditure responsibilities would be much diminished; the heavy reliance by the states on revenue sources that impose substantial distortions could be significantly reduced; and a number of regressive elements in the Australian tax system would be able to be eliminated. Whether the principles of tax assignment are seen in Musgravian allocative efficiency terms, or, Brennan and Buchanan style, in terms of promoting more competition among spheres of government, the Australian tax system would receive a much higher rating against those principles.

While the analysis on which this conclusion has been based has concentrated on Australia's peculiar federal fiscal arrangements, there are some aspects of it that have possible application to Canada — some of a general nature relevant to all federal systems others more specific to Canada. At the most general level, the possible lessons concern the linkages between the management of fiscal relationships in federations and the quality of intergovernmental relations more generally.

Brute fiscal force has a limited role — indeed, perhaps a self-limiting role — in securing truly national objectives in a federal system. The greater the force, the more likely the resistance and the greater the likelihood that subnational governments will seek creative ways of escaping its impact.

National objectives — in macroeconomic management or other policy areas — should not be regarded as exclusively the province of the federal government. The states, or provinces, as representatives of sub-sets of the citizens which together make up the federal government's political jurisdiction, have a legitimate interest in, and shared responsibility for, defining and promoting *truly national* objectives. Of course, the federal government is expected to take a broader view and to identify and take account of interdependencies: but it cannot be deduced from this that it has an exclusive role in relation to "national issues" to be exercised unilaterally and if necessary by force.

Recognition of the interdependencies of interests inherent in virtually all of the areas of activity that are, constitutionally speaking, the principal responsibility of one sphere of government, and the coordination or harmonisation of some aspects of state/provincial policies and activities to reflect broader national interests, requires a less ritualistic, more professional, system of intergovernmental relations. If the major features of the federal fiscal system and the peak institutions of the intergovernmental relations system are managed in a way that heightens conflict and offers little reward to voluntary cooperation and coordination, this is likely to infect much of the rest of the intergovernmental system with suspicion and resentment.

My suggestion for Australia that there should be established *National Fiscal Coordination Council* of treasurers and/or finance ministers possibly has application elsewhere, too — including Canada. As part of a negotiated *financial and fiscal accord or agreement* — an agreement between prime minister and premiers — it would symbolise and reinforce a thrust towards improved intergovernmental relations more generally. Apart from the details of mechanisms for securing fiscal policy coordination, the agreement might also include provision for the Coordination Council to regularly review progress on public sector microeconomic (structural) reforms and measures of efficiency in public sector spending. It also might encompass provision for regular reviews of federal and sub-national tax systems and for developing broad guidelines for the scope and design of conditional grants programs. The overall purpose would be to help to ensure that principle and negotiation dominate over expediency, conflict and unilateralism in federal fiscal arrangements.

At an even broader level, such a financial or fiscal agreement might be part of an even more encompassing *intergovernmental accord*, which would establish a set of guiding principles for relationships and for resolving issues about roles and functions, which would be agreed among political leaders as required to be respected in all intergovernmental forums and interactions. This is not the occasion to try to fill-out the details of the possible content of such an accord, although it is clear that, at the most general level, it would have to involve mutual recognition of the importance of both responsibility-sharing and autonomy and the value of diversity and experimentation, as well as the essential role of cooperation and consultation. At a more specific level, it would have to offer operational principles to guide deliberations about the roles and responsibilities of the different spheres of government.

Turning now to the more specific issue of tax powers — and at the risk of treading on Canadian sensitivities — the parts of my argument that might have most direct application to Canada concern the assignment of sales taxes and income taxes between federal and sub-national governments.

The general arguments that I offered earlier in favour of the federal level having the predominant, perhaps essentially exclusive, role in sales taxation (via a GST) because of the significance of this form of taxation, *inter alia*, for national savings and exports, and for interstate distortions, seem to me quite compelling. If it were accepted, an offer by the provinces to vacate the sales tax field in exchange for *both* the federal government making appropriate room for increased personal income tax collections by the provinces *and* an agreement to reform the provinces' personal income taxes to make them taxes on base (rather than taxes on tax, as they are now) might be of significant benefit, in my estimation, in improving the efficiency and equity of the Canadian tax system.

Given the size and scope of local government functions in Canada (compared with Australia) there might also be a case for a modest local government direct share in personal income taxation. The question of whether corporate income taxes might be harmonised, or even centralised, as part of a broader agreed reform package, would also be worth consideration. But I will not chance my arm further than these few speculative comments on these issues because of the need to recognise Canada's particular circumstances with respect to Quebec.

References

Barwise, K. and F.G. Castles. 1991. "The New Federalism," *Fiscal Centralisation and Public Policy Outcomes*, Discussion Paper No. 27, Canberra: Public Policy Program, Australian National University, September.

Evans, E.A. and I.M. McKenzie. 1989. "Some Macroeconomic Implications of Tax Reform," J. G. Head (ed.), *Tax Reform in Retrospect and Prospect*, Sydney: Australian Tax Research Foundation.

Evatt Research Foundation. 1989. "State of Siege: Renewal or Privatisation of Australian State Public Services," *Pluto Press: Sydney*.

Fletcher, Christine and Cliff Walsh. 1992. "Reform of Intergovernmental Relations in Australia: The Politics of Federalism and the Non-Politics of Managerialism," *Public Administration*, 70, (4), Winter, 591-616.

Freebairn, John, Michael Porter and Cliff Walsh (eds.). 1989. *Savings and Productivity: Incentives for the 1990s*, Sydney: Allen and Unwin.

Gerking, S.D. and J.H., Mutti. 1981. "Possibilities for the Explanation of Production Taxes: A General Equilibrium Analysis," *Journal of Public Economics*, 16.

Goodspeed, T. 1987. "A Re-Examination of the Use of Ability to Pay Taxes by Local Governments," *Journal of Public Economics*, 38.

Goss, Wayne. 1995. *Restoring the Balance: The Future of Australian Federation*, Canberra: Federalism Research Centre, Australian National University.

Keating, Paul. 1991. "The Commonwealth and the States and the November Special Premiers' Conference," *Address to the National Press Club*, Canberra, 22 October.

Mathews, R.L. and W.R.C. Jay. 1972. *Federal Finance: Intergovernmental Financial Relations in Australia Since Federation*, Melbourne: Nelson.

McLure Jr, C.E. 1986. "Tax Competition: Is What's Good for the Private Goose also Good for the Public Gander," *National Tax Journal*, 39.

Mieszkowski, P. and E. Toder. 1983. "Taxation of Energy Resources," C. McLure Jr, & P Mieszkowski (eds.), *Fiscal Federalism and the Taxation of Natural Resources*, Lexington, Mass: Heath-Lexington.

Moore, Des. 1991. "Federal-State Financial Relations — A Priority for Reform?" *Study Paper No. 17, Economic Policy Unit*, Melbourne: Institute of Public Affairs.

Musgrave, R.A. 1983. "Who Should Tax, Where and What?" C. McLure Jr., (ed.), *Tax Assignment in Federal Countries*, Canberra: ANU Press.

Premiers and Chief Ministers (of States and Territories in the Australian Federation). 1991. *Proposals for the Special Premiers' Conference in Perth*, November.

Report of the Working Party on Tax Powers. 1991. "Taxation and the Fiscal Imbalance Between Levels of Australian Government: Responsibility, Accountability and Efficiency," 4 October, Commonwealth and State Treasuries.

Walsh, Cliff. 1987. "The Riddle of Financial Relations," Mark Birrell (ed.), *The Australian States Towards a Renaissance*, Melbourne: Longman Cheshire.

Walsh, Cliff. 1987b. "The Distribution of Taxing Powers Between Levels of Government: The Possibility of a State Income Tax Reconsidered," G. Brennan (ed.), *Constitutional Reform and Fiscal Federalism, Occasional Paper No 42*, Canberra: Centre for Research on Federal Financial Relations, Australian National University.

Walsh, Cliff. 1990. "State Taxation and Vertical Fiscal Imbalance: The Radical Reform Options," Cliff Walsh (ed.), *Issues in State Taxation*, Canberra: Federalism Research Centre, Australian National University.

Walsh, Cliff. 1991. "Reform of Commonwealth-State Relations: No Representation Without Taxation," *Discussion Paper No. 2*, Canberra: Federalism Research Centre, Australian National University.

Walsh, Cliff. 1992. "Federal Reform and the Politics of Vertical Fiscal Imbalance," *Australian Journal of Political Science*, 27, Special Issue (November), 19-37.

Walsh, Cliff. 1993. "VFI: The Issues," D. Collins (ed.), *Vertical Fiscal Imbalance*, Sydney: Australian Tax Research Foundation.

Walsh, Cliff and Norm Thomson. 1994. *Federal Fiscal Arrangements in Australia: Their Potential Impact on Urban Settlement*, Canberra: Federalism Research Centre in association with SA Centre for Economic Studies.

Walsh, Cliff (with contributions by Jeff Petchey). 1993. "Fiscal Federalism: An Overview of Issues and a Discussion of their Relevance to the European Community," Cliff Walsh, Horst Reichenbach, and Roderick Meiklejohn (eds.), *The Economics of Community Public Finance*, published in *European Economy, Reports and Studies No 5*, Brussels: Commission of the European Communities.

Wildasin, D.E. 1984. "The Welfare Effects of Intergovernmental Grants with Distortionary Local Taxes," *Journal of Public Economics*, 25.

7

Assigning Responsibility for Regional Stabilization: Evidence from Canada and Australia

Paul Boothe and Jeffrey Petchey

The textbook conception of fiscal policy and the reality of fiscal stabilization in federal states are substantially different. In the textbook treatment, the economy is subject to random economic shocks, and governments respond to these shocks by adjusting spending and taxation to smooth flows of income and consumption. More sophisticated treatments distinguish between government actions which occur automatically (automatic stabilizers) and those that require conscious action on the part of government (discretionary policy). A substantial literature considers the relative efficacy of these two kinds of stabilization policy. Of course, in addition to "stabilizing" the economy, governments have other responsibilities such as providing public goods and redistributing income, but the focus of this paper is the stabilization role.

The reality of federations is that the assignment of taxing and spending responsibilities among the various levels of government is a major issue.[1]

---

* We are grateful to S. McPherson and J. Smythe for research assistance and to T. Courchene and C. Walsh for helpful discussions.
1. In this paper we will confine ourselves to considering two levels of government: the national (federal or commonwealth) government and the regional (provincial or state) government. Although very important in delivering services, local governments (such as municipalities) have a relatively small stabilization role and are therefore not included in this discussion.

Federal systems create two complications that are not usually considered in textbook treatments of fiscal policy: regions within a federation may be subject to substantially different random shocks and more than one level of government may be able to stabilize using automatic stabilizers or discretionary policy. In past literature, it has been tantamount to an article of faith that stabilization should be the responsibility of the national government. Recently, however, researchers (Oates 1972; Fisher 1993) have begun to question received wisdom, arguing that the existence of regional shocks means there is a legitimate stabilization role for regional governments. (Gramlich 1987)

The purpose of this paper is to look at fiscal stabilization policy in two federations, Canada and Australia, in an effort to answer the following policy question: does the need for fiscal stabilization imply anything about the assignment of expenditure and taxation responsibilities to national and regional governments? In answering the question we bring to bear analysis from Europe and the United States, as well as examining evidence from Canada and Australia.

The plan of the remainder of the paper is as follows: in Section 2, we review a number of issues that have been discussed in past literature: reasons for assigning the major role for stabilization; how big should a fiscal presence is required for stabilization; and the stabilization impacts of transfer systems primarily designed for redistributional purposes. In Section 3, we look at empirical evidence from Canada and Australia on the existence of region-specific shocks and the response of national and regional governments. Two specific case studies of discretionary policy are presented in Section 4, and Section 5 contains our summary and discussion of policy implications.

Previous Literature

In this section, we look at some issues related to fiscal stabilization in federations that have been discussed in the literature. A number of topics are covered, including reasons for assigning the major role for stabilization, the size of the fiscal presence required for stabilization, and the stabilization impacts of transfer systems primarily designed for redistributional purposes. Each of the topics are considered in turn.

Assigning the Role for Stabilization
Typically, the literature on fiscal federalism uses efficiency arguments to assign responsibilities for expenditures and taxation to national and regional governments. The principle of "subsidiarity" commonly invoked in

discussions in Europe suggests that to ensure responsiveness to local preferences and accountability to taxpayers, spending responsibilities should be assigned to national governments unless there are compelling reasons to pass them to the Community.[2] Compelling reasons generally fall into two categories. The first category is where there are significant "spillovers" from one region's expenditure to other regions and where the required coordination is too difficult or costly. The second category is where there are significant economies of scale in the provision of government services.[3]

The literature establishes a clear link between the assignment of expenditure and taxation responsibilities. The principle here is stated succinctly by Walsh (1993): "...governments which are responsible for expenditure decisions should be responsible for raising the revenue to fund them and should have control over, and responsibility for, revenue sources adequate to enable them to do so." (31) This principle flows directly from the need for government accountability. The mobility of certain tax bases and the possibility of tax shifting to residents of other regions are sometimes cited as reasons to modify this principle of tax assignment.

To this point, the discussion of expenditure and taxation assignment has been framed with the "allocation" role — the provision of government services — of government in mind. However, the other roles of government, redistributing income and stabilizing the macroeconomy, may also influence the assignment of these responsibilities. Early work in this area suggested that the stabilization role should be assigned to the national government. (Oates 1972) Oates gives three reasons for suggesting this assignment. The first is that regional economies are more "open" than national economies and thus leakages will render regional fiscal stimulus less effective than national stimulus. The second is that regional debt financing will result in liabilities that are more "external" (to the region), than national debt financing. The final is that regional shocks are likely to be highly correlated (i.e., national shocks dominate regional ones) and thus should be offset by a national stabilization effort.

The evidence in the literature does not support Oates' arguments. A 1977 study by the Economic Council of Canada found that for the four largest Canadian provinces, about 70 percent of the national effect of a fiscal stimulus was felt within the province initiating the stimulus. Later work by Miller (1980) and Fortin (1982) found that the effect of regional fiscal policy

---

2. In the European context, nations correspond to "regional governments" and the European Community corresponds to the "national government" of our discussion.
3. The possibility that stabilization could be acheived by coordination of regional government actions has received little attention in the literature. See Petchey and Shapiro (1995).

actions was significant and equal to 75 to 90 percent of national fiscal policy actions.

Oates' second argument is also open to debate. The argument essentially ignores redistribution (through repayment of bond interest and principal) within a jurisdiction and focuses on redistribution between jurisdictions. It could be argued that it is redistribution among individuals rather than among jurisdictions that is important. In this case, the important questions are related to who will benefit from the proceeds of borrowing and who will be responsible for repayment of interest and principal, rather than who will lend the funds. For Canada, it is clearly the case that much provincial borrowing is done outside the borrowing provinces. However, much of this borrowing is also external to the country. Indeed, a growing proportion of Canadian federal debt is now held externally. In any case, with highly integrated world capital markets, discussions of whether we "owe it to ourselves" seem to have little currency. The focus has now shifted to "how much to we owe?" and "can we repay?"

Oates' final argument is that regional shocks are dominated by national shocks, so that national attempts at fiscal stabilization will be most effective. Empirical evidence on this issue will be examined later in the paper. Recently, Gramlich (1990) has suggested that regional shocks may dominate. The core of Gramlich's argument is that as regional economies become more specialized due to globalization, they become more likely to respond differently to relative price shocks. Further support to this notion is given by Krugman (1993) who cites the case of Massachusetts in the New England region of the United States which suffered a particularly severe regional shock in the final years of the 1980s. Krugman argued that integration of the US market has led regional economies in that country to become highly specialized and thus vulnerable to relative price shocks. Increasing integration of the world economy (globalization) would suggest that specialization of regional economies will continue — together with increasing regional vulnerability to relative price shocks.

How Big a Fiscal Presence Is Needed for Stabilization?

Implicit in much of the discussion of assigning the role for fiscal stabilization, is the view that fiscal stabilization requires a substantial, indeed dominant, fiscal presence. Recently, however, research conducted to inform the debate over European integration has challenged this conventional wisdom. Using a macro simulation model to test their proposal, Italianer and Vanheukelen (1993) develop a stabilization scheme based on unemployment rates designed to deliver the same degree of stabilization to the EC as the US tax and transfer system delivers to that country. The cost of such a scheme is estimated at 0.2 percent of EC GDP.

How could so much stabilization stimulus be provided at such a low cost? Italianer and Venheukelen offer the following explanation:

> The main reason why such a high degree of stabilization can be achieved at relatively little cost is that, unlike in existing federations where stabilization properties are usually a by-product of the tax and transfer system, the mechanism proposed here is explicitly designed for stabilization purposes. Consequently, its efficiency in terms of the degree of stabilization obtained in relation to the costs of the system is much higher than that in existing federations. (505)

The impact of the transfer system on regional stabilization is addressed next.

The Impact of the Intergovernmental Transfers on Regional Stabilization

Because the textbook treatment of fiscal stabilization ignores the complications posed by federal states, it misses an extremely important factor in overall fiscal stabilization in Australia and Canada — the system of intergovernmental transfers. In considering the impact of these transfers, we turn to two recent papers by Courchene.

Courchene (1993) reviews the stabilization impact of the three major intergovernmental transfers in Canada: Equalization, Established Program Financing (EPF) and the Canada Assistance Plan (CAP).[4] Equalization is an unconditional grant which partially equalizes revenues across provinces. The equalization formula compares provincial revenues in 33 categories to a five-province standard and calculates payments to provinces (all but BC, Alberta and Ontario) whose aggregate revenues (in the 33 categories) are below the level of the five-province standard. Whether fiscal stabilization occurs depends on whether the province receives equalization payments, and whether the province is included as one of the five provinces used to calculate the standard.

Consider a situation where a province experiences a negative shock and all other provinces are initially unaffected by the shock. If the province receives equalization, the decline in its revenues is offset by increased equalization. In this case, provinces not included in the standard are better off than those included, since included provinces' decline in revenues will

---

4. The Federal Budget of 1995 proposed major changes in EPF and CAP. Since the exact nature of these changes are not yet clear, we confine our discussion to the current regime.

lower the standard as well. If a province does not receive equalization, there are obviously no stabilizing transfers, although if the province is included in the standard, equalization to all receiving provinces will decline.[5]

The effect of a positive shock will also depend on whether equalization is received and whether the province is included in the five-province standard. Provinces which receive equalization will lose a portion of it if their revenues increase, although less if they are included in the standard. Provinces which do not receive equalization will not lose revenue, but aggregate equalization may increase if they are included in the standard.

EPF is an unconditional grant which provides the federal contribution to two areas of provincial responsibility: health and post-secondary education.[6] EPF transfers are calculated as the sum of the value of provincial income points plus a cash transfer to a fixed ceiling. As the value of tax points grows, the cash transfer declines and vice versa. Because EPF tax points are included in the equalization calculation, these grants provide no additional active stabilization to equalization-receiving provinces facing shocks. However, EPF does have a passive stabilizing effect for provinces not receiving equalization since the sum of provincial tax points plus cash transfer does not change as regional economic circumstances change.[7]

The third major intergovernmental transfer, CAP provides conditional, cost-shared funding for social assistance programs. A number of conditions are attached to this transfer. The transfer is capped for the three provinces not receiving equalization, and thus may not act as an active stabilizer in the case of negative shocks in those provinces.

A final, special, transfer program deserves mention. Canada also has a special "stabilization fund" for provinces whose nominal revenues decline in a given year.[8] Until very recently, only three successful claims had been made for stabilization funds — all by provinces not receiving equalization. This illustrates the power of equalization in preventing a decline in revenue for provinces receiving equalization. The fund is designed to be an active stabilizer, but gaining federal approval for a payout has turned out to be such a protracted process that its value as a stabilizing transfer is questionable.

---

5. A distinction should be drawn between transfers that are "active" stabilizers (those that are counter-cyclical), "passive" stabilizers (those that are uncorrelated with economic fluctuations) and "destabilizers" (those that are pro-cyclical).
6. The Canada Health Act prohibits provinces from allowing "extra-billing" and ensures portability of health coverage between provinces. Provinces are not otherwise constrained in how EPF funds are spent.
7. Of course, this omits the effect a regional shock may have on national GDP. For the purposes of this discussion, we ignore this second-round effect.
8. Not all revenues (e.g. resource revenues) are treated in the same way. The 1995 budget changed the threshold from zero to a five percent decline.

The effect of transfers on regional stabilization in Australia is much simpler to describe. Transfers from the Commonwealth to states fall into two main categories: Special Purpose Payments (SPPs) which are conditional grants and Financial Assistance Grants (FAGs) which are unconditional. Unlike Canada, conditional SPPs are larger in magnitude than unconditional FAGs. Because they are relatively unresponsive to regional economic conditions, SPPs provide a measure of passive stabilization to state economies.

The FAGs are Australia's counterpart to equalization in Canada. However, there are a number of important differences. First, the Commonwealth Grants Commission, the body that administers the FAGs, calculates the "shares of the pie, not [...] the size of the pie." (Courchene, 1995:V-12). Thus, the overall size of the transfer is determined solely by the Commonwealth government. Second, forty expenditure categories as well as nineteen revenue categories are equalized. Third, both expenditure and revenue categories are fully equalized, i.e. states above the norm, are, in effect, brought down to the norm. Thus, both expenditure need and revenue capacity are equalized.

Like unconditional grants in Canada, the FAGs provide a powerful active stabilizer. Unlike Canada, full equalization of revenue and expenditure means that the stabilization effect of transfers is much more uniform across states. Because some SPPs are included in the CGC calculations, these are changed from passive stabilizers to active ones.

Evidence from Canada and Australia

One of the key practical questions to be answered in discussions of regional stabilization is how much do regional fluctuations differ? To answer this question for Canada, we have updated the evidence for Canada provided by Boothe and Davidson (1993). Regional fluctuations are calculated as deviations from a quadratic trend line drawn through real per capita output.[9] Correlations between regional fluctuations for a sample of Canadian provinces are provided in Table 7.1.

---

9. Methodology and data sources are provided in Boothe and Davidson (1993).

Table 7.1
Correlations of Real Per Capita Output Fluctuations: Canada 1961-93

Quebec	1.000				
Ontario	0.885	1.000			
Alberta	-0.144	-0.465	1.000		
British Columbia	0.447	0.135	0.358	1.000	
Canada	0.913	0.759	0.200	0.528	1.000
	Quebec	Ontario	Alberta	British Columbia	Canada

From Table 7.1, it is clear that there are substantial regional differences in economic fluctuations in Canada. For example, Alberta's fluctuations are negatively correlated with those in Ontario and Quebec and only weakly correlated with those in its western neighbour, BC. BC's fluctuations are weakly correlated with Quebec's and essentially uncorrelated with fluctuations in Ontario.[10]

We have repeated the same exercise (based on substantially fewer observations) for the Australian states in Table 7.2.

Table 7.2
Correlations of Real Per Capita Output Fluctuations: Australia 1980-94

Tasmania	1.000						
Western Aus.	0.892	1.000					
South Aus.	0.597	0.505	1.000				
Queensland	0.667	0.647	0.567	1.000			
Victoria	0.750	0.759	0.858	0.708	1.000		
New South Wales	0.836	0.848	0.468	0.809	0.773	1.000	
Australia	0.863	0.866	0.736	0.849	0.937	0.933	1.000
	TAS	WA	SA	QLD	VIC	NSW	AUS

For Australia, the situation is substantially different. Regional economic fluctuations are remarkably similar, with correlations ranging from 0.89 between Tasmania and Western Australia and 0.51 between South Australia and Western Australia.[11] Whether the degree of correlation between regional fluctuations in Canada and Australia differs because of the underlying structure of the economies or because of government policy (such as Australia's much more comprehensive equalization framework) is a question which deserves further attention by researchers.

---

10. With this number of observations, a significant difference (5 percent level) is approximately 0.34.
11. Given the small number of observations, significance tests are not meaningful.

Next, we examine Canadian federal and provincial fiscal policy in order to gauge its timing in relation to regional economic fluctuations. To do this, we first develop a measure of fiscal policy which can be divided into two components: automatic and discretionary. Our overall measure of fiscal policy is fluctuations of the normalized primary deficit (program expenditure less revenue normalized by program expenditure) around a quadratic trend. Discretionary stabilization policy is assumed to come from government spending on goods and services, subsidies, and capital assistance to business. The remainder of program spending and all of revenue is assumed to produce automatic stabilization policy. Again, these two components are measured as fluctuations around trend.

Looking first at federal fiscal stabilization by region, in Table 7.3 we present correlations between regional economic fluctuations and federal policy for a sample of provinces.

Table 7.3
Federal Fiscal Policy by Province 1961-93

Total	-0.471	-0.762	-0.611	-0.246
Discretionary	-0.037	0.111	0.505	0.124
Automatic	-0.472	-0.744	-0.696	-0.261
	Quebec	Ontario	Alberta	BC

We see that overall, fiscal policy is generally negatively correlated with regional economic fluctuations, although the negative correlation is relatively weak for British Columbia. This is exactly what one would expect from counter-cyclical fiscal policy. However, we see that the counter-cyclical properties of federal policy come primarily from the automatic component of the policy. Indeed, in the case of two provinces, the discretionary component of fiscal policy is weakly pro-cyclical, and, for Alberta, strongly pro-cyclical.

The same sort of analysis can be performed for provincial government fiscal policy. The results of those calculations are presented in Table 7.4:

Table 7.4
Provincial Fiscal Policy 1961-93

Total	-0.326	-0.688	-0.702	-0.223
Discretionary	-0.064	0.071	0.133	0.345
Automatic	-0.361	-0.726	-0.702	-0.382
	Quebec	Ontario	Alberta	BC

The results for provincial fiscal policy are generally similar to those for federal policy. However, overall stabilization policy is slightly more counter-cyclical than its federal counterpart for Alberta. Provincial discretionary policy is less pro-cyclical than its federal counterpart in Alberta, but substantially more so in British Columbia. Overall, it is clear that both federal and provincial governments run counter-cyclical automatic policy, but also that both run pro-cyclical discretionary policy.

Turning to Australia, lack of data on Commonwealth spending and revenue by region means that the methodology used above cannot be used to examine national policy in Australia. However, the similarity of economic fluctuations across regions makes this less important. An alternative methodology, based on dividing federal fiscal policy into its cyclical (automatic) and structural (discretionary) components allows us to examine Commonwealth policy relative to aggregate economic fluctuations.

By itself, the actual budget deficit, or Public Sector Borrowing Requirement (PSBR), is a misleading indicator of the stance of fiscal policy. This is because actual budgetary outcomes reflect both discretionary policy changes and the impact of automatic stabilizers and cyclical effects on the fiscal position. The two effects are often separated by dividing budgetary aggregates into their structural and cyclical components. The structural component reflects what the budget outcome would have been with the economy at full employment. Thus, estimates of the structural deficit attempt to "net out" the effect of cyclical factors, and automatic stabilizers, on budgetary outcomes. The structural deficit is a more meaningful estimate of the stance of discretionary fiscal policy.

The methodology used to compute the so-called "structural deficit" is based on estimates of the economy's NAIRU (non-accelerating inflation rate of unemployment), growth in the supply of labour and measures of total factor productivity. The presence of a structural deficit indicates that discretionary fiscal policy is expansionary while a structural surplus indicates that discretionary fiscal policy is contractionary. The cyclical component of fiscal policy is found by deducting this structural component from the actual budgetary outcome. It reflects the effects of automatic stabilizers and hence the economic cycle on the budgetary position. Though the structural deficit is seen as a relatively uncontroversial measure of the stance of fiscal policy there are still reasons to treat the concept with some degree caution (for a discussion see Pitchford 1995).

There are various estimates of the structural deficit available for Australia. For example, Neville (1993) derives an estimate of the structural deficit over the period from the late 1960s to the early 1990s. Table 7.5

provides OECD estimates of the structural and cyclical deficits for Australia over the period 1981 to 1996.

Table 7.5
Changes in the Cyclical and Structural Components of the Public Sector Deficit
(Percent of GDP)[1]

Year	Change in Actual Deficit	Change in Cyclical Deficit[2]	Change in Structural Deficit[3]
1981	0.9	-0.1	1.0
1982	0.2	-1.0	1.2
1983	-3.6	-1.1	-2.5
1984	1.0	1.4	-0.4
1985	0.3	0.7	-0.4
1986	-0.1	-0.4	0.3
1987	2.7	0.4	2.3
1988	1.3	0.2	1.1
1989	0.0	0.4	-0.4
1990	-0.7	-0.5	-0.2
1991	-3.3	-1.5	-1.8
1992	-1.1	-0.5	-0.6
1993	0.2	0.3	-0.1
1994	-0.3	0.6	-0.9
1995	1.1	0.6	0.5
1996	1.1	0.4	0.7

1. A positive sign indicates movement towards fiscal contractionary while a negative sign indicates a move towards fiscal expansion.
2. Captures the effect of automatic stabilizers, and hence the economic cycle, on the actual budgetary outcome.
3. Captures the effect of discretionary fiscal policy on actual budgetary outcomes.

Source: OECD, Economic Outlook, No. 56, December 1994, pp. A32-A33.

The data indicate that there have been five episodes (covering half of the sixteen-year period) since 1981 when the cyclical and discretionary components of the budgetary position have been moving in opposite directions. First, in 1981 and 1982, when the cyclical deficit was moving towards expansion, discretionary policy was becoming more contractionary. Second, in 1984 and 1985, discretionary policy was moving towards expansion while the cyclical component was moving towards contraction. Third, in 1986, discretionary policy was moving towards contraction when cyclical policy was becoming more expansionary. Fourth, in 1989, discretionary policy was becoming more expansionary while the cyclical deficit was becoming more contractionary.

Finally, in 1993 and 1994, discretionary policy was moving towards expansion while the cyclical component was becoming more contractionary. This indicates that discretionary policy over this period was pro-cyclical rather than counter-cyclical. As will be seen below, the main discretionary fiscal program responsible for this was the "One Nation" package.

One component of Commonwealth spending is disaggregated on a regional basis: Commonwealth transfers to State governments. In Table 7.6, we present the correlations between fluctuations in Commonwealth grants to States and regional economic fluctuations:[12]

Table 7.6
Correlation of Federal Grants with Regional Fluctuations: Australia 1980-94

0.294	-0.333	0.225	-0.453	0.094	-0.711
TAS	WA	SA	QLD	VIC	NSW

Although this is far from the whole story, since regional taxation and other Commonwealth spending are not considered, we see that Commonwealth grants are weakly pro-cyclical in three of the states and counter-cyclical in the other two, especially New South Wales. Once again, the small number of observations prevents us from performing any statistical tests.

Turning to state fiscal policy, it is possible to perform an analysis similar to the Canadian one for individual states. Again using the methodology described in Boothe and Davidson (1993), discretionary policy is assumed to be reflected by capital spending, while other spending and revenue are assumed to reflect automatic policy. The correlations between fluctuations in these policy variables and the regional economies are reported in Table 7.7:

---

12. In this table, we compare deviations of trend output by region with the fluctuations around trend Commonwealth grants.

Table 7.7
State Fiscal Policy: Australia 1980-94

Total	-0.200	-0.568	-0.462	-0.468	-0.261	-0.267
Discretionary	-0.498	0.115	0.359	0.193	-0.153	0.275
Automatic	0.049	-0.493	-0.430	-0.381	-0.129	-0.285
	TAS	WA	SA	QLD	VIC	NSW

Overall state fiscal policy is uniformly counter-cyclical, although in three of the states the correlation is less than -0.3. As in Canada, a number of the states run pro-cyclical discretionary policy which is offset by counter-cyclical automatic policy. The one anomaly seems to be Tasmania where a strongly counter-cyclical discretionary policy offsets a weakly pro-cyclical automatic policy.

In summary, despite substantial differences in regional economic fluctuations both federal and provincial governments in Canada run counter-cyclical fiscal policy. A fairly general result is that strongly counter-cyclical automatic components offset weaker, pro-cyclical discretionary components of policy. The (incorrect) perception that federal stabilization policy is insensitive to regional conditions in provinces like Alberta probably stems from the relatively strongly pro-cyclical federal discretionary policy in that region.

In contrast to Canada, economic fluctuations in Australian regions are much more highly correlated. Although data are not available to permit a full analysis of federal policy, federal automatic stabilizers appear to be counter-cyclical while discretionary policy seems to be generally pro-cyclical. Commonwealth grants to states are counter-cyclical in at least half of the states. Data are available to make a full analysis of state stabilization policy and we find a pattern very similar to that of Canada, where (except for Tasmania) the work of stabilization is done mainly through the automatic components of policy, with discretionary components being pro-cyclical in four of the six states.

Two Case Studies of Discretionary Fiscal Policy

In this section we focus on discretionary stabilization policy. As we saw in the previous section, discretionary policy tends to be pro-cyclical. Thus, a key issue is timing. There is a voluminous literature on the problems of discretionary policy dating back at least to Friedman (1968). To examine this issue concretely, we look at specific examples of discretionary policy in Canada and Australia. The Canadian example is the federal government's recent "Infrastructure Works" program.

The Canadian Infrastructure Works Program

The Infrastructure Works program was conceived as part of the federal Liberal Party's campaign platform and was included in the 1993 document "Creating Opportunity" commonly referred to as the "Red Book." The program was designed to be a partnership between federal, provincial and municipal governments with each party contributing one-third of a total of $6 billion. In a 1995 press release describing the program (Canada, 1995) nine criteria were listed for judging individual projects. The first two criteria listed were "incrementality and/or acceleration of investment" and "short- and long-term job creation." Thus, it seems clear that at least one of the program's objectives was fiscal stabilization. Federal funding was divided among provinces according to a simple formula:

(province i / Canadian total) = 0.5 [(province i population/ Canadian population) + province i unemployed / Canadian unemployed)].

In words, a province's share of Infrastructure Works funding is a simple average of its population share and its unemployment share. Thus, funding is specifically targeted to regions with above-average unemployment.

The timing of the program was initially that project approvals would be completed by March 31, 1996 and all projects would be complete by March 31, 1997. Indeed, 93 percent of the funds were committed by August 1995. Originally, the program was designed to run over three years to 1996-97, but the federal government announced in the February 1995 budget that the program would be extended with the original expenditure spread over five years instead of three.

The difficulty in timing a program with economic fluctuations is evident in Figure 7.1. The program was initially conceived in 1993 at the depth of the latest recession. However, by the time agreements with partner governments were signed in early 1994, the economy was already beginning to recover. By the time the bulk of projects were approved (summer 1995), the economy was operating above trend output. The actual spending will occur over the period 1995-96 to 1997-98, perhaps in time for the *next* recession in Canada. Thus, it may be that the program will actually be pro-cyclical. While stabilization was not the only goal of the program, it is safe to assume that it was never intended to accentuate rather than smooth business fluctuations.

Assigning Responsibility for Regional Stabilization   *155*

Figure 7.1
Canadian Deviations from Trend Output
(percent)

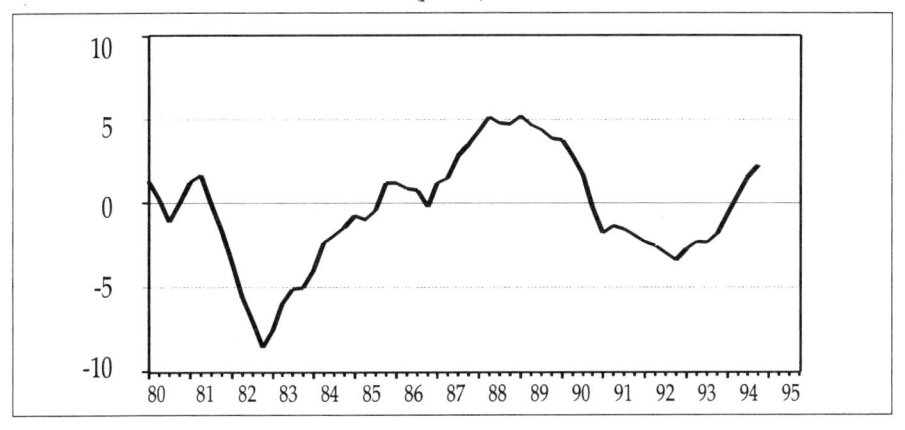

The Australian One Nation Program

During 1988, the Australian economy experienced an historically rapid rate of growth fueled by strong global aggregate demand. Growth was also accompanied by a sharply rising current account deficit. Both trends initially took policy-makers by surprise. Monetary tightening, the main policy response to both problems, was not implemented until April 1988 when the Reserve Bank of Australia (RBA) first raised interest rates.[13] By early 1989, the 90-day bank bill rate peaked at over 18 percent and growth turned negative by 1990-91. The extent of the ensuing recession is shown in Table 7.8.

Table 7.8
Changes in Real Per Capita GDP, 1988-89 to 1994-95

Year	Percentage Change
1988-89	4.6
1989-90	1.4
1990-91	-3.5
1991-92	-2.3
1992-93	1.2
1993-94	2.4
1994-95	3.7

Source: Estimated from Australian Bureau of Statistics (ABS) Government Finance Statistics data, the Australian Treasury's index of underlying inflation and ABS population figures.

---

43. Pitchford (1990) was strident critic of this approach.

The lowest point in the downturn was reached in 1990-91 and 1991-92. Growth was positive again in 1992-93 and in the two years since then has been relatively strong. In response to the return to growth, monetary policy was eased early on in the cycle (from 1990-91 onwards) with the 90 day bank bill rate being around 6 percent by December 1992.

The discretionary fiscal response, as indicated by the OECD data in Table 7.5, came later in the cycle when the structural deficit was already moving into surplus. And as is shown in Table 9 below, the spending effects of the major programs put in place have continued into 1995. Indeed, the late timing of these initiatives has been criticized by many (Indes, 1995:26). The major discretionary fiscal programs introduced included: the *November Economic Statement* (November 1991), the *One Nation* package (February 1992) and the *Working Nation* package (costing $1.2 billion over 2 years). These initiatives are summarized in Table 7.9.

Table 7.9
Major Discretionary Fiscal Initiatives (1991-95)

Program	Date Announced	Period over which funds to be spent	Intended Net Contribution to Actual Budget Deficit
One Nation	Feb 1992	1991-92 to 1994-95	2,300
Working Nation	June 1992 (1992-93 Budget)	June 1992-June 1994	1,200
Total			3,500

Source: Commonwealth Budget Papers (Various) 1990-91 to 1995-96.

The One Nation package was a combination of infrastructure and taxation policy initiatives while the Working Nation package has concentrated largely on labour market programs targeted in particular at the long term unemployed. Thus, it was the One Nation program that was intended to provide the main discretionary fiscal stimulus during the 1992-95 period. We now provide a brief summary of the main elements of the program.

The main elements of the One Nation program included fiscal initiatives, taxation reforms, wages and workplace reforms, education, training and labour market initiatives, changes to competition policy, industry based initiatives and infrastructure spending. Many of the initiatives announced were actually policies the government was already contemplating, but which were brought under the umbrella of the One Nation initiative.

Fiscal policy changes

The main fiscal initiatives included a once-off payment to families (under the Family Allowance Scheme) costing $317 million. In addition, the federal government restructured depreciation allowances for plant, equipment and infrastructure for income tax purposes. The other major fiscal initiative was the promise of a two-stage reduction in income tax rates, especially for middle income earners, the first of which was delivered in 1994. The second round was not introduced and instead the federal government increased its contribution, on behalf of employees, to the national superannuation scheme (also established as a part of the One Nation program - see discussion below).

Wages and workplace reforms

The shift to workplace bargaining as the basis of the industrial relations system, and a commitment to the Accord (an incomes policy which has been in place in Australia since the early 1980s) were accelerated though it should be remembered that these were policies which were already under way. Also, the federal government introduced a new scheme to provide for a national superannuation system to cover those employees not already in a private superannuation scheme. The new scheme was to be effective from July 1, 1992.

Education, training and labour market initiatives

A new system of vocational training and education was announced with additional spending of $720 million over the period 1993-95. Other reforms in entry-level training and training wages paid by the federal government were also announced. In addition, extra funding was provided to employers to keep on apprentices during the recession. Interestingly, there was no resort to "make work" schemes. Instead, a range of highly targeted measures were introduced (mostly job training) to increase the employability of the long term unemployed.

Competition policy and microeconomic reforms

During the 1980s, Australia had already gone through substantial deregulation of financial markets, tariff reductions and reforms in specific industries such as aviation, designed to enhance economic efficiency. These policies had been implemented under the broad banner of "microeconomic reform." One Nation continued with this program by introducing further commitments to liberalization in the aviation industry and in areas such as electricity generation.

Industry policy

The major industry policy initiative was the introduction of accelerated depreciation for plant, equipment and income producing buildings. But two additional spending initiatives were also introduced. The first was the establishment of a "Development Allowance" for large scale projects. This provided a pool of funds to be used to subsidize depreciation of equipment used in such projects. To be eligible projects had to have a capital cost of at least $50 million. The second initiative was the introduction of a "Pooled Development Fund." This was to provide for the establishment of concessionally taxed investment companies for investment in established small and medium sized firms.

Other measures were introduced to stimulate the development of offshore branches by domestic banks, establishment of an Australian Technology Group (ATG) to act as a small commercially focused company to invest in research with commercial potential and various export assistance measures.

Infrastructure

A substantial increase in infrastructure spending by the federal government provided much of the immediate fiscal stimulus in One Nation. In particular, $454 million was allocated over two years (up to the end of 1994) for major upgrading of the railway system, particularly on the eastern coast. An extra $602 million was allocated to road spending over the period from 1991-92 to 1993-94, mainly to the national highway system, while an additional $255 million was allocated to road maintenance over this period. Other projects were also hurried along, in particular, the Commonwealth's "Better Cities Program" which provides for inner city refurbishment, was included as part of the One Nation commitments.

In conclusion, there is evidence to suggest that there have been periods since at least the early 1980s when discretionary fiscal policy in Australia has been pro-cyclical. This is true, for example, of the period 1993 and 1994 when the major discretionary fiscal stimulus was provided by the One Nation program, the spending effects of which have continued into 1994-95 well after the automatic stabilizers, as reflected in the cyclical deficit, had begun to move towards contraction.

Conclusions

The evidence presented in this paper is easily summarized under three headings.

Regional fluctuations

Provincial economies in Canada exhibit substantially different economic fluctuations. Indeed some, like those of Alberta and Ontario, are negatively correlated. Others, like those of BC and Ontario, are essentially uncorrelated. In contrast, economic fluctuations in Australian states are relatively highly correlated. Thus, it appears that economic fluctuations in Australia are generally "national" in scope, while those in Canada are sometimes regionally based.

Automatic versus discretionary policy

In Canada, both federal and provincial governments run counter-cyclical fiscal policy overall. The bulk of this counter-cyclical stimulus comes from automatic stabilizers, which offsets their often pro-cyclical discretionary fiscal policy. Our case study of a Canadian discretionary policy illustrates the problems inherent in correctly timing discretionary policy.

Lack of data hampers our ability to make a similar judgment about the regional impact of Commonwealth government in Australia. At the national level, discretionary policy seems to be pro-cyclical. The results for the small portion of Commonwealth regional impacts we can examine is mixed. States seem to exhibit the same kind of behaviour as Canadian provinces, i.e., overall counter-cyclical policy, but with pro-cyclical discretionary policy.

Size of fiscal presence required

Research from the European Community indicates that the size of fiscal presence required for effective stabilization is quite small. The estimate presented above suggests that the same degree of fiscal stabilization enjoyed in the US could be achieved with outlays in the order of 0.2 percent of GDP. As we saw, the transfer systems in Canada and Australia have a significant impact on overall stabilization policy. In the case of Canada, the design of transfer programs makes this impact differ substantially by region.

Returning to the original question which motivated this paper, we can say with a fair degree of confidence that the need for fiscal stabilization does *not* have implications for the assignment of spending and taxation responsibilities within a federation — even those with substantial diversity among regional economies. Our judgment here is based on two factors. First, evidence from the European Community suggests that a reasonable degree of regional fiscal stabilization can be accomplished with quite a small fiscal presence. Thus, the relative size of governments should have little bearing on the assignment of stabilization responsibilities. Second, we have found that most effective fiscal stabilization takes place through the automatic stabilizers imbedded in government budgets. Thus, regionally-sensitive fiscal stabilization will occur regardless of which government is responsible for collecting taxes based on income and/or statutory spending programs which fluctuate with the level of economic activity. Discretionary fiscal policy, which receives the most public attention, is often pro-cyclical and should generally be avoided by *all* levels of government. The evidence provided by the two case studies reinforces this general point emphatically.

If the need to conduct stabilization policy does not provide reasons for dividing expenditure and taxation responsibilities between national and regional governments, what criteria should be used to assign these responsibilities? The answer to that question is to be found in looking at the other major roles of government: the provision of public goods and services, and the redistribution of income.[14] The debate over which level of government should take the lead in these areas continues.

---

14. For a new approach to the provision of public goods in federations, see Petchey and Shapiro (1995). See Wildasin (1991) for a recent look at the assignment of the income redistribution function.

References

Boothe, P. and M. Davidson. 1993. "Fiscal Stabilization in a Federal State," *University of Alberta Discussion Paper 93-12*.

Canada. 1995. "Media Release on Canada Infrastructure Works Program," August 16, 1995.

Commonwealth Budget Paper No. 1. Various. 1990-91 to 1995-96, Canberra: Australian Government Publishing Service (AGPS).

Courchene, T. 1993. "Reflections on Canadian Federalism: Are there Implications for European Economic and Monetary Union?" *European Economy*, 5.

Courchene, T. 1995. "Fiscal Federalism and the Management of Economic Space: An Australian-Canadian Comparison," unpublished manuscript, May.

Economic Council of Canada. 1977. *Living Together: A Study of Regional Disparities*. Ottawa: Government of Canada.

Fisher, R. 1993. "Macroeconomic Implications of Subnational Fiscal Policy: The Overseas Experience," D. Collins (ed.), *Vertical Fiscal Imbalance Proceedings from a Workshop*. Canberra: ANU Press.

Fortin, P. 1982. "Provincial Government Involvement in Regulating the Business Cycle: Justification, Scope and Terms," *Economic Council of Canada Discussion Paper 213*.

Friedman, M. 1968. "The Role of Monetary Policy," *American Economic Review*.

Gramlich, E. 1987. "Federalism and Federal Deficit Reduction," *National Tax Journal*, 40.

Gramlich, E. 1991. "A View from the Outside: The Relevance of Foreign Experience," M. McMillan (ed.), *Provincial Public Finances: Plaudits, Problems and Prospects*, Toronto: Canadian Tax Foundation.

Italianer, A. and M. Vanheukelen. 1993. "Proposals for Community Stabilization Mechanism: Some Historical Applications," *European Economy*, 5.

Krugman, P. 1993. "Lessons of Massachusetts for EMU," F. Torres and F. Giavazzi, (eds.), *Adjustment and Growth in the European Monetary Union*, Cambridge: Cambridge University Press, 241-261.

Miller, F. 1980. "The Feasibility of Regionally Differentiated Fiscal Policies," *Canadian Journal of Regional Science*, 3.

Neville, J. 1993. "Structural Deficits and Fiscal Policy Stance," P. Maxwell and S. Hopkins (eds.), *Macroeconomics, Contemporary Australian Readings (2nd ed.)*, Pymble, NSW: Harper Educational.

Oates, W. 1972. *Fiscal Federalism*, New York: Harcourt, Brace and Jovanovich.

Petchey, J. and P. Shapiro. 1995. "One People, One Destiny: Centralisation and Conflicts of Interest in Australian Federalism," forthcoming in D. Wildasin (ed.), *Fiscal Policy in Emerging Federations*, New York: Cambridge University Press.

Pitchford, J. 1990. *Australia's Foreign Debt: Myths and Realities*, Sydney: Allen and Unwin.

Pitchford, J. 1995. "Some Short and Long Run Issues for Australian Fiscal Policy," *Australian Economic Review*, First Quarter, 118-122.

State of Play: The Australian Economic Policy Debate. 1995. INDECS, Sydney: Allen and Unwin.

Walsh, C. 1993. "Fiscal Federalism: An Overview of Issues and a Discussion of their Relevance to the European Community," *European Economy*, 5.

Wildasin, D. 1991. "Income Redistribution in a Common Labour Market," *American Economic Review*, 757-74.

The Partisan Component in Intergovernmental Transfers

8

Robert Young and
Campbell Sharman,
with Andrew Goldstein

This is a study of whether the scale and direction of transfers from central to state and provincial governments in Australia and Canada are affected by partisan considerations. Both federations share the basic problem of vertical fiscal imbalance, a condition that has justified a very large and diverse set of transfers to sub-national governments. These transfers are justified in political discourse, normally, by their ostensible purposes. In Australia, for example, financial assistance grants are designed, as equalization is in Canada, to allow governments to provide services at standards comparable to those in other states, without having to impose appreciably higher taxes and charges.[1] And in both countries, specific-purpose payments (or "tied" grants) are justified by the objectives of particular programs — to improve infrastructure, boost spending on education or other social services, alleviate unemployment, promote industrial growth, and so on. The distribution of

---

* We acknowledge with thanks the contribution of research assistants, Christine Carberry and Cris de Clercy. For comments on an earlier version of this paper, we are grateful to Paul Boothe, Tom Courchene, Gwen Gray, J.R. Nethercote, Peter Self, Marian Simms, Cliff Walsh, and participants in the Edmonton conference, especially Stuart Landon and Al O'Brien.
1. For a recent review of the Australian system, see Walsh and Thomson (1994).

grants among the various states and provinces is justified with reference either to common "national" values that support federal aid (sometimes with a redistributive component) or else to the particular needs of individual states and provinces.

These are the publicly stated objectives of the transfers. In political discourse, the flows of money to sub-national governments are justified with reference to the goals the programs are designed to achieve. But in this paper, we throw this justification into question. We ask whether the scale and direction of transfer flows are affected by partisan considerations. In short, we ask whether federal governments are more likely to make transfers to state and provincial governments of the same partisan persuasion, or, conversely, whether they are less likely to direct funds towards governments controlled by their partisan "opponents." To anticipate, we find that the distribution of transfers is explained most by differences in the underlying conditions that are the explicit targets of the programs. But we also find some intriguing evidence that partisan considerations have some influence, at the margin. *Ceteris paribus*, political allies seem more likely than political enemies to receive transfers (of some kinds). What implications this may have for national or regional competitiveness, and for policy change, are questions that are addressed briefly in the conclusion.

Initial Considerations

In this paper we focus primarily on Canada, because — as will be discussed — some groundbreaking work has already been done on the Australian case. But in both countries, in the abstract, there are some good reasons to expect that central governments might tend to favour their party colleagues at the sub-national level. It is well understood that transfers to individuals can be beneficial in increasing the chances of re-election. What are the advantages of making transfers to certain provincial and state governments? The underlying assumption, first, is that such transfers provide funds that provincial governments can spend to increase their chances of re-election. Then there could be three favourable consequences. One is that relations with a province governed by a "friendly" party could be more cooperative in the general conduct of affairs than with the same province were it governed by a "opposing" party. The second is that an ally in power provincially could reciprocate the favour when a federal election loomed, not by making transfers, of course, but by facilitating whatever actions the central government thinks necessary to secure its re-election. The third consequence is that control of a provincial government not only strengthens the party organization but also provides resources and jobs for large numbers of partisans — especially the entourages that surround premiers and ministers - and these can be deployed to help in federal elections. Yet another consideration is sheer loyalty. At the margin, this factor may operate so that party colleagues tend to receive more transfers. A final consideration is ideology. It may be easier to negotiate new programs (or their winding up) with a provincial government that shares a similar governing philosophy, and this could justify biasing the distribution of funds towards it.

Of course there are counter-arguments to all of these hypotheses. An important one is structuralist in essence. It holds that provincial governments, and premiers in particular, come to represent their domestic constituencies and provincial interests and take the appropriate stance towards Ottawa, regardless of partisan considerations. As Donald Savoie put it, "when it comes to regional development policy, provincial premiers, no matter their political affiliation, stand where they sit." (Savoie, 1992:4) This is similar to J.R. Nethercote's observation that a common partisan complexion will never assure "friendly relations" between national and sub-national governments. We agree with both contentions, generally. But we still ask whether there is not some inflection in the provincial position when two governments are of the same stripe — whether relations would be "friendlier" than they would have been otherwise. In Canada, after an exhaustive study of regional ministers, Herman Bakvis concluded that it was hard to detect "the exercise of regional influence" on transfer payments:

> little evidence exists of ministers having tapped directly into the social transfer system for regional purposes. To put it differently: while the fortunes of provinces and specific ridings can vary dramatically in terms of regional development grants, discretionary projects, and defence expenditures with the arrival and departure of cabinet representatives, this is not the case with respect to old age pensions to individuals or transfer payments to provinces under EPF, the Canada Assistance Plan, or the fiscal equalization program. (Bakvis, 1991:290)

But here we are interested precisely in the "little evidence" (and in the actions of whole governments, not of regional ministers alone).

A more important objection is that the party systems are not integrated enough in either country to provide the partisan glue that — to mix metaphors — would grease the flow of grants. The big example in Australia consists of the various right-wing parties and their coalitions; in Canada, analysts often point to the complete organizational and financial separation of the federal and provincial wings of the Liberal party in Quebec (and to the non-existence there of a provincial Progressive Conservative party). And the tendency to disintegration of the central-subnational party systems has undoubtedly progressed over time. However, if this progression has occurred, it could well be captured and demonstrated in our analysis. More important, there is still substantial integration. The Australian Labour Party remains a relatively well integrated machine, albeit one based firmly in the state party organizations (Parkin and Marshall, 1994), and so does the NDP in Canada. And the Liberal party in Canada has an integrated organization in the six smaller provinces, along with a rule that provincial members cannot also be members of another national party. (Carty, 1994:139) Even if these organizations are state-based or confederal, so that most power does not reside at the federal level, and if the pattern of recruitment has changed so that service at the provincial level is now a terminal career, does it matter? If one seeks re-election at the sub-national level and if funding helps achieve this objective, the question remains whether provincial politicians are likely to get more funding if their cousins are in power at the centre, even if these are distant cousins.

Another argument is that central-government politicians animated by the desire for re-election should have a greater interest in direct spending than in transfers. Of course, it is a testable proposition whether there is an electoral cycle of direct expenditures — or of the ratio of transfers to direct expenditures. But it is also worth noting that there is a substantial sense of identification with the provinces and regions in Canada, and that highly publicized transfers to provincial administrations can boost the electoral fortunes of federal politicians. Such transfers — perhaps in the form of the photo-op handshake with the premier — can also be arranged more quickly than a flow of direct spending, especially of transfers to individuals.

There is a certain amount of anecdotal evidence concerning partisanship and transfers in Canada. Much concerns John Diefenbaker. It is well documented that before the 1957 election the Maritime premiers and MPs pressed him hard for a commitment to make special transfers for hydro-electric development and regional aid, and soon after his victory, these programs were announced.[2] Diefenbaker also made a commitment to Leslie Frost. The St. Laurent government had turned down Frost's proposal to increase the standard taxes in the first equalization legislation by $250 million, of which Ontario would receive $100 million. Diefenbaker "promised Frost that if he won the election Ontario would get this $100 million, and that promise no doubt influenced Frost and the Progressive

---

2. See Camp, 1970, pp. 324-41. The regional aid took the form of Special Atlantic Provinces Adjustment Grants. There was also special help for particular power projects: see Young, 1982.

Conservative organization to campaign actively in the election." (Pickersgill 1975) Even more striking, perhaps, was Diefenbaker's own recollection of his "good friend" Frost advising him to call an election in 1961. Frost apparently was prepared not only to stay on until after this election, but also to delay until it was over the implementation of an Ontario provincial sales tax which would be unpopular and which would "rebound unfavourably against the electoral fortunes of a Progressive Conservative government in Ottawa." (Diefenbaker 1977) But this relationship was by no means unique to Diefenbaker: the biographer of Louis Robichaud has noted how the province of New Brunswick relied on special-purpose transfers to bolster its economy, "particularly when the same political party held the majority position in both Ottawa and Fredericton." (Stanley 1984)

In Canada and Australia, there have been suspicions about a partisan component to special-purpose grants. As recently as 1991, for example, federal Liberals accused the Mulroney government of introducing the GRIP and NISA programs of agricultural supports in order to prop up the electoral fortunes of the Devine government in Saskatchewan. They noted in particular its timing and the fact that payments were accelerated for wheat farmers, the great majority of whom are Saskatchewan residents.[3] Similarly, many commentators have noted that Mr. Dingwall's recent diversion of road-building money from the Trans Canada Highway to the Fleur-de-Lis trail in his own riding was done with the co-operation of — indeed, at the behest of — his Liberal Nova Scotian counterpart. (Simpson 1995) Where there is a lot of discretion over particular agreements, it seems reasonable to suspect partisan collusion.

General-purpose grants, on the other hand, seem less politically permeable. Both Financial Assistance Grants and the equalization programme involve heavy bureaucratic input, highly technical measurements, and complex formulae. The discourse surrounding them is one of technocratic neutrality.[4] And yet, at least some provincial premiers have harboured suspicions. W.A.C. Bennett, whose province, granted, was

---

3. The GRIP and NISA programs for agricultural support were negotiated in 1991. Premier Devine managed to persuade the Tories in Ottawa to make interim payments before the crop yield statistics would arrive in November, so that the funds for crop insurance - about $6,000 per farmer - would flow before the October 21st election. Devine had to hold an election in October. The day the election was called, Ottawa announced that the headquarters of the Farm Credit Corporation would be relocated to Regina. See Redekop 1991; Roberts 1991.
4. See, for example, Canada, Department of Finance, 1994:2: "In order to calculate the provincial entitlements which will carry out the above-stated purpose of equalization, objective comparisons are made in respect of the relative capacities of provinces to raise revenues from taxes and other own-source revenues."

always on the sending end of equalization after 1962, and who, as a Social Credit premier, had no partisan allies, federal or provincial, once explained:

> The money was collected by the federal government and the provinces and they poured it out into the provincial governments. I'd go visit these provincial governments and I'd see in their offices the enormous staffs they had, all without money...I only opposed these equalization grants because they were going to the wrong people. They were going to the provincial governments so they could get political contracts — a lot of patronage for their party. (Mitchell 1983)

But more seriously, the determination of these general-purpose transfers involves a great deal of intense negotiation, even though the interests involved may have to cloak themselves in arcane measurements and formulae. And the fact remains that in Canada the equalization program has been far from immutable. Since its inception, the program has had nine major changes in the basic fiscal arrangements, five changes in the equalization standard, six changes in the formula relating to natural resource and energy resource revenues, six changes in the calculation of personal income tax revenues in the formula, and eight other changes in the calculation of the formula.[5] As Courchene obliquely put it, "Any program that has been in place for twenty-five years is likely to become subject to the political pressures of the hour." (Courchene 1984) He meant, of course, that a program designed for strict horizontal equity might find itself shaped by the urgent issues and priorities of the day — that equalization "is responsive to the economic and political environment." But with so much at stake, and with so many changes having been made, would we be quite remiss to ask whether some alterations were made, or made at particular times, in order to help achieve some partisan — as opposed to policy — objectives?

Previous Studies

In Canada, there have been few systematic studies of expenditures conducted in the public-choice perspective. Most have found a political component in spending programs. Munro showed that highway expenditures in British Columbia were allocated among provincial electoral districts according to a mix of economic and political considerations: the latter included whether the riding was held by a cabinet minister and how

---

5. Calculated from Canadian Tax Foundation, *The National Finances,* various years; and Courchene (1984).

close the preceding election had been in the constituency. (Munro 1975) Spafford found evidence of an electoral cycle in highway construction in the provinces, one that diminished over time — presumably as the opportunities for such primitive patronage as roadwork declined. (Spafford 1981) Blake showed that Local Initiatives Program funds were allocated among constituencies in the 1972-74 period according to partisan factors like percentage of Liberal support in the 1972 election as well as indicators of the "need" that justified the program and provided its explicit objectives — unemployment, low education levels, and large Aboriginal populations. (Blake 1976) MacNaughton and Winn demonstrated that Department of Regional Economic Expansion subsidies were correlated not only with a constituency's labour force participation rate and mean family income (to be expected because DREE was meant to alleviate unemployment and poverty), but also with political variables — the riding's volatility and whether it had a Social-Credit incumbent. (MacNaughton and Winn 1981) The standard technology for such studies is to set up a regression equation in which the "need" or "program objective" variables are integrated with the relevant political variables, and to see whether the political relationships are both in the predicted direction and also statistically significant.

In Australia, much more work has been done along these lines. Evidence can be found for all the partisan factors influencing intergovernmental transfers that were outlined in the initial section of this paper, including the subtle and not so subtle benefits of partisan similarity between federal and state governments. (See Parkin and Marshall 1992 and Parkin and Marshall 1994:31), and also the importance of partisanship in negotiating intergovernmental agreements.[6] In a recent study, Sharman has built upon Riker's work to construct an index of partisan disharmony. This is simply the number of state governments that do not share the partisan complexion of the Commonwealth government. (Sharman 1994) A depiction of this relationship is found in Figure 8.1. Interestingly, this simple index of partisan disharmony corresponds rather well with that of Riker and Schaps for Australia. But a qualitative assessment of genuine disharmony in the system produced mixed results. It was true that partisan dissimilarity was associated with Commonwealth-state tensions. But there were also sharp tensions in two post-war periods of high similarity. The conclusion was that complete similarity, "far from reducing tensions, removes the force of partisan loyalty that will normally operate to restrain overt conflict when the

---

6. Much of the literature on the period of the Whitlam Labor Party government (1972-1975) stresses the importance of partisan factors in intergovernmental relations. For an excellent case study, see Stevenson, 1987:65-67. Note also Sharman, 1976:34-37.

governmental units in the federation are of mixed partisan colour. ... Once partisan differences between governments are removed, the states are less constrained from forming coalitions against the Commonwealth." Apart from offering an insight into how partisanship might moderate Commonwealth-state tensions, this historical analysis suggests more fundamentally that the Australian party system is sufficiently integrated that partisan complexion does indeed make a difference in governmental behaviour.

Figure 8.1

State Governments with the Same Partisan Colour as the Commonwealth, 1910-95

The most systematic examination of partisanship and intergovernmental grants in Australia was conducted by Bungey, Grossman and Kenyon (1991). In some respects, this analysis has served as a model for our own investigations. Bungey, Grossman and Kenyon set up two competing models that might explain the distribution among the states of Commonwealth grants. One was a welfare-maximizing model that assumed a benevolent government. The dependent variable was the real grant received by each state, and the explanatory variables were the unemployment rate, the taxable income per capita, the population density in rural areas (an indicator of service-delivery cost differentials), the population, and the percentage of the population in school. This model also included an ideological dummy variable, on the assumption that federal Labor governments would be more predisposed either to spend directly or to intervene more through grants. There were also dummy variables for each of the states. The second model was a "public-choice" one, in which a government concerned with its own self-interest made grants in order to generate loyalty: "[g]rants are paid for by the receiving politician endorsing the grantor and delivering to the politician the votes of local supporters and of interest groups with which he is associated. With state-based political parties this importantly includes the financial and other support of the state party's political machine." In the public-choice model, the key explanatory variables were the percentage of House of Representative seats held by the federal government in the state, the squared value of this variable, the percentage of House seats held with less than a 5 percent two party preferred vote, the percentage of the population living in urban regions, an indirect measure of Catholic religiosity, and a dummy variable — LIKE — scored 1 if the federal and state governments were led by the same political party and 0 otherwise.

Bungey, Grossman and Kenyon found that the benevolent-government model performed rather well, with unemployment and rural population being significantly associated with higher grants of all forms: special purpose recurrent, special purpose capital, total special purpose, and total general purpose. The public-choice model performed less well. In particular, the sign on the LIKE variable was negative. What did count in the public-choice model were the two variables about the percentages of representatives from the state, and the urbanization variable. Arguing that the two models' initial estimations showed that Ordinary Least Squares regression was inappropriate (because of first-order autocorrelation and heteroskedasticity problems), Bungey, Grossman and Kenyon used a Generalized Least Squares estimation procedure, and then employed the J test procedure to decide which model was superior. They concluded that the welfare-maximizing model best fitted the data.

There are some problems with this analysis, however. First, some of the variables in the public-choice model are rather odd: it is not at all obvious that the proxy for Catholic religiosity (proportion of school pupils in the state attending non-government schools) makes any sense in terms of a support-maximizing government. Neither should urbanization: to say that this factor "picks up the vote-buying potential in urban areas" is simply odd. Second, the welfare-maximizing results have some curious elements. The signs on both personal income per capita and proportion of the population in school are in the wrong directions: contrary to their results, the federal government should be dispensing more grants when per capita income is low and more of the population is in school. More seriously, these analysts seem to confuse pork-barrelling with assistance to state governments. There is a big difference. Grants to sub-national governments permit them to engage in pork-barrelling, patronage, or spending without raising taxes — all of which should be returned to the federal government in the form of loyalty and support. Direct spending, on the other hand, would be undertaken to shore up the support for the Commonwealth government. It makes perfect sense that pork should flow to states with a high percentage of government representatives, but this is not at all true of grants. Indeed, their finding is that grants tend to flow to states where the percentage of representatives is relatively low. Obviously, the call can be made either way: what is required is an integrated consideration of direct spending and grants to sub-national governments. Fourth, the dummy variables for the states carry a lot of the explanatory freight. This must be because Bungey, Grossman and Kenyon use the absolute size of the grant as the dependent variable, and they need to "mop up" the gross differences in scale between the states. But it would be better to run a direct test in which all the other factors that differentiate between states were not also picked up in the dummy variables' values. The dependent variable might better be "percentage change in grants" from one year to the next, or, better yet, "percentage change in grants for state A minus the average percentage change in grants to all states." Finally, the J test run by these analysts is odd. Rather than run the two models in isolation, the normal technique is to integrate competing explanatory variables (or sets of variables) into a single equation, to see which prevail with explanatory power. This is what we have done.

The Results

Our approach is relatively simple. We employed data for the 1953-85 period. We are interested in several types of Canadian federal-provincial grants, and these are the dependent variables in sets of regression equations. These variables are:

1. Equalization payments,
2. Total general-purpose transfers (1 and all others),
3. Social welfare transfers,
4. Natural resource and industrial development grants,
5. Total specific-purpose transfers (3 and 4 and all others), and
6. Total transfers to local governments in the province.

Rather than use the absolute size of the transfers, we concentrate on first differences (percentages) and also the percentage change in transfers to one province minus the average percentage change in transfers to all provinces. The latter is our main dependent variable: it captures the relative favoritism of the treatment of any one province.

The objectives of all transfer programs are multifarious. In general, however, transfers to the provincial governments are justified on redistributive grounds — unlike direct spending, which may have some purpose related to efficiency or to positive economic integration, and unlike tax expenditures, which may reinforce regional inequalities. Our social-welfare-regarding or "economic" explanatory variables are:

1. per capita income and
2. unemployment.

At first, we did not concentrate on changes in these variables over time or in their values relative to a national average, simply because the objectives of most transfer programs — especially equalization — are framed in terms of absolute values. On the other hand, formula-driven programs should be responsive to changes in these variables, and so we also ran equations with first-difference values for them.

The question of lags also arises here. The dependent variables are payments actually made in particular fiscal years (and they are corrected ones at that). So when do changes in income and employment register, either through the political process or the figures that enter the formulae determining payments under programs like equalization and CAP? We experimented, but took the view that a one-year lag was most appropriate. For example, a precipitous drop in per capita income in Newfoundland in the calendar year of 1970 (fiscal year 1970-71) should result in increased transfers in fiscal year 1971-72.

The third set of variables includes the "public-choice" or "political" factors that might underlie transfers. Here we were interested in several factors, including:

1. whether it was a pre-election year in the province,
2. whether it was a pre-election year federally,
3. the number of years remaining before the next provincial election,
4. the number of years remaining before the next federal election, and
5. whether the provincial and federal governments were of the same partisan complexion (LIKE).[7]

---

7. All variables and sources of data are listed in Appendix I.

Obviously, the last is the crucial factor. The others were included primarily because they might interact with LIKE in various ways. (As long as the dependent variables are measured as differences from the national average, stable factors like whether it was a federal pre-election year could not affect them — they would influence the total amount of transfers, perhaps, but not their relative distribution. For this reason, we also ran regression equations using percentage changes in the transfers with dummy variables for each province.)

Here too the issue of lags arises. We took the position that a one-period lag on the political variables was appropriate. Although it is arguable that a federal government aiming to assist a provincial government of the same partisan stripe could get monies flowing more quickly than this, our assumption is that the announcement of most transfers would be more important than the concrete effects they might have; as for equalization and other formula-driven grants, the argument given above about "economic" variables applies.

We find several sets of results. First, in regression equations where the dependent variables were the provinces' differences from the average provincial change (in social transfers, general-purpose transfers, and so on), neither the economic nor the political variables have much explanatory power. None of the classes of federal-provincial transfers was found to be significantly affected by changes in unemployment and per capita income or by the political factors. Results were slightly more suggestive when the percentage changes in transfers were taken as the dependent variables, and provincial dummy variables were incorporated into the regression equations. It was found, for example, that specific-purpose transfers were related to the (lagged) change in provincial unemployment (t=2.646, sig. < .009). There was also some evidence of political-cycle effects. The closer was a federal election, other things being equal, the higher were the percentage changes in specific-purpose transfers (on FEDYRTO, t=-1.744, sig. < .08). There were also glimmers of a cyclical effect on changes in equalization payments. But the relationships were not strong, and there was some instability when separate equations were run for Liberal and Progressive Conservative federal governments, for the pre-1975 and post-1975 periods, and for all provinces and the nine non-Quebec provinces.

More interesting results emerged through the analysis of two ratios: the ratio of direct expenditures in a province to all transfers to the provincial government, and the ratio of total transfers to a province to total revenues derived from the province. The hypotheses here were simple. First, we expected that a federal government with confidence in its partisan colleagues at the provincial level might be more inclined to make transfers rather than engaging in direct expenditures (pork-barrelling). Hence, when the governments were of the same partisan stripe, the EXPTRAN ratio should be smaller. Second, what might count in the overall distribution of costs and benefits might be not the relative magnitude of transfers made to a province, but the net benefits conferred through a two-way flow of funds — transfers to the provincial government and tax revenues taken out of the province. When governments were alike, we would expect the ratio of total transfers to total revenue (TOTREV) to be larger.

Table 8.1
The Impact of Political and Economic Factors on the Ratio of Direct Expenditures to Total Transfers (for all provinces)

Concept	Variable	Unstandardized Coefficient	Standard Error	t-value
Unemployment	LPUNEMP	-.713	.241	-2.952**
Per capita income	LPPERCAP	-3.300	.804	-4.104***
Federal election cycle	FEDYRTO	-.011	.037	-.288
Federal pre-election	FEDPRE	.079	.097	.816
Provincial election cycle	PROVYRTO	-.012	.038	-.327
Provincial pre-election	PROVPRE	.039	.094	.415
Liberal federal government	LFEDLIB	-.132	.112	-1.170
Partisan similarity	LLIKE	-.282	.089	-3.150**
Constant		1.709	.139	
R^2 (adj.)		.12		

* sign # .05
** sign # .01
*** sign # .001

Note: for data sources and variable definitions, see Appendix.

The first results are shown in Table 8.1. Here the economic variables are significant. Increased unemployment and increases in per capita income are both associated with decreases in the ratio of expenditures to transfers. That is, direct expenditures decline or transfers increase, or both. But partisan considerations are also significant. When governments are alike, benefits are more likely to flow into a province in the form of transfers; when they are not, direct expenditures take on greater weight. This relationship was found not to be fully consistent, however. It does not hold for Progressive Conservative federal governments; nor does it persist after 1975. On the other hand, it does hold (in a form very close to that displayed in Table 8.1) when Quebec is excluded from the equation.

Further results are found in Table 8.2. Here, the dependent variable is the transfer/revenue ratio. Although the explanatory power of the variables involved here is not great, the political factors are important. Liberal governments are associated with higher ratios. More striking, partisan similarity is highly significant in affecting the transfer/taxation ratio. This result does not hold for Progressive Conservative federal governments — though the electoral-cycle effect is significant for such governments. But the result does hold for both the pre- and post-1975 periods, and also when Quebec is excluded from the equations.

Table 8.2
The Impact of Political and Economic Factors on the Ratio of Total Transfers to Federal Revenues (for all provinces)

Concept	Variable	Unstandardized Coefficient	Standard Error	t-value
Unemployment	LPUNEMP	.086	.189	.454
Per capita income	LPPERCAP	.757	.628	1.206
Federal election cycle	FEDYRTO	-.029	.029	-.980
Federal pre-election	FEDPRE	.013	.076	.171
Provincial election cycle	PROVYRTO	.013	.029	.446
Provincial pre-election	PROVPRE	-.007	.073	-.101
Liberal federal government	LFEDLIB	.168	.088	1.920*
Partisan similarity	LLIKE	.436	.070	6.24***
Constant		.241	.109	
R^2 (adj.)		.12		

* sign # .05
** sign # .01
*** sign # .001

Note: for data sources and variable definitions, see Appendix.

Our last result concerns the equalization program. As stated, there were some signs in the general equation that equalization payments might be affected by partisanship. But in any overall analysis, such effects might be washed out as governments changed after the equalization formula was amended. As a result, we limited our analysis to the years immediately following major renegotiations of the formula (that is, 1958, 1963, 1968, 1973, 1978, and 1983). The dependent variable was the percentage change in equalization payments. Table 8.3 presents the results.

Table 8.3
The Impact of Political and Economic Factors on Percentage Change in Equalization Payments (years after renegotiations only)

Concept	Variable	Unstandardized Coefficient	Standard Error	t-value
Unemployment	LPUNEMP	-.019	.659	-.029
Per capita income	LPPERCAP	-3.195	1.130	-2.825"
Federal election cycle	FEDYRTO		(excluded)	
Federal pre-election	FEDPRE	.665	.417	1.595
Provincial election cycle	PROVYRTO	.087	.149	.580
Provincial pre-election	PROVPRE	-.339	.378	-.897
Liberal federal government	LFEDLIB	5.650	1.358	4.160'''
Partisan similarity	LLIKE	1.228	.344	3.573'''
Constant		-3.867	.977	
R^2 (adj.)		.40		

* sign # .05
" sign # .01
''' sign # .001

Note: for data sources and variable definitions, see Appendix.

As would be expected, changes in provincial per capita incomes are significantly associated with the percentage change in equalization payments. So are two political variables. Obviously federal Liberal governments are associated with big increases in equalization transfers. But so is partisanship. The LIKE variable is highly significant in affecting the percentage increase in these transfers. It might be thought that this is an artifact of the "donor" provinces being predominantly Progressive Conservative, or at least not Liberal: the contributors include Ontario throughout the period, B.C. after 1962, and Alberta after 1965. But when these data points are excluded, the LIKE variable remains significant. It is hard not to conclude that partisanship plays at the margin amidst the arcane formulae and heavy bureaucratic involvement that characterize the equalization program.

Conclusions

More work is needed on this topic. In particular, it would be worthwhile to assemble a fully comparative data-set, so that differences in the characteristics and evolution of the Canadian and Australian transfer systems could be more systematically explored.

Unfortunately, there are few concrete policy implications that flow from these findings. On the one hand, the distribution among provinces of year-to-year changes in transfers is not well explained by either the political or the economic variables examined here. That the relationship is not powerful suggests that programs have a strong momentum (or inertia) that renders them relatively impervious to economic and political fluctuations. Arguably, this stability is salutary for Canadian economic competitiveness; or, it may represent a competitive drag: only close examination of the effectiveness and efficiency of each program could illuminate this issue.

On the other hand, there is clear evidence that partisan factors play a role in the choice of instruments through which benefits are distributed among provinces (transfers or direct expenditures), and also in the level of benefits relative to tax flows to Ottawa. Moreover, equalization negotiations produce outcomes that are inflected at the margin by partisanship. These striking findings certainly require further study. But if partisanship is inefficient — a view we do not necessarily share - then these programs need to be questioned on grounds other than the ones normally used to assail them.

References

Bakvis, Herman A. 1991. *Regional Ministers: Power and Influence in the Canadian Cabinet*, Toronto: University of Toronto Press, 290.

Blake, Donald C. 1976. "LIP and Patisanship: An Analysis of the Local Initiatives Program," *Canadian Public Policy*, 2, 17-32.

Bungey, Mel, Philip Grossman and Peter Kenyon. 1991. "Explaining Intergovernmental Grants: Australian Evidence," *Applied Economics*, 23, 659-68.

Camp, Dalton. 1970. *Gentlemen, Players and Politicians*, Toronto: McClelland and Stewart, 324-41.

Canada, Department of Finance, Federal-Provincial Relations Divisions. 1994. "The Equalization Program," *MS*, April 1994, 2.

Carty, R.K. 1994. "The Federal Face of Canadian Party Membership" Campbell Sharman (ed.), *Parties and Federalism in Australia and Canada*. Canberra: Federalism Research Centre, 137-52

Courchene, Thomas J. 1984. *Equalization Payments: Past, Present and Future*, Toronto: Ontario Economic Council.

Diefenbaker, John G. 1977. *One Canada: The Memoirs of the Right Honourable John G. Diefenbaker*, Toronto: McMillan, 3, 112.

MacNaughton, Bruce D. and Conrad J. Winn. 1981. "Economic Policy and Electoral Self-interest: The Allocations of the Department of Regional Economic Expansion," *Canadian Public Policy*, 7, 318-27.

Mitchell, David J. 1983. *W.A.C. Bennett and the Rise of British Columbia*, Vancouver: Douglas & McIntyre, 398.

Munro, John M. 1975. "Highways in British Columbia: Economics and Politics," *Canadian Journal of Economics*, 8, 192-204.

Parkin, Andrew and Vern Marshall. 1992. "Federal Relations," Andrew Parkin and Allan Patience (eds.), *The Hannon Decade: The Politics of Restraint in South Australia*, Allen and Unwin.

Parkin, Andrew and Vern Marshall. 1994. "Frustrated, Reconciled or Divided? The Australian Labor Party and Federalism," *Australian Journal of Political Science*, 29, 18-39.

Pickersgill, J.W. 1975. *My Years with Louis St. Laurent*, Toronto: University of Toronto Press, 311.

Redekop, Bill. 1991. "Devine's GRIP politics upsets farm leaders," *Winnipeg Free Press*, July 22, 1991, 17.

Roberts, David. 1991. "Devine prepares for Oct. 21 election," *Globe and Mail*, September 21, 1991, A-6.

Savoie, Donald J. 1992. *Regional Economic Development: Canada's Search for Solutions*, 2nd ed., Toronto: University of Toronto Press, 4.

Sharman, Campbell. 1976. "The Bargaining Analogy and Federal-State Relations," R.M. Burns et al., *Political and Administrative Federalism*, Canberra: Centre for Research on Federal Financial Relations, Australian National University, Research Monograph No. 14, 34-37.

Sharman, Campbell. 1994. "Discipline and Disharmony: Party and the Operation of the Australian Federal System," *Parties and Federalism in Australia and Canada*, Sharman (ed.), Canberra: Federalism Research Centre, 23-44.

Simpson, Jeffrey. 1995. "In Nova Scotia at least, all roads lead to pork barrels," *Globe and Mail*, June 21, 1995, A-10.

Spafford, Duff. 1981. "Highway Employment and Provincial Elections," *Canadian Journal of Political Science*, 14, 135-42.

Stanley, Della M.M. 1984. *Louis Robichaud: A Decade of Power*, Halifax: Nimbus Publishing, 112.

Stevenson, Garth. 1987. *Rail Transport and Australian Federalism*, Canberra: Centre for Research on Federal Financial Relations, Australian National University, Research Monograph No. 48.

Walsh, Cliff and Norm Thomson. 1994. *Federal Fiscal Arrangements in Australia: Their Potential Impact on Urban Settlement*, Canberra: Federalism Reserach Centre.

Young, R.A. 1982. "Planning for Power: The New Brunswick Electric Power Commission in the 1950s," *Acadiensis*, 12, 73-99.

Appendix: Variable Definitions And Sources

EQUAL Equalization payments (formerly tax-rental and tax-sharing agreements). Data for the year 1953, for example, is from the fiscal year beginning April 1, 1953 and ending March 31, 1954. Source: Statistics Canada, *Federal Government Finance*, cat. #68-211.

FEDLIB Dummy variable: scored 1 if the federal government is Liberal (majority or minority), and 0 if otherwise. Source: Kathryn O'Handley, ed., *Canadian Parliamentary Guide*, (Toronto: Globe and Mail Publishing, 1994).

FEDPRE Dummy variable: scored 1 if the year is a pre-election year (i.e., there was an election in the next fiscal year), and 0 if otherwise. Source: *Canadian Parliamentary Guide*.

FEDYRTO Years until the next federal election. Note: elections occurred on June 10, 1957 and March 31, 1958: each of 1957 and 1958 was considered to be an election year, although 1957 was also considered a pre-election year. Similarly, elections occurred on May 22, 1979 and February 18, 1980, and both were considered as election years, with the former also being a pre-election year. Source: *Canadian Parliamentary Guide*.

GENERAL General purpose transfers to the provinces. Includes all non-shared-cost or tied-aid programs, notably (as of 1986-87), statutory subsidies, federal corporation income tax on privately owned public utilities, payments in respect of reciprocal taxation, equalization, and grants in lieu of taxes. Source: *Federal Government Finance*.

LIKE Dummy variable: scored 1 if the federal and provincial governments had the same party in power, and 0 otherwise. In an election year, if the election was held before October 1, the party that won was considered to be the party in power for that year (taking the mid-point of the fiscal year as the pivot point). If the election was held after October 1, then the incumbent party was considered to be the party in power for the year. In Manitoba, from 1953-58, the Liberal Progressive Party was considered to be "like" the federal Liberal Party. Source: *Canadian Parliamentary Guide*.

LOCAL Total transfers to local governments. Source: *Federal Government Finance*.

MINOR Dummy variable: scored 1 if there was a minority federal government, and 0 otherwise. Source: Frank Fiegert, *Canada Votes*, (Durham: Duke University Press, 1989).

NATRES Transfers to provinces in respect of natural resource development and industrial development: as of 1986-87, includes agriculture, fish and game, forests, oil and gas, mines, trade and industry, water, and other. Source: *Federal Government Finance*.

PERCENT Percentage of total seats won by the party forming the provincial government. Source: *Canadian Parliamentary Guide*.

PERINC Provincial personal income, in millions of dollars. Source: Statistics Canada, *National Income and Expenditure Accounts, Annual Estimates 1926-1986*, cat. #13-531.

POP Provincial population, in thousands, estimates as of June 1st. Source: Statistics Canada, *National Income and Expenditure Accounts*.

PROVPRE Dummy variable: scored 1 if a provincial pre-election year (i.e., there was an election during the next fiscal year), and 0 otherwise. Source: *Canadian Parliamentary Guide*.

PROVYRTO Years to next provincial election. In an election year, PROVYRTO = 0. This variable is scored according to the federal fiscal year. For example, for 1953 to be considered an election year in some province, an election had to take place between April 1, 1953 and March 31, 1954. In Newfoundland, there were elections on October 28, 1971 and March 24, 1972: only 1972 was considered to be an election year.

SOCIAL Total transfers to a province for social welfare. As of 1985-86, includes Canada Assistance Plan, vocational rehabilitation of the disabled, and other social welfare. Source: *Federal Government Finance*.

SPECIFIC Total specific-purpose transfers to a province. Includes total social welfare, total natural resources and industrial development, and all other tied transfers except those to local governments. Source: *Federal Government Finance*.

UNEMP Provincial unemployment rate. For years 1966-86 (except for P.E.I. [1975-86]), the source is Statistics Canada, *Canadian Economic Observer*, cat. #11-210. For 1953-65 (1953-74 for P.E.I.), the source is Urquhart and Buckley, *Historical Statistics of Canada*, 2nd ed., and the data for each province are those for the relevant region - Atlantic, Quebec, Ontario, the Prairies, and British Columbia.

9

Preserving and Promoting the Internal Economic Union: Australia and Canada

Thomas J. Courchene

With the advent of Europe 1992 and its 300 or so integration "directives," attention has been focussed on the degree to which the national markets of federal nations (and even unitary states) are integrated. For example, Canadian politicians and business leaders are fond of claiming that goods and capital can flow more freely across member states of the EC than across the Canadian provinces. Presumably, this can also be said of the U.S. and Australian federations, among others, at least in terms of selected types of goods and capital.

However, this should not be surprising: federal constitutions are essentially *political blueprints*, whereas Europe 1992 is primarily an *economic blueprint*. Thus, the overwhelming rationale for Europe 1992 is to free up European markets, or, more positively, to create a "single market" where disputes with respect to adherence to the directives are largely a matter to be settled in the arena of *administrative law*. On the other hand, while all federations have constitutional provisions relating to securing their internal economic unions, disputes relating to barriers or impediments to the internal economic union tend to be resolved, initially at least, in the *political* arena, although resort to the courts is always a back-up option. In this sense, achieving a single or unified market for certain goods or factors in federal systems may well be more difficult than in arrangements like Europe 1992, which were *explicitly* designed for this purpose. More interesting, perhaps, is that the types of instruments capable of delivering unified markets are likely to differ as between economic unions and federal nations.

At the most general level, one can speak of two types of integration — *negative integration* and *positive integration* (Leslie 1991). Negative integration, an admittedly awkward term, refers to the imposition of a series of constraints or, if one prefers, a set of "thou shalt nots" on the behaviour of governments. In other words, negative integration facilitates the creation of a single market by removing the ability of governments to impede the flow of goods, services and factors of production across political boundaries. Typically, the constitutional provisions relating to internal free trade, and the associated judicial interpretation, provide the framework for the exercise of negative integration. Beyond some point, however, more is needed to secure a unified market. Thus, positive integration relates to legislative or regulatory action designed to coordinate or harmonize policy across boundaries; e.g., to ensure full portability of social benefits across jurisdictions. While, as noted, federal systems may well fall short of the European Union in selected aspects of negative integration, they are typically well ahead of the EU in terms of positive integration, particularly in the social policy areas.

The purpose of this paper is to direct attention to the variety of ways in which Australia and Canada manage their internal economic integration. Specifically, part two focuses comparatively on the relevant constitutional provisions relating to securing the internal common market. Part three then focuses on the manner in which international agreements are not only influencing the division of powers in federal nations but also serving to free up domestic markets, particularly in Canada's case. In part four, I focus on some innovative ways in which Australia has proceeded with positive integration. These include the European model of "mutual recognition," the recent Commonwealth-state agreement on the so-called "Hilmer" microeconomic reforms which submit state public enterprises (electricity, railways, etc.) to enhanced competition and the manner in which the Australian federation achieved effective uniformity in company law. Part five then reproduces this exercise for Canada, with principal focus on the *Agreement on Internal Trade* (AIT). Included also are a series of innovative integration measures, largely on the taxation side, that have no counterpart in Australia because of the restricted scope, *de facto*, of the taxation powers of Australian states. Part six addresses the trade-off that exists between the pursuit of an internal economic union on the one hand and the ability to engage in "competitive federalism" on the other. In particular, data are presented which demonstrate that parts of Canada and Australia are becoming integrated more with the rest of the world than with the rest of their federation. This complicates the pursuit of a thorough-going internal economic union.

Constitutional Provisions Relating to the Internal Economic Union

Table 9.1 contains the relevant constitutional provisions, for Australia and Canada respectively, relating to securing the internal economic union. These provisions are grouped into three categories: the "free trade" clauses, the federal regulatory power and provisions relating to individual mobility. All federations have some version of the federal regulatory power, typically in the form of a trade and commerce clause. Not all, however, have what I have referred to, following Hayes (1982), as a free trade clause which is, in effect, a free enterprise provision because it constrains both levels of government. For example, the U.S. and German constitutions do not have a free trade clause.

The Free-Trade Clause

The Australian free trade guarantee (Section 92, from Table 9.1) was initially interpreted in a manner which hindered government control of trade and commerce. Essentially, the "absolutely free" aspect of section 92 was deemed to be synonymous with liberal, *laissez-faire* philosophy. As a result of this interpretation, the High Court struck down Commonwealth legislation seeking to nationalize banking and air transport. However, in *Cole v. Whitfield* (1988) 165 CLR 360, 78 ALR 42 the High Court rejected this "individual rights approach" to section 92. From Zines (1992:121):

> The court declared that the object of s.92 in its application to trade and commerce is the elimination of protection. The section only prohibits measures which discriminate against interstate trade and commerce and which have the purpose or effect of protecting the intrastate trade or industry of a State against competition from other states.

Table 9.1
Selected Constitutional Provisions Relating to Securing the Internal Economic Union

AUSTRALIA
1. Free Trade Clause:
    - Section 92: ... trade, commerce, and intercourse among the States, whether by means of internal carriage or ocean navigation, shall be absolutely free.
2. Federal Regulatory Power:
    - Section 51: The Parliament shall, subject to the Constitution, have power to make laws for the peace, order and good government of the Commonwealth with respect to:
    (i) Trade and commerce with other countries, and among the States:
    - Section 99: The Commonwealth shall not, by any law or regulation of trade, commerce or revenue, give preference to one State or any part thereof over another State or any part thereof.
    - Section 96: ... the Parliament may grant financial assistance to any State on such terms and conditions as the Parliament thinks fit.
3. Individual Mobility:
    - Section 117: A subject of the Queen, resident in any State, shall not be subject in any other state to any disability or discrimination which would not be applicable to him if he were a subject of the Queen resident in such other State.

CANADA
1. Free Trade Clause:
    - Section 121: All Articles of Growth, Produce or Manufacture of any one of the provinces shall, from and after the Union, be admitted free into each of the other Provinces;
2. Federal Regulatory Power:
    - Section 91: Parliament has the exclusive authority to make laws with regard to: ...
    (2) The Regulation of Trade and Commerce.
3. Individual Mobility from the Canadian Charter of Rights and Freedoms
    - Section 6: ... (2) Every citizen of Canada and every person who has the status of a permanent resident of Canada has the right a) to move and take up residence in any province; and b) to pursue the gaining of a livelihood in any province. (3) The rights specified in subsection (2) are subject to a) any laws or practices of general application in force in a province other than those that discriminate among persons primarily on the basis of province of the present or previous residence; and b) any laws providing for reasonable residence requirements as a qualification for the receipt of publicly provided social services. (b) Subsections (2) and (3) do not preclude any law, program or activity that has as its object the amelioration in a province of conditions of individuals in that province who are socially or economically disadvantaged in the rate of employment in that province is below the rate of employment in Canada.
    - Section 15 (Equality Rights): (1) Every individual is equal before and under the law and has the right to the equal protection and equal benefit of the law without discrimination ... (2) Subsection (1) does not preclude any law, program or activity that has as its object the amelioration of conditions of disadvantaged individuals or groups ...

Source: Adapted from Hayes (1982), among other sources.

Arguably this frees up the legislative scope of the states in intrastate areas, provided of course that the laws cannot be interpreted as discriminatory. Commentators have noted that this also frees up the scope for Commonwealth legislation. In all likelihood, the earlier cases relating to nationalizing banks and airlines would, under *Cole v. Whitfield*, not be ruled *ultra vires*. But the Commonwealth remains constrained in terms of fragmenting the internal economic union by section 99 which expressly prohibits it from giving preference to any particular state or group of states. This provision appears to be unique to the Australian constitution, at least among mature federations. However, section 96 provides the Commonwealth with a wide loophole here in terms of Commonwealth-state grants. (Both sections 99 and 96 are reproduced in Table 9.1).

In contrast, the Canadian version of the free trade guarantee (Section 121) has been subject to much less judicial review and has been interpreted much more narrowly. As the wording indicates ("All Articles of Growth, Produce or Manufacture ..."), it obviously applies to "goods," but has not been interpreted as encompassing services, capital or persons. As Hogg (1992:1015) notes, "in both *Gold Seal v. A-G Alta* (1921) 62 S.C.R. 424 and *Atlantic Smoke Shops v. Conlon* (1943) A.C. 550 arguments based on s.121 were rejected on grounds that s.121 prohibited only customs duties between provinces and no other kinds of impediments to interprovincial mobility of goods." And s.121 has not proved that effective even in terms of generating a customs union for goods. For example, Ontario has long had special taxes on foreign wines (relative to Ontario wines), which are in effect "customs duties" established at the provincial level. The challenge to this practice has come more from international agreements (GATT) than from s.121. Moreover, again from Hogg (1992:1016), when the federal government has enacted barriers to the mobility of goods, either alone or in concert with the provinces, the laws have been upheld. In terms of the former, *Caloil v. A-G Can* [1971] S.C.R. 543 upheld the prohibition on the shipment of imported oil west of the Ottawa Valley. In terms of the latter, namely Ottawa and the provinces acting in concert, both in the transportation (trucking) area, where Ottawa's power to regulate has been delegated to provincial agencies, and in agricultural commodities (eggs), where Ottawa and the provinces have passed complimentary legislation, provincial barriers have been erected. One reason for the paucity of cases under s.121 (as compared with the extensive recourse to s.92 under the Australian constitution) may be that Ottawa preferred to challenge provincial free trade impediments under s.91(2), the federal trade and commerce power, rather than under s.121. This is so because any judgments arising from the latter would be binding on *both* levels of government whereas, almost by definition, Ottawa could not be bound by one of its own powers. In any event, the free trade clause appears to have been much more binding in Australia and, in particular, served to limit recourse to "Commercial Crowns" in Australia.

The Trade and Commerce Power

This is an appropriate lead into the comparison of the federal regulatory powers. The Commonwealth trade and commerce power (Section 51(i)) has also been broadly interpreted by the courts to extend far into intrastate matters, although probably not quite as far as the U.S. interstate commerce clause. In contrast, s.91(2) in Canada has been interpreted as having a far narrower reach. One obvious reason for this is that the Canadian constitution, unlike its Australian counterpart, contains a lengthy list of exclusive provincial powers (which are reproduced in the appendix). If the Fathers of Canadian Confederation anticipated a broad reach for s.91(2) they would not have detailed the list of exclusive provincial powers, or so the argument goes. Indeed, the force of some of these provincial powers (especially s.92(13), "property and civil rights in the province") is such that the residual power in the federation for many areas was effectively vested in the provinces.

This leads to an important detour on the comparative reach of the federal powers. Perhaps influenced by the Canadian cases, the early Australian judges read the Constitution as if the powers reserved to the states (that is, all the powers except those which the Constitution expressly enumerates as belonging to the Commonwealth) were also expressly granted to the states. This is the principle of immunity or implied limitation. The *Engineer's* case (1920) 28 CLR 129 completely altered this interpretation. The key issue in the *Engineer's* case was the implied limitation of the exercise of the legislative powers of the Commonwealth and, specifically, whether Parliament had power under s.51(xxxv) to make binding laws on the states.[1] *Engineer's* held that it had and, in the process made *Engineer's* "probably the most important case in Australian constitutional law, at any rate, from the point of view of principles of general interpretation" (Zines, 1992:7). Zines then reflects:

> The immediate result of the *Engineer's* case was that the Commonwealth power was to be interpreted broadly and *without regard to what amount of power should be left to the States*. The States

---

1. Section 51(xxxv) reads: "The Parliament shall, subject to this Constitution, have power to make laws for the peace, order, and good government of the Commonwealth with respect to - ... (xxxv). Conciliation and arbitration for the prevention and settlement of industrial disputes extending beyond the limits of any one state."

and their "instrumentalities" could, generally speaking ... be made subject to Commonwealth law. The *Engineer's* case clearly enabled the growth of Commonwealth power that many would regard as commensurate with its increasing national responsibilities. It also, to an extent, freed the court from the problems that have bedevilled the interpretation of the Canadian Constitution in forcing the court to decide within which of two different subject matters an Act belongs when it can be regarded as reasonably coming within both (Ibid., 13, emphasis added).

The most recent High Court decision relating to s.51(xxxv) would be quite incomprehensible to Canadians: under (*Victoria v. Commonwealth* (1995), ALR pending) the state of Victoria could not force its employees to come under the provisions of a Victoria industrial relations statute. In terms of minimum wages and working conditions, state of Victoria employees have the right to opt into federal awards. From the High Court's decision:

It seems to us that critical to that capacity [the capacity to function as a government] of a State is the government's right to determine the number and identity of the persons whom it wishes to employ, the terms of employment of such persons and, as well, the number and identity of the persons it wishes to dismiss with or without notice from its employment on redundancy grounds. An impairment of a State's rights in these respects would, in our view, constitute an infringement of the implied limitation. On this view, the prescription by a federal award of minimum wages and working conditions would not infringe the applied limitation ... (26).

This sweep of Commonwealth legislation resonates much more closely with what is happening in the U.S. than with the Canadian experience.[2] In Canada, not only are industrial relations pertaining to sub-national

---

2. Traditionally, the U.S. anti-trust laws applied to private individuals and not to the activities of the states. In *National League of Cities v. Usery* (426 U.S. 833 (1976)) the Supreme Court, relying on the Tenth Amendment which reserves certain rights to the states, invalidated an attempt by Congress to apply a minimum wage and maximum hour standard. However, in a landmark decision, *Garcia v. San Antonio Metropolitan Transit Authority* (469 U.S. 528 (1985)), the Supreme Court overturned *Usery*: "We therefore now reject, as unsound in principle and unworkable in practice, a rule of state immunity from federal regulation that turns on a judicial appraisal of whether a particular governmental function is 'integral' or 'traditional'" (*Ibid.*, pp. 546-47). Perhaps it is not surprising that this ruling resonates much more closely to the application of s.51(xxxv) of the Australian Constitution than any interpretation under the Canadian Constitution - both Australia and the U.S. constitutions share the feature of having no enumerated powers assigned to the states.

governments in provincial jurisdiction, but so are minimum wages and working conditions for private sector operations in the respective provinces except for those industries that explicitly fall under federal regulation (e.g., banking and nuclear plants). Indeed, in the summer of 1995 the Canadian federal government announced that, henceforth, federal minimum wages would track provincial minimum wages. At the time of the announcement, the federal minimum wage was $4.00 per hour, lower than any provincial minimum wage. From now on, federal minimum wages will differ across provinces, in accordance with the respective provincial minimum wage. This is almost at the opposite pole from the Australian reality.

More generally, and presumably strongly influenced by the sweep of s.51(i) and (xxxv) among other provisions, aspects of Australia's economic space are akin to a unified market. For example, wages for university professors are essentially identical across universities (and, therefore, across states). Much of this is traceable to the operations of the Industrial Relations Commission and its various predecessors and, in particular, to the Commission's 1907 *Harvester* judgment which granted a man, his wife and three children a "living wage." Henceforth, remuneration had more to do with accessing an appropriate share of the societal surplus than with productivity. Australia utilizes wages (i.e., the allocative system) as a vehicle for redistribution. The general point here is that this is way off side with Canadian experience.

By way of summary to this point, the manner in which the High Court has interpreted the Australian Constitution has generated an environment where there are far fewer differences in wage/rental or labour/leisure ratios across economic space than is the case in Canada. This is not just the result of the provinces having greater powers than the Australian states: the Canadian federal government also has more ability to fragment the internal market than does the Commonwealth government. For example, during the 1980s, the federal income tax incorporated different tax write-offs for R and D expenditure in different provinces: i.e., there is no equivalent in Canada of s.99 of the Commonwealth Constitution. Indeed, s.36(1) of the *Constitution Act, 1982* can be interpreted as a call for pro-active regional policy to ensure "equality of opportunity."[3] I leave to constitutional scholars whether the

---

3. Section 36(i) reads: "Without altering the legislative authority of Parliament or of the provincial legislatures, or the rights of any of them with respect to the exercise of their legislative authority, Parliament and the legislatures, together with the government of Canada and the provincial governments, are committed to promoting equal opportunities for the well-being of Canadians; further economic development to reduce disparity in opportunities; and providing essential services of reasonable quality to all Canadians."

Canadian-type UI system, replete with regional benefits, would be ruled *ultra vires* in Australia.

I hasten to note that the thrust of this section is not to argue for "constitutional determinism" in terms of the evolution of the internal economic union. For example, the presence of Quebec in the Canadian federation — a province that is culturally, linguistically and legally (civil law, rather than common law) distinct — does presumably have an influence on how the written word of the Constitution is interpreted.

Individual Mobility

Turning, finally, to the third category of Table 9.1, namely individual mobility, these rights in Australia are guaranteed by s.92 (because "intercourse" has been interpreted to include the movement of people) and, more explicitly, by section 117 (see Table 1). Portability of social services across states is much less of a challenge in Australia because, as will be elaborated later, many of these services are delivered by the Commonwealth government.

Until 1982 there were no specific provisions in the Canadian Constitution relating to mobility of individuals. However, the *Constitution Act, 1982* enshrined the Canadian Charter of Rights and Freedoms which, among many other features, incorporates mobility provisions. Yet, in part to obtain provincial support for the Charter, the federal government also agreed to enshrine several *impediments* to the internal economic union:

- the right of some provinces to discriminate against out-of-province residents in terms of land ownership (in the Charter);
- the right of low-employment provinces to discriminate in favour of hiring residents (in the Charter); and
- the right of energy-producing provinces to enact indirect taxes in energy (not in the Charter but in the *Constitution Act, 1982*).

Enshrining the right of provinces to fragment the internal economic union is nothing short of incomprehensible and probably makes the Canadian Constitution unique in this regard.

The message from the individual mobility side is consistent with that from the free movement of goods, services and capital, namely that Australia has a freer internal market than does Canada.

Nonetheless, in both countries there is need for further integration and both have responded, although in quite different ways, to promote this enhanced integration. Prior to dealing with these initiatives in "positive integration," it is useful to focus on how the international sector and, in particular, international free trade is impinging on domestic free trade.

International Influences

One obvious implication of enhanced economic and political integration is that, in the process, nations are giving up aspects of sovereignty (Courchene 1995a; Courchene and Walsh 1995). In turn, this is likely to have important implications for the internal balance of power in federal nations. The courts in Canada and Australia have, to this point, taken diametrically opposed positions on the application of international agreements and treaties to subnational governments. In Australia, the High Court has given an expansive reading to the Commonwealth's external affairs power (s.5(xxix)): it has struck down provisions of a Queensland racial discrimination act (*Koowarta v. Bjelke-Petersen* (1982) 153 CLR 168) and prevented the construction of a dam in Tasmania (*Franklin Dam* case (1983) 158 CLR 1) on the basis of the Commonwealth's adherence to the Racial Discrimination Convention and the World Heritage Convention, respectively. As Zines (1992:240) notes in connection with the *Franklin Dam* case: "It was clearly established by a majority of the court that under the external affairs powers the Commonwealth could give effect to any international obligations imposed by a *bona fide* international agreement or by customary international law in relation to any subject."

Note that the issue at stake here goes well beyond the implications for preserving and promoting an internal common market. As University of Melbourne's Greg Craven (1993:11) notes, the core issue is the following: "Can the central [federal] government, simply through the exercise of its capacity in the field of foreign relations, significantly alter what otherwise would be the constitutional balance of power?" The answer for many federal systems is "Yes." Whether via the executive power and/or the foreign relations power (the power to enter into treaties), it seems clear that in the American, Swiss and Australian federations, the federal governments have relatively free reign to manoeuvre here and, in the process, enforce compliance by sub-national governments (Courchene and Walsh 1995). The countervail, to the extent that it exists, is political, not constitutional. For example, there is a move afoot in Australia to establish a "treaties council" as an official agency of the Council of Australian Governments (their more formal equivalent to Canada's First Ministers' Conference) in order to allow the Australian states to have some input into Commonwealth treaties.

Canada appears to be an exception here. Prevailing constitutional precedent in Canada points in the other direction. In the *Labour Conventions*

Case (1937), A.C. 326 (P.C.), the Judicial Committee of the Privy Council decided that Canada's signature to the International Labour Organization Convention did not give Parliament the power to implement those aspects of the Convention relating to matters coming under provincial constitutional responsibility. This is a particularly useful case for comparative purposes, since the earlier Australian case relating to federal awards for minimum wages and working conditions dominating Victorian awards was presumably influenced because the federal awards were embodying ILO principles or conventions.

Things may be about to change in Canada. Article 103 of the FTA states: "The Parties to this Agreement [i.e. the federal governments of Canada and the United States] shall ensure that all necessary measures are taken in order to give effect to its provisions, including their observance, except as otherwise provided in the Agreement, by state, provincial and local governments." As Peter Leslie (1995) points out, the words "all necessary measures" are much stronger than the GATT obligation where a federal state need take only "such reasonable measures as may be available" to ensure compliance by state or provincial governments. While the provinces are exempt from some provisions of the FTA and, now, NAFTA, the likelihood is that they will find themselves bound by other provisions, even if they are within their own constitutional areas. Phrased differently, the ruling arising from the *Labour Conventions Case* may not be sustained. Already, the FTA has generated anomalous situations with respect to the Canadian economic union. The FTA principle of "National Treatment" means that the province of Ontario, for example, is allowed to legislate as it pleases in certain areas, subject to the requirement that it treats American firms on the same basis as Ontario firms.[4] But it need not treat Alberta firms identically. This obvious anomaly has, in part, led to the recent (1994) *Agreement on Internal Trade*, more on which later.

As already noted, aspects of the reach of the combined executive/external affairs powers relate to the broader issue of the balance of internal powers in a federation and not only to internal economic union issues. But the latter are likely to become increasingly significant. In the EU, reference is frequently made to "environmental dumping" and "social policy dumping" and there are labour/social policy and environmental "riders" to NAFTA. These are likely to bite more on federations like Canada, where much of the responsibility for social policy and the environment remain in provincial jurisdiction, than on more centralized federations such as Australia.

---

4. Essentially "national treatment," or its internal equivalent "provincial treatment," is a non-discriminatory clause which bears considerable resemblance to the non-discrimination test arising in the wake of the above-noted *Cole v. Whitfield* case in Australia.

However, the FTA and NAFTA are also affecting the Canadian internal economic union in "commercial" dimensions — dimensions that have not yet had anywhere near the impact on Australia. With goods able to flow freely across the Canadian-U.S. border, this is beginning to unwind some of the east-west (internal) impediments. Once U.S. beer can flow into Canada, what sense does it make to maintain the former prohibition against east-west flows? While marketing boards for agricultural products are "grandfathered" under the FTA, these will be increasingly difficult to sustain when feedstocks and foodstocks can flow north-south. Analytically, this is exactly what one would expect. Much of the reason provinces were enticed to mount internal trade barriers related to the fact that the Canadian-U.S. border was closed (or tariff-ridden) — open the border and the advantage to provinces of mounting internal barriers disappear because north-south "by-pass" is now possible. Thus, the FTA and NAFTA are serving (even apart from the *Agreement on Internal Trade*, to be dealt with later) to free up the Canadian economic union, at least in terms of goods, services and capital.

Finally, there is an important relationship between the *commercial* implications of free trade as it influences the internal economic union and the *constitutional* implications. Specifically, now that trade is flowing freely north-south, it is only natural that judges will take this into account in any deliberations. One would expect, for example, that the federal trade and commerce power, s.91(2), will be given a more expansive reading. The recent Supreme Court decision decreeing that the federal government has the right to regulate telephones may be the beginning of this trend.

Therefore, while the Australian Constitution and its interpretation have delivered a freer internal market than is the case for Canada, this is offset to some extent because greater north-south interaction and particularly the direct and indirect impacts of the FTA and NAFTA, are serving to erode internal barriers in Canada.

However, in neither country have these constitutional or trade measures delivered a fully effective internal market. To do this requires pro-active measures, measures that fall under the rubric of "positive integration." To these I now turn.

Positive Integration
Australia
Mutual recognition
In the Commission of European Communities' 1985 White Paper (*Completing the Internal Market*) there was an important conceptual distinction between matters or areas where full harmonization was essential and those where

there would be "mutual recognition" of the equivalences of various basic requirements laid down under national law.[5] In the context of Europe 1992, mutual recognition was applied not only to goods, but as well to regulated professions and to selected services (banking, for example). As Majone (1994:83) notes:

> Mutual recognition is a sophisticated and flexible instrument of regulation, especially appropriate for federal type systems where state rights are jealously guarded ... The method is so attractive because it promises to achieve economic integration while preserving national and regional characteristics; to reduce the burden of centralized regulation without sacrificing essential safety requirements; and to promote experimentation and learning, but not unrestricted laissez-faire.

Underlying any meaningful process of mutual recognition must be some effective harmonization of essential health and safety requirements, but the dynamic within a mutual recognition agreement tends to generate such harmonization.

Australia was quick off the mark in recognizing the potential for mutual recognition. In October, 1990, the Australian Heads of Government agreed in principle to introduce a program providing for mutual recognition of regulations and standards relating to the sale of goods and the registration of occupations. By May, 1992, they agreed on draft legislation and signed off on the "Mutual Recognition Agreement" (MRA). But the states needed the Commonwealth to give effect to this legislation to ensure that it would be binding on all signatories. Thus, utilizing section 51(xxxvii), the states requested that the Commonwealth legislate and implement the MRA.[6] The MRA was proclaimed in February 1993 and commenced on March 1, 1993. All states and territories have passed legislation to join the scheme, except Western Australia, which is committed to doing so in the near future.

---

5. The principle of mutual recognition was given prominence by the European Court of Justice decision in the famous Cassis de Dijon case in 1979. Majone (1994:70) notes: "The court had stated that a member state may not in principle prohibit the sale in the territory of a product lawfully produced and marketed in another member state even if this product is produced according to technical or quality requirements which differ from those imposed on its domestic products — except when the prohibition if justified by the need to ensure effective fiscal supervision, to protect public health or the environment, or to ensure the fairness of financial transactions."
6. Section 51(xxxvii) reads: "51. The Parliament shall, subject to the Constitution, have power to make laws for the peace, order and good government of the Commonwealth with respect to: ... (xxxvii) Matters referred to the Parliament of the Commonwealth by the Parliament or Parliaments of any State or States, but so that the law shall extend only to States by whose Parliaments the matter is referred, or which afterwards adopt the law."

Prior to addressing some of the provisions of Australia's MRA, it is instructive to stand back a bit and focus on some of the underlying political, even constitutional, implications. Gary Sturgess, a prime mover in the MRA process, elaborates as follows (1993:10):

> ... the Commonwealth is obtaining no power from the States under this very limited reference, other than to pass a single Act of Parliament once-for-all. It cannot pass further legislation in the same area, nor can it establish a bureaucracy through which to regulate the States. In that sense, there is no reference of powers at all.
>
> In effect, the States are using the Commonwealth to jointly make an amendment to each of their constitutions at the one time. In practice, what the States are doing is ceding sovereignty to each other.
>
> And if you look at the underlying relationships of trust upon which this integration is built, it becomes obvious that the Commonwealth is merely a bystander in the process, and not a player at all. It is the States that have had to recognize each others' regulatory systems, not the Commonwealth. The Commonwealth's regulatory systems are, by definition, already national in scope.

The MRA has two key principles.[7] The first (section 9) is that goods which can be sold lawfully in one jurisdiction may be sold in any other, even though the goods may not comply with all the details of the regulatory standards in the second jurisdiction. The second (section 17) is that if a person is registered to carry out an occupation in one jurisdiction, he or she can be registered to carry out the equivalent occupation in any other jurisdiction without the need for further assessment of qualifications.

Henceforth, therefore, the MRA means that goods will not have to comply with many regulations relating to the sale of goods in the host jurisdiction such as:
- the standards of goods themselves: for example requirements relating to their production, composition, quality or performance (together referred to as *product standards*);
- the way goods are presented: for example requirements relating to packaging, labelling, date stamping of age;

---

8. Much of what follows is taken directly from an excellent overview of the MRA, both in its own right and how it might be extended to New Zealand (*A Proposal for the Trans-Tasman Mutual Recognition of Standards for Goods and Professions*), a discussion paper circulated by COAG and the Government of New Zealand (April 1995).

- a requirement that the goods be inspected, passed or similarly dealt with [by the host country]; (COAG/New Zealand Discussion Paper:3).

But MRA will not affect other regulations, such as registration of sellers (e.g. liquor licences), franchise licences (e.g. tobacco licences) and certain conditions relating to circumstances in which goods may or may not be sold (e.g. health requirements). In all such cases, however, these regulations would have to apply equally to goods produced within a jurisdiction and goods imported into a jurisdiction.[8]

On the occupational mobility side, for automatic registration in the host jurisdiction, all that is required is evidence of registration in an equivalent occupation in any participating jurisdiction. The host state can refuse registration on grounds that an occupation is not equivalent to the occupation registered in the origin state, but this can then be appealed under the *Administrative Appeals Tribunal Act, 1975*.

The COAG/New Zealand discussion paper notes that "by reducing, and often eliminating, regulatory impediments to trade in goods and the movement of skilled labour within Australia, mutual recognition has resulted in a number of benefits for consumers, business, skilled personnel and the regulatory practices of government." (6) Of particular interest is that mutual recognition has accelerated the development of national standards in areas with significant implications for public health, safety and the environment. Moreover, the existence of the MRA will impose greater discipline in the introduction of standards and regulations. For example, manufacturing regulations will only affect companies in the regulatory jurisdiction. Goods produced to more efficient and less costly requirements elsewhere can still be sold in that jurisdiction. Obviously, an underlying premise is that the parties are confident that the standards set by other jurisdictions are acceptable. Finally, one of the virtues of MRA is that it avoids the "extremely slow and painstaking" traditional approach to removing regulatory impediments, namely developing national standards (2).

---

8. Canadians would refer to this last principle as "provincial treatment."

While Australia's mutual recognition initiative is still in its infancy, it represents an excellent example of "positive integration" and one that the Canadian federation should be monitoring closely.[9]

Micro-economic reform (The Hilmer Report)

On April 11, 1995, the Council of Australian Governments (COAG) meeting delivered on the long-debated, micro-economic-reform agenda, frequently referred to as the Hilmer Report after its author, Professor Fred Hilmer, who headed the independent review of national competition policy which reported in August of 1993. The *Competition Principles Agreement*, signed by all the Heads of Government, establishes agreed principles on structural reform of public monopolies and state enterprises (e.g., gas, electricity, water, rail, urban transit (including taxis), ports, self-regulating professional organizations, agricultural marketing boards and so on), on competitive neutrality between public and private sectors; on prices oversight of utilities and other corporations with significant monopoly power; on a regime to provide access to essential facilities; and on a program to review legislation restricting competition. This is truly landmark reform/legislation, well beyond the fondest dreams of even the most ardent centralists in Canada.

What made this exercise so fascinating from the perspective of a federal system is that while an estimated 80 percent of the reforms fell under state jurisdiction, the states would, budgetary-wise, be big losers. This was so for two reasons. First, various fees and revenues from the (frequently monopolized) state-owned or state-run enterprises account for an important proportion of their own-source revenues and these would decrease under the proposed reforms which will bring more competition into these areas. Second, while the potential benefits are huge (estimated by the Industry Commission to be $9 billion a year to consumers within four to eight years and a further $8.9 billion a year windfall to governments), the states' share of the government revenue component is estimated to be only $3 billion out of

---

9. Note, however, that the role of the COAG/New Zealand Discussion Paper is to broach the possibility of extending MRA to New Zealand. This raises an intriguing set of issues. For example, if extended to New Zealand, would this be an international agreement between the Australia states and New Zealand? Or is there some way in which it could be an Australia-New Zealand agreement? Sturgess (1993:10) argues that "if mutual recognition is extended across the Tasman, it will be because the States are satisfied with New Zealand's regulatory systems, and vice versa, and not because of any unilateral action on the part of the Commonwealth." I think that this is right as far as it goes. But there is a further complication that goes beyond the states, namely that the Commonwealth has to be satisfied with New Zealand's regulatory system and standards in the Commonwealth's sphere of competences. At the formal level, however, it seems clear that any agreement with New Zealand would be negotiated by the Commonwealth under its external affairs power.

this $8.9 billion. In large measure, this is due to the vertical fiscal imbalance that characterizes the Australian federation (see Courchene 1995b or Dahlby and Wilson, this volume). For example, to the extent that benefits take the form of enhanced personal or corporate income taxation, this is a Commonwealth budgetary benefit because the states do not share in the proceeds of either personal or corporate income taxation. Accordingly, right from the beginning of the Hilmer Report deliberations it was recognized and accepted that the states would receive some financial compensation in return for implementing these reforms. The figure agreed to at the COAG meeting was $600 million annually (in 1994-95 dollars) in the steady state. This figure would be achieved in terms of three tranches of $200 million each, which would have to be "earned" by the states in terms of their implementation performance. Another important concession won by the states is that the appointments to the oversight bodies (the National Competition Council and the Australian Competition and Consumer Commission, NCC and ACCC respectively) will require the support of the Commonwealth and a majority of parties (six states, two territories and the Commonwealth). Relatedly, and of even more significance, is that COAG agreed on a mechanism for voting on amendments to the Competition Code. The Commonwealth will have two votes and a casting vote with each of the other parties having a single vote. As the COAG communique notes: "this will provide meaningful State and Territorial participation in changes to the competitive conduct rules while maintaining a consistent national scheme" (COAG, Communique, April 11, 1995:2).

Finally, as an important related measure, the earlier provision for an indefinite real per capita guarantee for the total of financial assistance grants (under the Commonwealth Grants Commission) was maintained and, in addition, the eventual annual $600 million in competition payments would be "quarantined from assessment by the Commonwealth Grants Commission" (COAG:3).[10]

The implications of these agreements/arrangements are potentially so far-reaching that some comment is warranted. The first point relates to the manner in which all of this co-exists with the earlier assessment of the way in which Australia and the High Court have implemented the internal economic

---

10. The reference here is to Australia's "equalization program," administered by the Commonwealth Grants Commission. Unlike Canada's equalization formula, the CGC approach equalizes for *both* revenue means and expenditure needs. In Courchene (1995b), the point is made that excluding this $600 million from entering revenue equalization may not "quarantine" this $600 million from the very egalitarian Australian equalization program. One would *also* have to exclude this $600 million from the *expenditure side* of the CGC model. Conceptually, as well as practically, this is likely to be very difficult to accomplish. See Courchene (1995b, chapter 4).

union. It seems to me that these proposals resonate much better with the *early* interpretation of s.92, namely an emphasis on individual rights and *laissez-faire* liberalism which serves to rid the system of monopolies wherever they exist. Whereas some of these state monopolies presumably could have been struck down under this early interpretation of s.92, this became much less likely after *Cole v. Whitfield*, with its emphasis on non-discrimination. It may well be that *Cole v. Whitfield* is, indirectly, the author of these proposals, since the sort of consumer-driven or efficiency-oriented economic liberalism that characterizes these micro-economic reforms must now be accomplished *via intergovernmental agreement* rather than pursued through the courts.

Second, the procedure relating to appointments to the NCC and the ACCC as well as the process for amending the competition code seems strange given the proclivity of the High Court to narrow the sphere of state authority that is exempt from the reach of Commonwealth legislation. As such, this may be a major victory for the states, especially if the experience can be replicated in other areas.

The third point is somewhat related. This agreement appears to tilt Australian federalism in the Canadian direction of "executive federalism." Amendments to the Competition Code will be hammered out in executive (COAG) forums and then submitted to legislatures for a "yes" or a "no," with little or no flexibility for altering any "back-room" deal. While this may not be new to the Australian federalism — the mutual recognition agreements at the interstate level were essentially of this variety — it does represent a constraint on Commonwealth legislative autonomy that is, I think, quite atypical.

My final point is more down to earth. Will all these promised benefits appear? At one level, it is possible to challenge the benefit projections of the Industry Commission. I leave this to others. The more fascinating, although related, issue is the politics of the implementation process. It is one thing to focus on the aggregate benefits from this reform, whether in terms of overall consumer benefits or efficiency gains or benefits accruing through increased taxation. It is quite another to personalize these benefits *and costs*. Eroding the value of a taxi medallion will inflict large losses on a small group of people. Likewise, achieving the projected gains from introducing greater competition in the provision of electricity and gas, etc., have to imply removal of the existing set of cross subsidies, many of which have become quasi-property rights in the eyes of the beneficiaries. It is at this level — the level where citizens will assess the costs and benefits — that in my view the major challenge to these reform measures will lie. But this is somewhat far afield from the focus of this study.

As a concluding comparative comment on the Canadian reality, while this degree of cooperative intergovernmental deregulation of provincial monopolies is probably not in the cards, the forces of globalization are nonetheless wreaking havoc on some provincial monopolies. Consider the hydros. In effect, they are independent fiefdoms within the respective provinces. To the extent that they exported electricity, these exports were to the U.S., not to adjacent provinces. Yet Ontario Hydro has recently undergone an unprecedented and very substantial restructuring and downsizing in order to forestall some cities in the grid from opting for cheaper local power generation. While these hydros may have immunity from the reach of the internal market provisions of the Canadian Constitution, they have no such immunity from the powerful forces of the market. Nor do the commercial crowns in the transportation area (CN and Air Canada), which are in the process of being privatized.

Company law

The recent developments in the Australian company law area shed further light on the role that positive integration can play in creating freer internal markets. Section 51(xx) of the Australian Constitution would appear to provide enough scope for the Commonwealth to forge a uniform approach to company law. Section 51(xx) reads:

> 51 ... The Parliament shall, subject to this Constitution, have power to make laws for the peace, order and good governments of the Commonwealth with respect to
>
> > (xx) Foreign corporations, and trading or financial corporations formed within the limits of the Commonwealth.

However, in the *Corporations Case* (1990), the High Court held that s.51(xx) did *not* empower the Commonwealth to legislate in terms of the formation or incorporation of companies but only in terms of companies *already* "formed" or incorporated. This means, in effect, that company legislation relating to the formation of corporations is to be regarded as a state matter.

In terms of the phraseology adopted earlier, this means that "negative integration" was thus stymied, so that the pursuit of a unified company law had to proceed via the positive integration route. Aided no doubt by a series of high-profile bankruptcies in several states, the solution came in the form of the so-called Alice Springs Agreement in 1990 which effectively "federalized" company law. Under this Agreement, the Commonwealth amended its *Corporations Act, 1989* and the *Australian Securities Commission Act, 1989* to apply only to the ACT (Australian Capital Territory). That is, federal law would no longer apply to the states. However, for their part, each of the states (and the Northern Territory) would adopt, verbatim, the text of the Commonwealth law and then enact it as their *own* legislation or law. As Lipton and Herzberg (1993:10) point out, "each resulting state corporation law act, while technically legislation of a particular state or territory, has the characteristics of, and is treated for all practical purposes within each jurisdiction as if it were, a Commonwealth rather than a state law." In more detail, from the Explanatory Memorandum of the *Corporations Legislation Amendment Act, 1990*:

> The legislative framework ... will enable Commonwealth and State laws regulating companies, securities and futures industries to operate to the greatest extent possible as national laws ... There will be a uniform text of companies and securities law applying throughout Australia and companies and persons dealing with companies will be able to operate on the basis that there is a single national law. Companies will be able to lodge documents, including an application for incorporation, with the A.S.C. (Australian Securities Commission) anywhere in Australia and, in effect, operate as if they were incorporated Australia-wide.

This is a very innovative approach to creating a single market for those areas where uniformity is becoming essential.

This is in stark contrast to Canadian practice. First of all, Canada is surely unique among federations in that the securities industry is almost entirely provincially regulated. The stock markets are provincial and the regulatory apparatus, including the accreditation of brokers, is also under the control of the relevant provincial securities commissions. Were one to design the Canadian constitution anew, it would surely be the case that this most mobile of areas would be put under federal control. Nonetheless, the various provincial securities commissions have harmonized their operations to such a degree that Canada has a very effective capital market for a country of its size — indeed, for a country of any size. One way of rationalizing why this occurred is that *because there was no federal role*, the provinces were forced to deliver a national capital market. Analytically, one can probably make a case that this is probably an early example of "mutual recognition," although it is typically not viewed as such in Canadian circles. One final note with respect to the Canadian securities industry. As a result of changes in Ontario legislation in the mid-1980s, the Canadian securities firms have largely been taken over by the Canadian banks. Since these banks are federally regulated, it is probably only a matter of time before federal regulation begins to "follow the banks," as it were, into their securities business. Hence, the status quo may, over time, be undermined.

More generally, in terms of company law, the Canadian experience is a far cry from the harmonized, even uniform, Australian regime. More for comparison purposes than any attempt on my part to draw implications, the following excerpt from Hogg (1992:23.1-23.2) is warranted:

> ... Canadian constitutional law draws a distinction between the power to incorporate a company and the power to regulate its activities. ... it is clear that the incorporation power does not imply a power to regulate the activity of a company once it has been brought into existence. This follows from the fact that both the federal Parliament and a provincial legislature may create a company with objects whose subject matter is outside the regulatory power of the incorporating jurisdiction.
>
> The power to regulate corporate activity is distributed in accordance with the classes of subjects listed in the constitution, especially in ss91 and 92. Once a company has been incorporated, its activity will be subject to the legislation of whichever order of government has validly enacted laws in respect of that activity. In ascertaining the appropriate regulatory jurisdiction, as opposed to the appropriate incorporating jurisdiction, the territorial extent of a company's objects is not decisive. The mere fact that a company's activity extends beyond the limits of any one province will not by itself bring the activity within federal regulatory jurisdiction. If the activity wears an aspect within provincial legislative jurisdiction such as "property and civil rights" [s.92(13)] — and most business activity does — then each province will have the power to regulate that part of the company's activity which occurs within the province's borders. Conversely, if the activity wears an aspect which is within federal jurisdiction, then it will be under federal control even if it is local. ... An insurance company may be incorporated federally, but will be subject to provincial laws as to the terms and conditions of its contracts of insurance, and as to the classes of business in which it may engage. An interprovincial telephone company may be incorporated provincially, but its rates will be subject to federal regulation. A hotel may be owned and operated by a federally-incorporated company, but its labour relations will be subject to provincial regulation.

The point is that the jurisdiction of incorporation has the power to confer on a company its legal personality, its organization, and its essential powers; but its business will be regulated by whichever jurisdiction possesses and exercises the power to regulate that kind of business.

It should come as no surprise, then, that Canadian company law and regulatory practices can create major problems for some firms and some industries. One good example relates to the financial sector. Quebec's philosophy with respect to the role of financial institutions (excluding banks which are under federal control) is quite offside with that in the rest of Canada. Not to put too fine a point on this, Quebec has embraced a continental European approach to the financial sector — one that allows much more flexibility in terms of ownership, one that allows the financial sector to own commercial sector assets and, in terms of specifics, one that allows the caisses populaires (i.e., credit unions) to own insurance companies and to merchandise insurance products on caisses premises. The rest of Canada (including Ottawa) is more in the Anglo-American mold, which prefers a separation of the financial and commercial sectors. While the evolution of federal legislation is beginning to broach this divide by moving toward a continental universal banking approach, it is nonetheless the case that significant philosophical differences remain. What this means is that, short of adopting a completely flexible framework that accommodates *all* philosophical positions, there can be no single vision emanating from the center that can reconcile these divergent positions. One obvious approach is to embrace mutual recognition, subject to host province (non-discriminatory) provisions relating to such things as consumer protection and conduct-of-business practices. Indeed, this was the proposal of the 1990 Senate report *Canada 1992: Toward a National Market in Financial Services*.

This discussion of comparative Australian and Canadian approaches to company law is illustrative of a more pervasive issue or problem. Simply put, because Canada is far more decentralized, the challenges in terms of preserving and promoting its internal economic union are likewise more daunting. Thus, areas where harmonization is essentially automatic in Australia frequently require substantial creativity in the Canadian context. The purpose of the next section is to focus on some approaches that Canada has undertaken to enhance its internal economic union. The section will conclude with a discussion of the recent *Agreement on Internal Trade*.

Canada
Integration initiatives: muddling through
Income Taxation

Because corporate and personal income taxation are centralized in Australia, they do not present challenges for the internal economic union. Not so in Canada, where roughly 40 percent of personal income tax revenues accrue to the provinces. Nonetheless, Canadians have been quite creative in ensuring substantial harmonization within decentralization. Specifically, Ottawa collects the provincial portion of the personal income tax free of charge provided that the provinces accept the federal definitions for income and deductions/credits and the provinces limit themselves to applying a single rate of tax against federal tax owing. While the tax rates differ considerably by province (45.5 percent for Alberta and 69 percent for Newfoundland) and, therefore, the combined federal-provincial marginal tax rates vary across provinces, this single-tax-rate-approach preserves the underlying progressivity defined by the federal tax rates.[11] The federal government also collects, this time for a small fee, various provincial tax credits and surcharges. The proviso is that these credits/surcharges cannot serve to fragment the internal economic union. The result minimizes compliance cost (only one form to file) ensures a common tax base (although not tax *rates*), prevents fragmentation of the economic union and, in the process, allows the provinces, as noted, to collect roughly 40 percent of total personal income tax revenues. Note that this shared-tax arrangement does not apply to Quebec — it has its own separate provincial income tax system.

On the corporate side, a similar arrangement applies although three provinces (Alberta, Ontario and Quebec) have their own corporate tax systems. For these three provinces, tax basis can diverge not only from each other but as well from the federal corporate tax base. But all provinces have agreed to a common formula which allocates profits across provinces for firms operating in more than one province. This ensures that corporate profits are neither double-taxed nor are zero-taxed which, in turn, serves to ensure that decentralized corporate taxation is rendered consistent (or as consistent as possible) with maintaining an internal economic union.

---

11. The three federal marginal tax rates are 17 percent, 26 percent and 29 percent. For a province with a 50 percent tax on federal tax owing, the combined (federal-provincial) marginal tax rates are the federal rates multiplied by 1.5. For Newfoundland, with a 69 percent tax rate, the aggregate marginal tax rates are the federal rates multiplied by 1.69. Thus, higher provincial tax rates mean higher overall marginal rates but maintain the federal progressivity.

On the sales tax side, however, Canada's tax system has little to recommend it. Ottawa levies a 7 percent GST (essentially a VAT), while nine of the provinces levy their own provincial sales tax. The result is excessive compliance and collection costs since the tax bases are not harmonized and there are ten collection agencies where one "national" agency would probably be appropriate (Boothe and Snoddon 1994). Recently, the province of Ontario has signalled its willingness to harmonize its PST with the federal GST, so that there may be room for optimism here.

The Federal Spending Power
Because areas like welfare fall under provincial jurisdiction in Canada (unlike Australia, where responsibility rests with the Commonwealth), there is a need to ensure that these benefits are portable across provinces. Canada's way of ensuring this is to prohibit residency requirements for access to provincial welfare. The instrument for ensuring compliance is the federal-provincial grant system: federal cash transfers to the provinces in support of provincial welfare expenditures are conditional on their being no residency requirements. Similar portability provisions exist with respect to federal cash transfers for health. In effect, this is the exercise of the federal spending power and its role is to convert the various provincial programs into "national" programs. However, Australians would be excused if they questioned what passes as "national" in a decentralized federation, namely that welfare benefits for single individuals in Ontario are more than double what they are in New Brunswick. I shall address aspects of this issue a bit later. For now, the main message is that the exercise of the federal spending power plays a critical role in preserving and promoting the Canadian economic union.

Provincial Retaliation
The final, but hardly exhaustive, example of the various ways in which Canada enhances its economic union is, admittedly, somewhat bizarre — namely provincial retaliation. Quebec has long applied restrictions on the ability of out-of-province construction workers to ply their trade within the province. For reasons that are difficult to fathom, Ottawa stayed clear of all of this. In late 1993, an exasperated Ontario retaliated with a set of rather draconian measures levied against Quebec workers in Ontario. This initiative "worked" in the sense that almost immediately the two provinces agreed to a set of common principles that served to enhance the provincial mobility of construction workers. Obviously, one hesitates to suggest that retaliation ought to be an important instrument in promoting a Canadian economic union, let alone to recommend it to other federations. But it can

serve, and has served, as a last-ditch instrument for freeing up markets since it focuses attention on the negative-sum aspects of fragmenting the internal union. Moreover, I do not think that we have seen the last of the exercise of provincial retaliation as an "integration" instrument. For example, were Alberta or Ontario to attempt to "export" their welfare recipients to other provinces, retaliation from other provinces would be swift and harsh. In a sense, retaliation is negative integration at the horizontal (provincial) level.

The underlying message in this section is that a decentralized federation has no choice but to resort to an incredibly wide-ranging set of instruments and conventions to preserve and promote its unified economic space. The most recent and most significant of these is the 1994 *Agreement on Internal Trade*.

The Agreement on Internal Trade (AIT)

In July, 1994, Canada's First Ministers signed the *Agreement on Internal Trade* designed to eliminate barriers to trade, investment and mobility within Canada. The structure of the AIT includes:

- general principles which, among other things, prevent governments from erecting new trade barriers and which require reduction of existing ones in areas covered in the Agreement. These principles, with examples, are reproduced in Table 9.2.
- specific obligations in ten economic sectors — procurement, investment, labour mobility, consumer-related measures and standards, agricultural and food goods, alcoholic beverages, natural resource processing, communications, transportation, and environmental protection;
- provisions for the streamlining and harmonization of regulations and standards;
- a formal dispute resolution mechanism that is accessible to individuals and businesses as well as governments;
- a commitment to further liberalized trade through continuing negotiations and specified target dates;
- a ministerial-level committee on Internal Trade to oversee the implementation and operation of the Agreement and a Secretariat to provide administrative and operational support.

Table 9.2
Agreement on Internal Trade: General Principles

Principle 1: Reciprocal Non-Discrimination

- Establishes equivalent treatment for all Canadian persons, goods, services and investments by requiring governments to provide treatment that is no less favourable than the "best-in-Canada" treatment.

    Examples:
    Governments cannot charge businesses from other provinces higher fees than they charge their own businesses.

    Provinces cannot require products manufactured in another province to meet higher safety standards than those manufactured within the province.

Principle 2: Right of Entry and Exit

- Prohibits governments from adopting or maintaining measures which prevent or restrict the movement of persons, goods, services or investments across provincial or territorial boundaries.

    Example:
    A province cannot impose minimum processing requirements on mineral resources before they can leave the province.

Principle 3: Prohibition Against Creating Obstacles to Trade

- Requires governments to ensure that their policies and practices do not have the effect of creating obstacles to trade.

    Example:
    Governments will have to ensure that the tendering of contracts covered under the Agreement does not favour suppliers of a particular province.

Principle 4: Legitimizing Derogations

- Recognizes that, in pursuing certain non-trade objectives, it may be necessary to deviate from the three preceding trade rules. Governments would then need to meet a 4-part test designed to minimize any adverse trade impact. Specifically, the measure must:

    - be intended to achieve a "legitimate objective" — a defined term that includes specified objectives like consumer protection, environmental protection, public health and safety;
    - not operate to "impair unduly" the access of persons, goods, services or investments which meet that legitimate objective;
    - not be more trade restrictive than necessary to achieve that legitimate objective; and
    - not create a disguised restriction on trade.

    Example:
    A province can prohibit the transportation of hazardous goods through its territory in unsafe containers. But insisting on a particular container design rather than a performance standard for the containers may be more trade restrictive than necessary and could be a disguised trade barrier, e.g. if the only firm manufacturing that particular design is located in-province.

Principle 5: Reconciliation

- Provides the basis for eliminating trade barriers caused by differences in standards and regulations across Canada.

    Example:
    Governments will be required to harmonize standards and related measures on a range of issues such as labelling and direct selling.

Principle 6: Transparency

- Contains a number of provisions — such as publication and notification — to ensure that information is fully accessible to interested businesses, individuals and governments. It exposes potentially unacceptable policies and practices to public scrutiny.

    Examples:
    Governments must identify a place where businesses and individuals can get information about their policies.

    All proceedings before dispute resolution panels must be open to the public.

Source: The 1994 Agreement on Internal Trade.

This is a comprehensive and complex agreement, indeed far too comprehensive and complex to allow for any meaningful assessment in the context of the present paper. However, in a recent volume drawing on the views of experts in the various areas, editors Michael Trebilcock and Daniel Schwanen (1995) are cautiously optimistic that the AIT can become a milestone in the promotion of Canada's internal economic union. Their caution relates, among other things, to the fact that the agreement leaves much to further negotiations and to the fact that the respective governments must ensure that the dispute settlement procedures and the oversight function of the secretariat are made to deliver on their obvious promise.

While an overall assessment is ruled out, there are two features that merit highlight in the context of an Australian-Canadian comparison. The first of these relates to the AIT's provisions on labour mobility and, more generally, on mutual recognition. Basically, this part of the Agreement establishes two principles:

1) a limitation on the use of residency requirements as a condition of licensing, certification, and registration or as a condition on eligibility for employment and allows local hiring preferences to be used only in certain defined circumstances; for example, provinces will not be able to require electricians to live in the province in order to get a license to work there;
2) a process for the recognition of occupational qualifications of workers in regulated occupations and an opportunity for governments to move toward even greater uniformity of occupational standards.

My reading of these provisions is that they are much weaker than the principles under Australia's MRA. Indeed, it is not even clear that has much at all to do with mutual recognition. Rather, the text appears to point towards the development of national standards for occupations and professions, which is at the opposite pole from mutual recognition of standards in other jurisdictions. If my reading is correct, then full occupational mobility across provinces may be a long way off, since it will require a time-consuming process of defining "national" standards as principles for each occupation. The Australian approach, with appeal to some national (interprovincial) arbitrator, seems much the preferable route.

The second area for highlight relates not only to an old Canadian chestnut but as well to my introductory remarks in this volume, namely the provision for a regional economic override. Subject to a few caveats, article 1801:2 specifies that the provisions of the AIT, as they relate to the principles outlined in Table 9.2 of this paper and to the ten economic areas, do not apply to a measure (adopted or maintained by the Federal Government or any other Party to the Agreement) that is part of a general framework for regional economic development. There are two provisos: the measure does not operate to impair *unduly* (my emphasis) the access of persons, goods, services, or investments of another Party; and the measure is not more trade restrictive than necessary to achieve its specific objective. This is an outrageous provision and it has the potential for undermining the entire Agreement. Almost by definition, all barriers are interregional (or interprovincial). And, again by definition, all have-not provinces (*and Ottawa*) will be free to claim that any offending provision is enacted in the name of regional development. There are no appeals to these initiatives under the AIT. All that the provinces have to do is proclaim or assert that the initiatives are part of a regional development strategy. This is the very philosophy that has undermined a "national market" in Canada for decades and we now see it front and centre in the AIT. Unless and until we bury this regional preference philosophy and recognize that regional-disparities policy should be limited to the formal equalization program, agreements like the AIT will fall into the category of pious rhetoric which implicitly, if not explicitly, actually *sanction* the mounting of interprovincial barriers. As already noted, this is what we did in the *Constitution Act, 1982* and we appear to be up to our traditional tricks once again.

Competitive Federalism and the Internal Economic Union

At this juncture, it is appropriate to focus on the relationship between federalism (especially competitive federalism) on the one hand and the promotion of an economic union on the other. The tension between these two is straightforward: a thorough-going economic union is, in an important sense, the very antithesis of competitive federalism since the former implies that wage/rental, labour/leisure and tax/price ratios should not differ across economic space. Yet the exercise of competitive federalism implies that different jurisdictions will and should experiment with alternative design, delivery and incentive procedures which, almost by definition, means fragmenting the internal economic union on a geographical/jurisdictional basis. Because Canada is more decentralized than Australia, the scope for the exercise of competitive federalism is likewise much greater. Indeed, the range of experimentation across the provinces in the health and welfare fields is quite staggering. Presumably, design and delivery features that prove to be "winners" in any one province will spread to other provinces.

Based on an admittedly limited experience with things Australian, my view is that competitive federalism is less appreciated both in theory and practice in Australia. One rationale for this comes from my introductory paper to this volume, namely that Australia appears to be more interested in devolution (to the markets) rather than in Canadian-style decentralization, so that market competition substitutes for competitive federalism. Examples are easy to come by — workers' compensation is paid, in some states, to private insurance, some prisons are privatized, the Australian equivalent of Canada Pension Plan flows through market intermediaries and so on.

However, there are important voices for competitive federalism in Australia. The following are excerpts from a paper by Alan Wood (1994) the economics editor for *The Australian*:

> ... the model we should adopt or more accurately, improve upon — is competitive federalism. Far from being an impediment to the new globalized Australian economy, the States can have quite an important role to play. In fact, and within broad limits, the appropriate internal counterpart of our national strategy of globalization is competition among the States and between them and the Federal Government to deliver the most efficient model of governance (2).

> ... the real value of the States in a modern federal system is that they offer a means, via differing policy approaches, to test alternative policies and via competitive federalism to spread the best system. Had [the State of Victoria] been able to introduce wage flexibility it would have offered the opportunity for Australia to test an alternative to the clearly unsatisfactory federal government model, and one that worked remarkably well in New Zealand. Attempts to set up alternative wage bargaining systems in other states such as West Australia have also been compromised by federal intervention.

> If we are to get the value from a federal system, it must be allowed to operate as such and not be overriden by a power-hungry commonwealth motivated by political rather than economic considerations. (5)

Wood goes on to note that aspects of mutual recognition and the Hilmer reform proposals may go too far in that they will serve to stifle the exercise of competitive federalism. The underlying point is that there is, *at the theoretical level*, a trade-off between the benefits of pursuing an internal economic union and the benefits of executive federalism.

The rest of this section focusses on some issues that arise *at the practical level*. In Canada's case, a key factor is that Canada should no longer be viewed as a single economy. Rather, it is increasingly a series of quite distinct, north-south (cross-border) economies. For example, if one classifies Canada into 4 regions — Western Canada (the four western provinces), Ontario, Quebec and Atlantic Canada (the four eastern provinces) — the exports of shipments of manufacturing and primary products for 1989 are as follows:

Canada West:	33.7% to rest of world; 11.8% to rest of Canada;
Ontario:	33.6% to rest of world; 18.7% to rest of Canada;
Quebec:	26.5% to rest of world; 27.1% to rest of Canada;
Atlantic Canada:	37.5% to rest of world; 15.9% to rest of Canada;

where the residual was sold within the region (Statistics Canada, 1993).[12] More recent data will surely reveal even more international exports, relative to exports to the rest of Canada, particularly since 1989 was the first year of the Canada-US Free Trade Agreement. These data complicate the pursuit of an internal economic union, since the east-west internal union provisions will be superimposed on an increasingly north-south trading system. For example, a narrow interpretation of the "appropriate" framework for corporate income taxation may and probably will run afoul of Alberta's desire to ensure that its corporate tax provisions as they relate to energy are "competitive" with those in the Texas Gulf. On the other hand, whereas trade can cross borders, it is much more difficult for labour to do so. This suggests that it is more important to have a thoroughgoing internal economic union with respect to labour mobility (including the mobility of occupation licensing) than it is to have an effective internal economic union with respect to policies which impact on trade. Note that this is not an argument against the recent AIT. Rather, it is an argument to the effect that special emphasis should be placed on the mobility of human capital, that is on factors where the east-west market *is* the relevant one.

Somewhat similar challenges exist in Australia as well. Figure 9.1 contains graphics relating to Western Australia's interstate and international trade. From Panel A, Western Australia's net imports from the rest of

---

12. John Helliwell and John McCallum have recently published a series of articles (e.g., Helliwell and McCallum, 1995) which assess these data. Based on estimates obtained from a gravity model, they demonstrate that, for cities that are of equal size and equi-distant, the presence of a border substantially reduces trade flows (by a factor of 20). For an evaluation of these results, as well as an argument that this does not invalidate the above claim that Canada is best viewed as a series of cross-border, north-south economies, see Courchene (1995a).

Preserving and Promoting the Internal Economic Union 215

Australia have remained fairly constant at roughly $4 billion ($A) over 1985/86 to 1992/93. On the other hand, Western Australia's international net export surplus was $11 billion ($A) in 1992/93, up from a low of $4 billion ($A) in 1986/87. What this means is that Western Australia is progressively integrating internationally rather than nationally. Table 9.3 presents similar data for Queensland. This state also has a substantial export surplus with the rest of the world and a substantial import surplus with the rest of Australia

Figure 9.1
Australia's Trade Balance

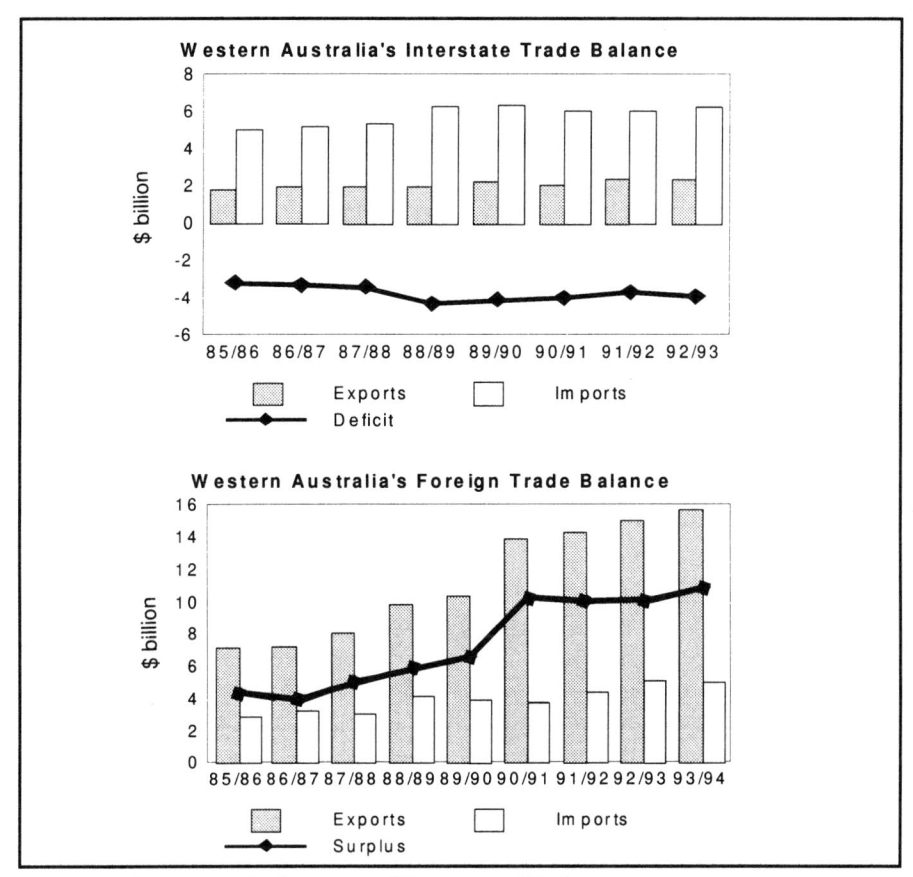

[Chart: Western Australia's Interstate Trade Balance, $ billion, 85/86–92/93, showing Exports, Imports, and Deficit]

[Chart: Western Australia's Foreign Trade Balance, $ billion, 85/86–93/94, showing Exports, Imports, and Surplus]

Source: Western Australia, Department of Commerce and Trade, *Western Australia's Trade Performance* (1995).

Table 9.3
Queensland Trade
($ billion Australia)

Panel A: Interstate Trade		
	1988/89	1993/94
Exports	3.638	4.627
Imports	8.318	11.426
Net *Imports*	4.680	6.799
Panel B: International Trade		
	1988/89	1993/94
Exports	9.089	12.276
Imports	3.788	6.869
Net *Exports*	5.301	5.407
Overall Balance	.621*	1.392**

* net exports
** net imports

Source: Australian Bureau of Statistics.

(presumably, much of the latter arises from tourism). For the largest states, New South Wales and Victoria, the situation is reversed. They have large import surpluses with the rest of the world and large export surpluses with the rest of Australia.[13]

This trade data for both Canada and Australia suggest the following hypotheses in terms of how centralization/decentralization, trade flows and the internal common market interact. Consider Canada first. The increasing north-south trade orientation and the decentralized nature of the country suggest that the Canadian federation has the needed flexibility on the competitive federalism front to ensure that the Canadian regions remain competitive vis-à-vis their cross-border counterparts. However, with the devolution of the social envelope embodied in the 1995 budget, there are

---

13. Data for NSW and Victoria were kindly provided by ECONTECH, an economic consulting company headquartered in Canberra.

genuine fears in the citizenry that competitive federalism on the social policy front could lead to the unravelling of the east-west social safety net. My view taken on this (1995a) is that this degree of decentralization is consistent with maintaining national programs only if the provinces begin to "internalize" the externalities of their actions on the social and economic policy front. In other words, the internal economic union and particularly the internal socio-economic union may not be strong enough to maintain the bonds that tie, east-west.

Arguably, the opposite is the case for Australia. A strong centralized government replete with a thorough-going economic union (including nationwide pay scales and narrow unskilled/skilled wage grids) may be inconsistent with the forces of globalization. Granted that Australians are more regionally homogeneous than Canadians in terms of their preferences, the fact is that their regions are beginning to differ sharply in the manner in which they are integrated inward and outward, trade-wise. To me, this suggests that Australia may have gone too far with the pursuit of centralization and the internal economic union.

In other words, Canada may have become too flexible on the social union side, whereas Australia may be too inflexible on the economic union front.

Conclusions

Australia and Canada have had little choice but to take quite different routes and to rely on quite different instruments in preserving and promoting their respective internal economic unions. In Australia, the Constitution and the High Court have done most of the work — the combination of the Court's expansive reading of the Commonwealth's legislative powers and the sweep of the internal market provisions in Table 9.1 has, of and by itself, gone most of the way in generating an economic union. Indeed, the Court has had to back off the interpretation of s.92 (as it did in *Cole v. Whitfield*) for fear of creating a version of classical *laissez-faire* individualism. Beyond this, Australia has further enhanced its internal economic union by means of a series of Commonwealth-State agreements (Hilmer, company law) or interstate agreements (mutual recognition).

In contrast, the Courts left Canada with a decentralized and fragmented internal economic space. External forces (north-south trade and agreements like the FTA and NAFTA) have played a much greater role in freeing up domestic markets in Canada than in Australia. Moreover, Canada has had to become quite creative in order to even attain the degree of internal integration that the constitution delivered to Australia. Nonetheless, the earlier observation still remains the internal economic union is more fragmented in Canada. This arises not only because of provincial actions: Ottawa also mounts important barriers, such as the regionally-variable entry requirements and benefit periods under the operations of the unemployment insurance program. Indeed, the productivity of the Canadian federal government to fragment the economic and social union in the name of addressing regional disparities may well emasculate the recently signed *Agreement on International Trade*.

My concluding observation is that preserving and promoting the internal economic union in both countries must now embrace the reality that the *external* forces of globalization may not be consistent with the long-standing *internal* societal preferences on this issue. Specifically, Canada may be overdoing the role of competitive federalism on the social front whereas Australia may be stifling competitive federalism on the economic front.

References

Boothe, Paul and Tracy Snodden. 1994. *Tax Collection in Canada: Prospects for Reform*, Commentary 63, Toronto: C.D. Howe Institute.

Courchene, Thomas J. 1995a. *Celebrating Flexibility: An Interpretive Essay on the Evolution of Canadian Federalism*, C.D. Howe Benefactors Lecture, Toronto: C.D. Howe Institute.

Courchene, Thomas J. 1995b. *Fiscal Federalism and the Management of Economic Space: An Australian-Canadian Comparison*, unfinished manuscript, School of Policy Studies, Queen's.

Courchene, Thomas J. and Cliff Walsh. 1995. "Globalization and the Knowledge/Information Revolution: Implications for Constitutional Federalism," in Brian Galligan and Peter Russell (eds.), *Redesigning the State: The Politics of Constitutional Change*, London: Oxford University Press.

Craven, Greg. 1993. "Federal Constitution and External Relations," Brian Hocking (ed.), *Foreign Relation and Federal States*, London and New York: Leicester University Press, 9-27.

Hayes, John A. 1982. *Economic Mobility in Canada: A Comparative Study*, Ottawa: Ministry of Supply and Services, Canada.

Helliwell, John and John McCallum. 1995. "National Borders Still Matter for Trade," *Policy Options*, 16 (July/August), 44-48.

Hogg, Peter. 1992. *Constitutional Law of Canada*, 3rd edition, Scarborough: Carswell.

Leslie, Peter. 1991. *The European Community: A Political Model for Canada?* (Ottawa: Supply and Services Canada).

Leslie, Peter. 1995. "Constitutional Restructuring by Stealth," Brian Galligan and Peter Russell (eds.), *Redesigning the State: The Politics of Constitutional Change*, London: Oxford University Press.

Lipton, P. and A. Herzberg. 1993. *Understanding Company Law*, Sydney: The Law Book Company Limited.

Majone, Giandomenico. 1994. "Mutual Recognition in Federal Type Systems," Anne Mullins and Cheryl Saunders (eds.), *Economic Union in Federal Systems*, Melbourne: The Federation Press.

Senate of Canada. 1990. *Canada 1992: Toward a National Market in Financial Services*, Ottawa: Senate of Canada.

Statistics Canada. 1993. *Daily*, cat. no. 11-001E, August 24.

Sturgess, Gary L. 1993. "Fuzzy Law and Low Maintenance Regulation: The Birth of Mutual Recognition in Australia," Conference of the Royal Institute of Public Administration on Mutual Recognition, Brisbane, Queensland, February 12.

Trebilcock, Michael J. and Daniel Schwanen (eds.). 1995. *Getting There: An Assessment of the Agreement on Internal Trade,* Toronto: C.D. Howe Research Institute.

Wood, Alan. 1994. "Australian Federalism in the 1990s," paper prepared for presentation at the conference on *Australian Federalism: Future Directions,* Centre for Comparative Constitutional Studies, University of Melbourne.

Zines, Leslie. 1992. *The High Court and the Constitution,* 3rd edition, Sydney: Butterworths.

Appendix
Section 92:
Exclusive Powers of Provincial Legislatures

92. In each Province the Legislature may exclusively make Laws in relation to Matters coming within the Classes of Subject next hereinafter enumerated; that is to say,—

1. Repealed.

2. Direct Taxation within the Province in order to the raising of a Revenue for Provincial Purposes.

3. The borrowing of Money on the sole Credit of the Province.

4. The Establishment and Tenure of Provincial Offices and the Appointment and Payment of Provincial Officers.

5. The Management and Sale of the Public Lands belonging to the Province and of the Timber and Wood thereon.

6. The Establishment, Maintenance, and Management of Public and Reformatory Prisons in and for the Province.

7. The Establishment, Maintenance, and Management of Hospitals, Asylums, Charities, and Eleemosynary Institutions in and for the Province, other than Marine Hospitals.

8. Municipal Institutions in the Province.

9. Shop, Saloon, Tavern, Auctioneer, and other Licences in order to the raising of a Revenue for Provincial, Local, or Municipal Purposes.

10. Local Works and Undertakings other than such as are of the following Classes:—

    (a) Lines of Steam or other Ships, Railways, Canals, Telegraphs, and other Works and Undertakings connecting the Province with any other or others of the Provinces, or extending beyond the Limits of the Province;

(b) Lines of Steam Ships between the Province and any British or Foreign Country;

(c) Such Work as, although wholly situate within the Province, are before or after their Execution declared by the Parliament of Canada to be for the general Advantage of Canada or for the Advantage of Two or more of the Provinces.

11. The Incorporation of Companies with Provincial Objects.

12. The Solemnization of Marriage in the Province.

13. Property and Civil Rights in the Province.

14. The Administration of Justice in the Province, including the Constitution, Maintenance, and Organization of Provincial Courts, both of Civil and of Criminal Jurisdiction, and including Procedure in Civil Matters in those Courts.

15. The Imposition of Punishment by Fine, Penalty, or Imprisonment for enforcing any Law of the Province made in relation to any Matter coming within any of the Classes of Subjects enumerated in this Section.

16. Generally all Matters of a merely local or private Nature in the Province.

10

A New Federalism for Canada

The Honourable Jim Dinning

In preparing this paper, I could not help but think back to a Conference Board of Canada session I attended last year. Canadian business men and women were joined by American CEOs and the Ambassadors to Canada from the U.S., Japan and Argentina. One after another, the non-Canadian speakers commented on how hard we Canadians are on ourselves. We are forever thrashing ourselves, especially in comparison with our mighty neighbours to the south or abroad, both east and west.

Why do we do this? It's the Canadian way. It's our way of saying: we're good, and we have a very good country here, but good isn't good enough. We're tough on ourselves because we want to be better, and we want to make our country better. Our aspirations are revealed not by flying the flag higher and mouthing our national anthem louder, but by self-analysis and criticism. Only in Canada, I am told, do people act this way. Only in Canada would we bring people all the way from Australia to join us in debating the internal squabbling and struggles of this diverse Canadian family. It is the Canadian way to debate our weaknesses rather than crow about our strengths, to struggle with diverse aspirations, and to bend, shape and recast the way we work together — provinces and the federal government — to make this country better.

The key message of my paper is that we can make a good country better if we change the way we manage our fiscal affairs so that they reflect the reality of Canada today. Not Canada in 1867 or even 1977, but the distinctly different Canada of 1995. The relationship between our federal and provincial governments is woefully out of date.

As Alberta's Premier Ralph Klein often says, "That was then ... this is now." Our current approach to fiscal federalism was defined in an earlier time when resources were plentiful, when governments thought there were few problems they could not fix, when we could boast about effort and not have to be accountable for achievement. Now is a different time. Three realities make it imperative that we recast our fiscal arrangements: the federal government is faced with continuing deficits and mounting debt; the global marketplace will not wait while we sort out our difficulties; and the provinces have grown up.

We all know the federal government's fiscal situation is a mess. The federal debt is 73 percent of GDP. Despite the steps the federal government is taking, the problem of Canada's debt situation will get worse before it gets better. The reality is that the federal government must reduce its spending across the country and across the board. Reductions must include transfers to provinces. And that reality runs smack into our cherished social programs and the inevitable wailing and gnashing of teeth about the effect of reduced federal spending on the future of Canada's social programs.

It seems we are only now waking up to the fact that our social programs were also developed in a different time, to meet yesterday's needs (supposedly). We have a tangled and overlapping web of government programs with few clear lines of accountability. What is the bottom line for Canadians? It is not the amount governments spend but the results they achieve. Canadians expect results and our governments are falling short of their expectations.

It is not easy for the federal government to reduce its spending. Nor is it easy for any of the provinces to respond to the inevitable impact. However, it must be done. Canada simply cannot compete in a global marketplace if we are known as a place that is mired in debt and taking only timid steps to fix it. This is the second reality. Our ability to compete globally, to attract new industries and new capital, is directly affected by the fiscal shape of our country.

Each year when rating agencies pass judgment on our federal and provincial budgets, it has a direct impact on Canadians and on Canadian businesses. Each time we are forced to increase interest rates, it adds to the cost of doing business in Canada and to the weight of government that Canadians must shoulder. Investors want to see a stable and secure fiscal environment. They want to see governments that have their fiscal houses in order and provide a positive environment for business to do what it does best: invest, grow and create jobs for Canadians.

The third reality we face in Canada today is that the provinces have grown up. If we think of the Canadian federation as a family, the children of 1867 and 1905 are now adults. Since the 1950s, the federal government has been "father knows best" of the federation. Ottawa used fiscal levers and a well-experienced public service to influence the priorities of the provinces and implement programs considered to be in the national interest. There was a sense by some that the provinces needed the guiding hand of the federal government in order to get things right.

However, times have changed and the kids have grown up. The relationship between the federal parents and the provincial offspring has to change when dad is 128 and even this Alberta kid is 90 years old! More and more, we see the provinces straining against the old guiding hand of the federal government. Today, we see the provinces working together in cooperation, often finding common ground and reaching consensus on important national issues without Ottawa's help.

Provinces have led the way in returning to fiscal responsibility. Ottawa is just beginning on a very difficult fiscal course while most of the provinces have balanced their budgets and others are on the way. While many of the federal government's social policy reforms are stalled, the Premiers agreed in August 1995 to act. Provinces are coming together to spell out a common action plan on national social policy issues, and to provide the means for ensuring consistency and greater flexibility in the design and delivery of social programs.

While provinces come together to discuss much-needed reforms and new approaches to the delivery of health care consistent with the principles of the Canada Health Act, all the federal government is doing is drawing lines in the sand, making threats and setting deadlines. While the provinces work together to define responsibilities in the area of the environment, the federal Minister decides she will "just say no," precipitating a fundamental breakdown in relations between the provinces and the federal government. While the federal Minister clings to the past, the rest of the world races by. Clearly, it is time for change.

Let me turn now to Alberta's approach to a new fiscal arrangement. Over the past two-and-a-half years, Alberta has been on a mission to balance its budget and fundamentally change the entire public sector. The result is smaller government focused on core businesses, abandoning a direct interventionist role in the economy, and moving more direct services and responsibilities to municipalities, school boards and regional health authorities.

We understand that change is absolutely essential to position Alberta in the global marketplace. We must change in order to secure and improve our essential social programs, and in the end, to make our province better and stronger for the future. The approach we have taken in Alberta definitely colours our approach to new fiscal arrangements. We see four key challenges in reforming fiscal federalism. They are all related:

- Sorting out who does what to achieve smaller and more efficient governments.
- Developing flexibility in the design and delivery of programs.
- Defining national standards and deciding where they are needed.
- Establishing a true partnership between federal and provincial governments.

Let us begin with sorting out who does what. Simply put, our objective has to be smaller governments that produce better results. To achieve this objective, we need to decide who does what, and then leave Canadians to hold their governments accountable for the results. In Alberta, we are looking for leaner, lighter governments which do not sit so heavily on the shoulders of taxpayers. Most Canadians want the same thing. We have been through the old times when governments tried to be all things to all people. Remember that old adage about government, "There's no problem we can't make bigger."

We are trying to put those days behind us, not just because we cannot afford them any more, but because people will no longer tolerate the lack of results. They are no longer content with governments saying, "We tried hard and spent money. What more can you expect?" People want to know what results we got for the dollars we spent — their dollars. In Alberta, "government lite" means getting back to core businesses. We are looking at everything we do and asking basic questions: Is this the business we should be in? If it is not, let someone else do it. If it is, how can we do it better and at less cost?

Together, the provinces and the federal government need to have that same discussion. Surely there is more than enough government to go around. As one of my colleagues says, "It's a good thing we don't get all the government we pay for." Our Constitution provides us with specific guidance in some areas and a lot of opportunity for flexibility in others. Where the Constitution gives clear lines of responsibility, the provinces and the federal government need an understanding that the other government will not be involved. We do not need two levels of government doing the same thing. Where the Constitution is fuzzy, Alberta's view is that an *ad hoc* approach will not do. We need a coordinated plan and an understanding that each level of government should do what it does best and the other level should get out of the way.

Before too many academics get visions of sugar plums dancing in their heads must tell you, this is one more area where Canadians are way ahead of their politicians. Canadians are tired of political gamesmanship and who can score the most points. In federal-provincial relations, the only people keeping score are the politicians, the media and academics writing about fiscal federalism. Canadians don't care about score-keeping. They are just asking us to sort things out so they get the right services, from the right people, at the right place, at the right price — which, by the way, is a much lower cost.

I am convinced that if we put a group of ordinary Canadians in a room and said, putting politics aside, who should handle manpower training or immigration or roads or culture -- they could work it out in a weekend. The tough part would be getting politicians to stick to it. The key point is that we need to sort out responsibilities and then let those decisions drive fiscal arrangements, not the other way around. We need to do it in the simplest, most practical and efficient way. That is all Canadians really want.

The second challenge is flexibility. Here, I am talking about the need for Canada's fiscal federalism to accommodate differences in needs, and therefore in programs across each of the provinces. The days of "one size fits all" are gone. As we have seen in health and we are seeing in other social programs, things change. People's needs change. Within our own province, we know that politicians sitting in Edmonton are not the best ones to say what is needed in Okotoks or Smoky Lake. Nor are we in the best position to say how those needs should be met.

The need to be flexible has caused us to change the way we do business. Instead of tying strings to municipal grants or saying that all regional health authorities should operate in the same way, we are trying to say, "Here are the expectations and high standards we have set on behalf of Albertans, and here are the dollars. Now get on with the job and then tell us, and the people you serve, what results you achieve." That is what we mean by flexibility.

In a decentralized, flexible approach, some will argue that we could create a patchwork of programs and services across the country. But a patchwork quilt has many common threads. Basic principles, such as guaranteed mobility of people across provinces, and mobility of trade and business, must be in place. If they are, those principles could capture the unique features and needs of Canadians in each of the provinces and still bind the country together.

This brings me to the third challenge: national standards. If we allow flexibility, enabling each province to respond to needs in its own unique way, what happens to national standards? Where will those common threads come from? Alberta is a strong supporter of national standards. We believe there are common threads that bind us together and that they should be preserved in all provinces. Canadians want to know that wherever they go in Canada, to live, work or raise their families, there are some basic things we all hold in common. The question is, how do we decide on common threads, especially in a changing environment where the needs and expectations of one province do not necessarily match those of its neighbours? The answer is, we weave those new threads not through federal dictates, but through a national consensus among the provinces and the federal government.

In many areas like education or environmental protection, provinces have worked together to find common ground and common solutions which provide consistency and set national standards across the country. A clear distinction needs to be made: national standards do not equal federal standards. National standards are forged through consensus, through discussions and debates among Canadians, not through the dictates of the federal government.

This brings me to the last challenge: establishing a true partnership among the provinces and the federal government. With cuts to federal transfers, we all know that the traditional role of the federal government is changing. In Alberta alone, cash transfers will decline from $1.5 to $1 billion, a cut of one-third. With decreasing fiscal transfers to the provinces, the question becomes, how can the federal government continue to legitimately prescribe social policy, especially in areas of provincial responsibility? As the old adage says, he who pays the piper calls the tune.

In Alberta, we believe Ottawa has an important role to play. Precisely how it will evolve, I don't know. However, I will guarantee that it will no longer be "father knows best." The federal government's role is that of a partner in a changed Canada — not always the senior partner, but one of eleven partners. Its role in international affairs is unquestioned, as is its role in defense and in monetary policy. But many of its traditional roles are open for debate. Just like here in Alberta, where we are getting out of some businesses we have been in for decades (and we still have much more to do), the federal government must do likewise. Changing the roles of governments does not weaken Canada as a nation. It makes us stronger, leaner and better able to move quickly, respond and adapt to the global marketplace.

In summary, Alberta wants to see a new and improved brand of fiscal federalism with five essential characteristics:

- Responsibilities sorted out so that Canadians will have smaller governments with clearly defined roles and better accountability.
- Flexibility — "no more one size fits all."
- National standards forged through national consensus.
- A new partnership where the provinces and the federal government work together to move this country forward to the 21st century.
- All this accomplished within the framework of our current Constitution.

It is time for Canada's fiscal federalism to catch up with the reality that Canada faces today. It is time to recognize that the kids have grown up. It is time for a new partnership among the federal and provincial governments.

An important question remains. If we achieved the new federalism I have described above, would that be sufficient to meet the expectations of Quebec? I remember as a wide-eyed Alberta kid visiting Montreal in 1967. Expo helped us to define what it meant to be a proud Canadian. I lived in Quebec in 1975 and 1976 and I remember the first referendum, the rounds of Constitutional debates and the strong desire of so many Canadians to find a way to make our country work.

As I said in the introduction to this paper, we Canadians are incredibly hard on ourselves, questioning our basic existence and how we work together. But we do it in order to make this country better. If Quebec were to leave the federation, Canada would not be better, nor would Quebec. Going through the struggles to make Canada better is not an easy task. But our history shows that we do not take the easy way out. There is a strong streak of unreasonableness among us. It prevents us from saying, it can't be done.

I am reminded of a quote from George Bernard Shaw. Shaw said, "Reasonable people adapt themselves to their environment. Unreasonable people adapt their environment to themselves. Thus all progress is the result of the efforts of unreasonable people." Shaw describes Canadians to a T.

Canadians are known as reasonable people. We bend, we compromise and we adapt. But to move ahead, to position Canada to compete and succeed in a global marketplace, we need unreasonable people across Canada to accept that the country has changed. We need to listen to Canadians when they say, "Quit with the games. Give us the results, inexpensively, and then stay out of our hair." Unreasonable people taking that simple approach will help to make our country better. And who knows, we might even stop mouthing the words to our national anthem and actually sing them gloriously and freely. It's worth a try.